Boat Building Master Course

By Naval Architect Morten Olesen

A few words about the boat plans

You can use the boat plans included in this book to build your own boat. However they are reduced in size to fit the pages so they may be difficult to read. You can order the boat plans in this book plus boat plans for many more designs in original size from Boatplans.dk by visiting my website at:

http://www.boatplans.dk/

The boat plans are originally developed for delivery by email and self-printing. So this is the first time they are presented in printing. It is my sincere hope that you enjoy this master course and the boat plans. Please feel free to contact me if you have comments, ideas and suggestions.

All the best,

Morten Olesen
Boatplans.dk
http://www.boatplans.dk/

Copyright © 2011 Boatplans.dk / Naval Architect Morten Olesen
All rights reserved.
ISBN: 1461145716
ISBN-13: 978-1461145714

 **Boat Building Master Course**

Dedication

This book is dedicated to the customers that have supported me via my website over the last many years. I wish I would be able to thank each and every one of you in person. Thank you for all your input and support and for trusting me enough to buy the boat plans and build the boats.

Boat Building Master Course

1 Table of Contents

1 Table of Contents 5
2 Beginner's Guide to Boat Building 7
3 Lofting Manual 25
4 Assembly Manual 41
5 Laminating Manual 67
6 Epoxy Manual 81
Appendix A, Boat plans for the 10' Rowboat 111
Appendix B, Boat plans for the 13' J – Skiff 139
Appendix C, Boat plans for the 16' Ozarks float boat 167

2 Beginner's Guide to Boat Building

Boat building has a long history, and ever since the first dugout was made there has been a great desire for better, prettier, larger and faster boats. Some special periods stand out in this long history.

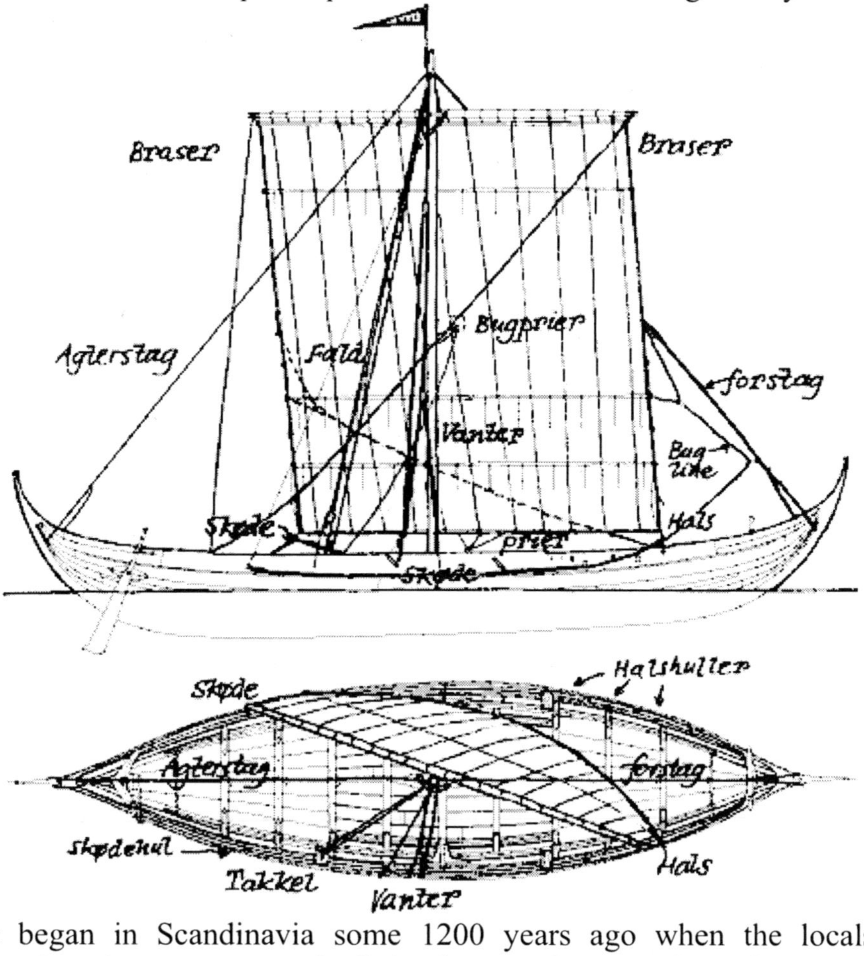

It began in Scandinavia some 1200 years ago when the locals developed some extremely light, long and seaworthy ships. With these boats the Vikings were able to cruise all over the Atlantic Ocean, from Greenland and Newfoundland in the north to Gibraltar in the south.

What began with the Vikings was a true success. It is possible to trace the influence these excellently designed ships have had on boat design. Here at Boatplans.dk we are proud to be a part of the Scandinavian boat building tradition, which for so many years has stood for true and original boat designs.

2.1 Boat building like our grandfathers did

If we go back just a few generations, boat building was a specialized profession. To become a boat builder it was necessary to serve one's apprenticeship for many years. Building boats required patience and a great deal of skill. Back then, boats were built with solid timber and every piece needed was cut out from large planks.

Since then, modern materials have been developed. The development of epoxy and fiberglass made it possible for people without any skills to build boats. That's why we at Boatplans.dk have made this 'Boat Building Master Course'. We believe it should be possible for everybody to build his or her own boat. Our boat plans are developed to give you, a first time builder, the best possible starting point for making the dream of building your own boat come true.

 **Boat Building Master Course**

Our boat plans are developed for immediate download when purchased via the website. This special feature has many advantages, and we were the first to develop it.

When you get your plans, the first thing you want to do is print them. You don't need any special hardware, just a standard printer capable of making black and white prints. It is not even necessary to print with color. The paper size is letter or A4, so no matter what the standard size is in your country, you will be able to easily print our plans.

There are many advantages to printing the plans yourself. Not only are you able to print as many copies as you like, but you will also be able to print new plans if the ones you are using get damaged or torn.

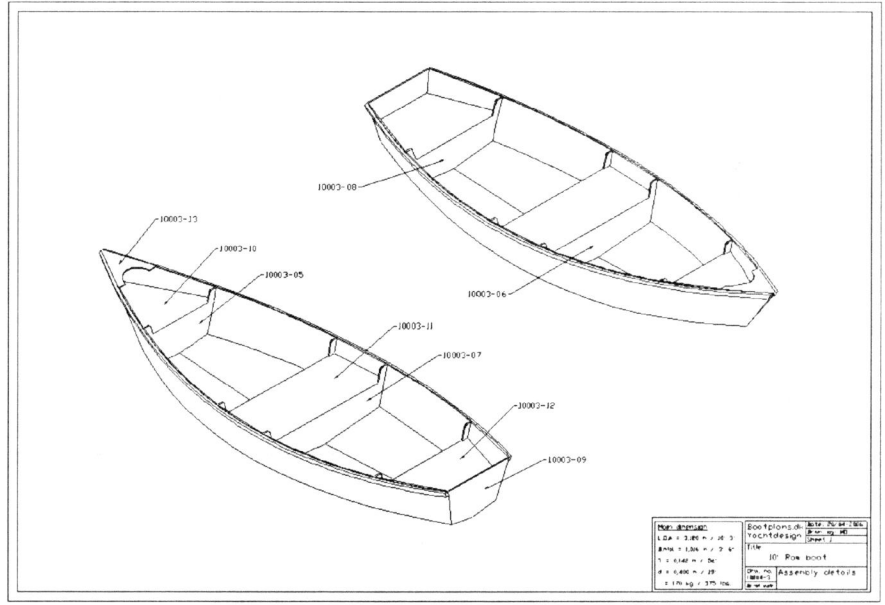
12' Row boat - Assembly detail plan

The boat plans you receive consist of several types of plans. Not only do you receive plans for the different parts you will need to build your boat, but you also receive plans showing you how the parts should be laid out on the plywood to ensure the best possible utilization of the plywood, and plans showing you assembly details so you know exactly how every part should fit together. You also receive a part list, building instructions and a list of materials. In addition to the plans you will receive this 'Boat Building Master Course' as PDF file.

2.2 Building your new boat

After studying the boat plans it is time to start building your new boat. The building process involves some steps that will be described below.

2.3 Tools

You won't need a lot of special tools for building your first boat. Actually you won't need any special tools at all. You can cut out and assemble the parts for the boat with just a handsaw, a screwdriver and a drill. Of course it is nice to have an electrical or saber saw, but it is not a must.

Besides the hand tools you will need a measuring tape and a pencil, plus some tools for working with epoxy and fiberglass.

2.4 Building materials

Before starting the building process you will need some building materials. The building instructions, along with the boat plans, will tell you what materials you need for the specific design.

You will need to buy some plywood. We normally recommend buying marine or exterior plywood, but other plywood types may also do. One thing, however, is to make sure the plywood you buy is water and boiling proof (WBP). Ordinary waterproof plywood is simply not good enough for boat building.

We know that many of our builders have used plywood types other than marine or exterior with good results. However, it is important to take a good look at the plywood your supplier offers you. Some less expensive plywood might be suitable for boat building and some might not. Quality is the important issue here.

For the gluing and glassing of your new boat you will need epoxy. The amount is stated in the building instructions, and is for an average builder. Depending on your boat building skills, you might need more or less. We always recommend you round up the amount of epoxy to the nearest can size your supplier can deliver. It is often also cheaper to buy one larger can than two or three smaller ones.

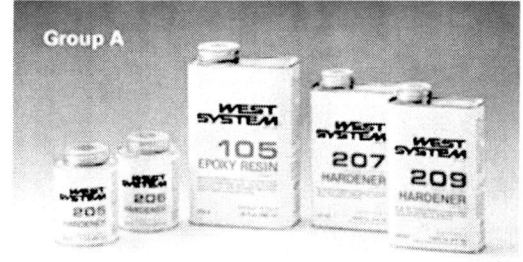

The hull of your boat will need some reinforcements at the seams where the plywood is assembled. For that purpose you should use fiberglass tape. The tape can be bought in many different widths and qualities, but again your building instruction will show you the amount as well as the width and quality. In most places you can buy the fiberglass tape by the yard, but it is much cheaper to buy a whole roll of tape. So check out your supplier's prices to see what will be best for you.

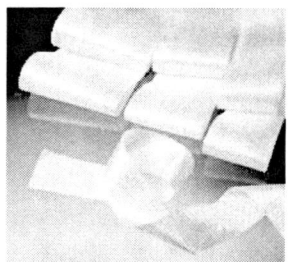

For some of the gluing jobs you will need some filler for the epoxy. The filler is used to thicken the epoxy so it will be possible to apply it evenly on vertical surfaces. Most times you will use wood flour for the thickening, but sometimes the building notes specify some special filler. This is due to the fact that some designs need especially strong glue.

2.5 Building places

Building your new boat does not require a large workshop with all the newest tools. Most of our builders use whatever they have around: a garage, a shed, a pent roof or even a tent can be used.

 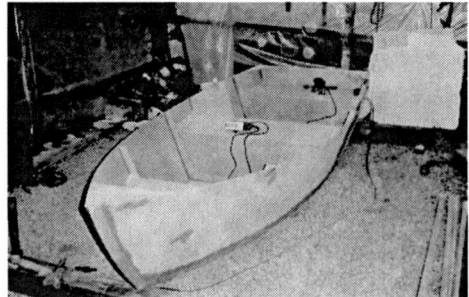

17' Norwegian pram built in a tent   13' J-Skiff built in a home made tent

When deciding where to build your boat it is important to have a few things in mind. First, it would be good if the place where you plan to build were a little larger than the boat itself. One meter [3 feet] around the boat is great, and less can do, but it is best if you can walk freely all the way around.

Second, you should keep in mind that when using epoxy the temperature has to be higher than 5°C [41F]. Therefore, if you are not able to heat your work place, and it gets below these temperatures in the winter where you live, you will have to wait until the temperatures rise outside before using the epoxy.

You can start building in the winter with low temperatures. Then you can loft and cut the pieces needed to build your new boat. Next, assemble the pieces then wait until the weather gets warmer before gluing and applying fiberglass tape and epoxy.

2.6 Lofting

When you have bought the plywood it is time to start lofting. Lofting is the process where you transfer the dimensions from your plans to full scale on the plywood. Our 'Boat building Master Course' has an entire section dedicated to this process, so after reading this section you will be well prepared to perform this task.

Lofting a curved panel

Depending on the part you are lofting, you will set out the different dimensions on the plywood. This will give you some points that you connect, either by using a slender trim to form a curve if it is a side panel you are lofting, or by connecting the points with straight lines if it is a frame.

Boat Building Master Course

Lofting a frame

After you have lofted the panels you will cut them out using a circular or saber saw.

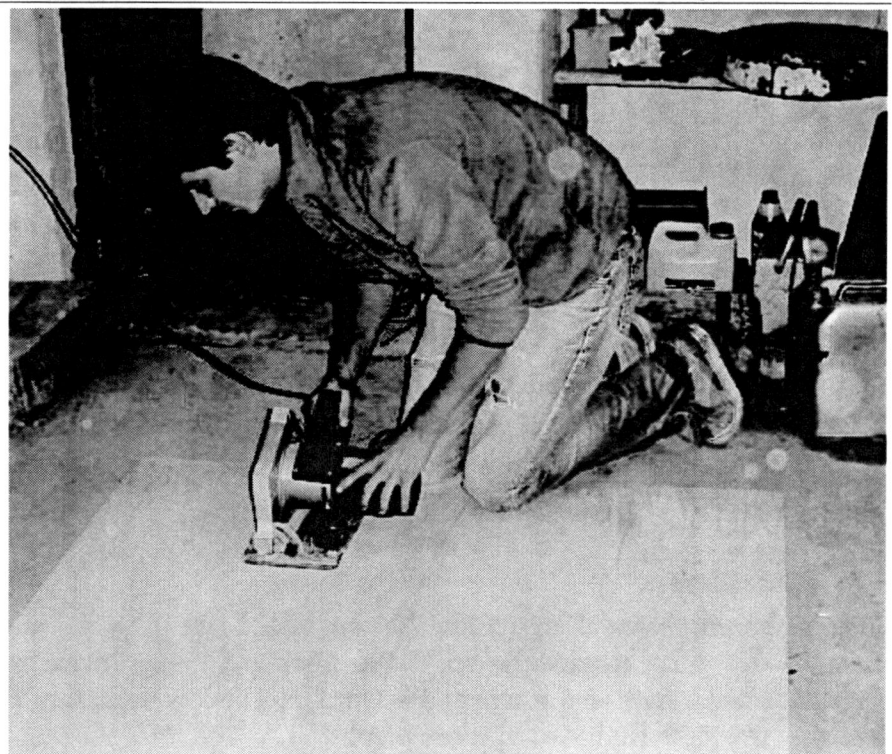

Cutting plywood

Since the boat is symmetric you will have some parts that are identical, only mirror inverted. Here we recommend you first cut out one of the parts and then use this part as a template to make the others. First of all, this is the most rational way since you will only have to loft once. Secondly, it makes sure the parts are really identical, since the parts are just copies of each other.

Boat Building Master Course

A 'pile' of parts for a 15' Dinghy

So after lofting and cutting all the parts, you will have a whole 'pile' of parts and are ready to start assembling the boat.

2.7 Assembly

Since standard plywood sheets are 244 cm x 122 cm [8' x 4'] and some of the parts needed to build the boat are longer than the plywood sheets, such as the side and bottom panels, it is necessary to assemble the parts from two or more pieces.

Joining panels with fiberglass tape

The assembly is easier when you use fiberglass tape and epoxy over the joints. By doing so you will get a strong joint of the panels. The joint also has the advantage of being almost invisible and will not add much to the thickness of the panel, which will be of greater advantage later on in the assembly process.

The first thing to do when starting the assembly is setting up the frames. Even though some of our builders manage to assemble the boat without a building jig, we always recommend making one. The 'Boat Building Master Course' contains detailed information on how to perform this task. Keep in mind it is not as difficult as it might seem. The building jig is simply a rack built from timber that gives you a way to hold the frame in place in a vertical position.

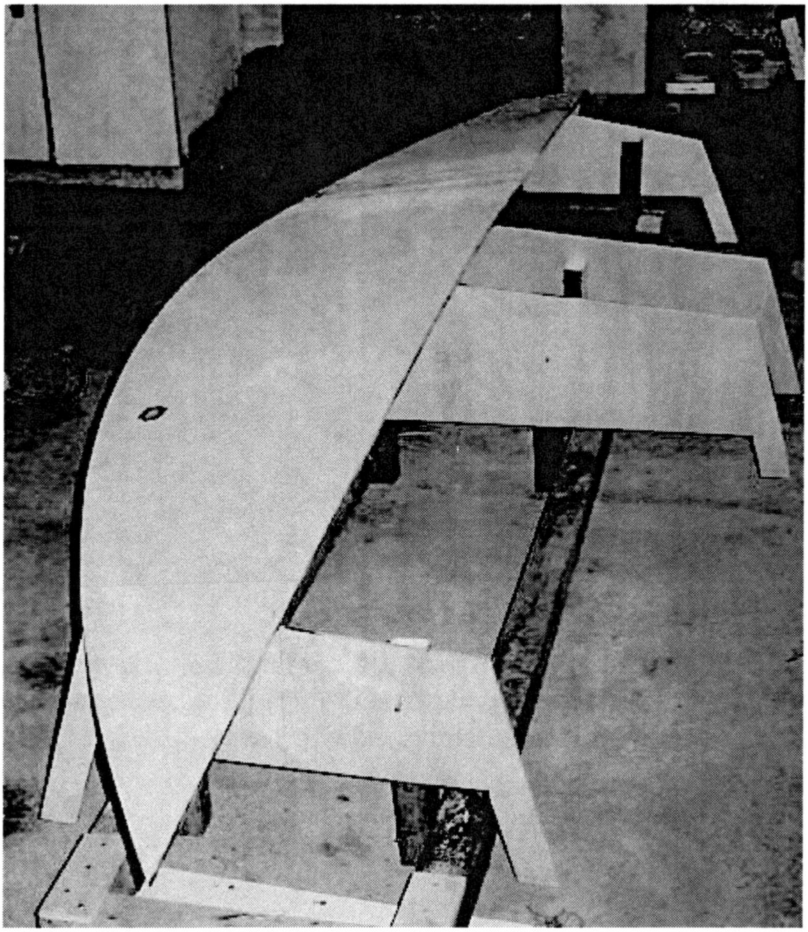

12' Row boat - Frame set up

 **Boat Building Master Course**

After setting up the frame you can start assembling the side and bottom panels. Now you can really start to feel and see the beautiful shape of your new boat. There is still some work to be done, but as the hull comes together you can begin to admire your boat.

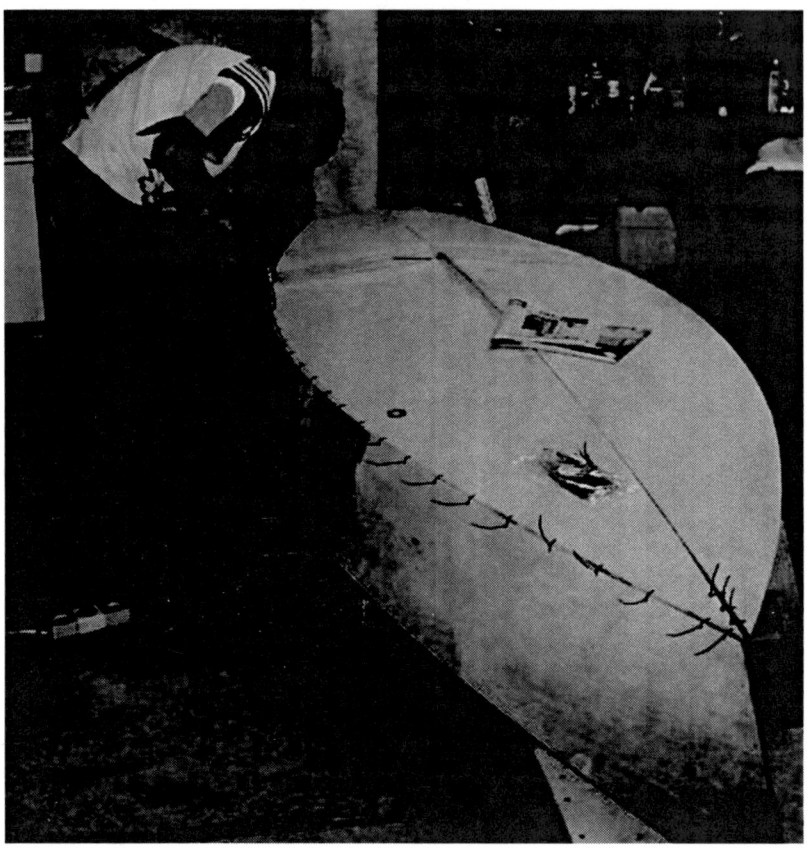

Stitching a 12' Row boat

When the side and bottom panels are coming together, it is time to start stitching. Stitching is done by simply drilling some small holes along the seam and then stitching the two panels together. You can use metal wire or cable ties to do this.

15' Dinghy fully stitched

2.8 Gluing and fiberglass tape/epoxy

The next step in finishing your new boat will be to glue everything together with thickened epoxy and fiberglass tape. This is usually done from both outside and inside, and handling the epoxy is often the most difficult part of this step. While the epoxy is quite tolerant of errors, carelessness in this area will require extra grinding and fairing later on.

Boat Building Master Course

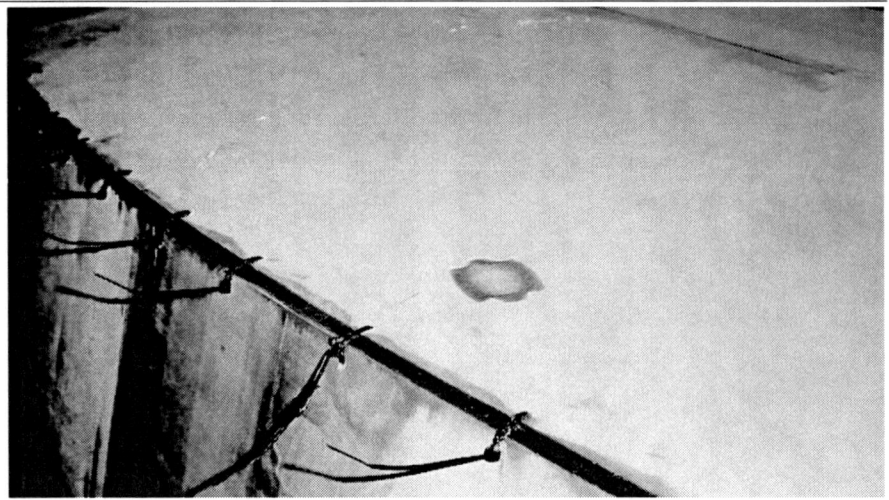

Gluing the seams of a 12' Row boat

When all the panels are assembled and stitched you can start gluing the seams. For the gluing you will use epoxy thickened with wood flour or whatever the building instruction states to use. The process is quite simple. After the glue is dry, remove the stitches and apply glue where the stitches have been.

A 12' Row boat glued and glassed outside

Boat Building Master Course

After grinding and fairing the seams you will apply fiberglass tape and epoxy. Our 'Boat Building Master Course' describes this process in details.

Sanding and fairing a 12' Row boat

The only thing left to do on the outside is to fill and grind the outside of the hull. Doing that is very hard work, but doing a good job at this phase is very important for the appearance of the boat. The better you prepare the surface, the nicer your boat will look when finished.

Now everything on the outside of the hull is finished. The next thing to do is to turn the hull and start working on the inside.

Filleting the inside of a 12' Row boat

When the hull is turned you will glue the frames and inside seams with thickened epoxy. The fiberglass tape does not fit well in sharp corners; therefore, use some large fillets inside so the tape will be able to fit nicely and without any sharp folds. After the glue is dry, grind and fair the fillets so any unevenness is removed.

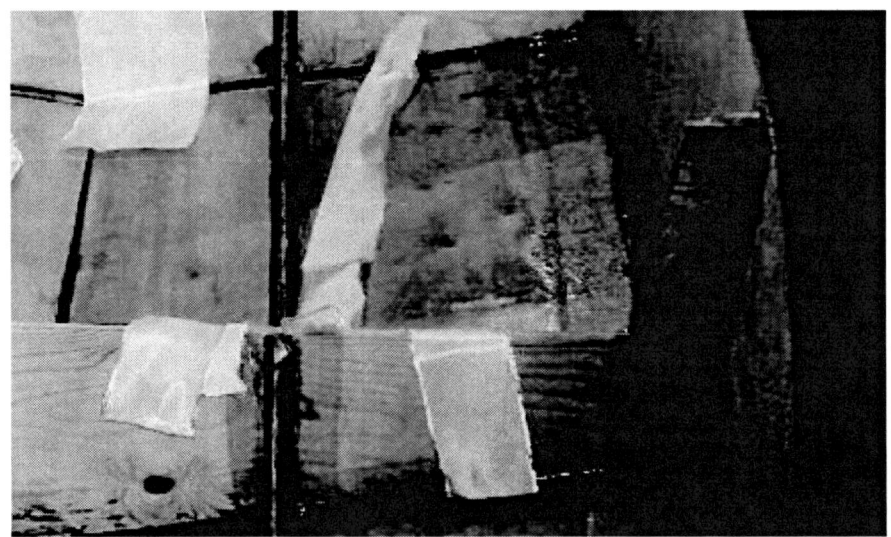

Applying fiberglass tape at the inside of a 14' Garvey flex

Now it is time to apply fiberglass tape to the inside. All corners should be glued with fiberglass tape and epoxy, unless your building instructions tell you otherwise. By applying the tape you will ensure a good strong connection between the hull side, bottom panels and the structural frames.

A 10' Garvey flex glued and glassed inside

Finish the inside by assembling the seats and thwarts. The seats and thwarts are also glued with thickened epoxy and fiberglass tape. Now the only thing left to do is grind and fair the inside of the boat so the result inside will be as nice as the outside.

 **Boat Building Master Course**

A 12' Row boat ready for trial

Now the building is about to come to an end and the only thing left to do is painting or varnishing the boat. You may need to assemble some fittings for oars or an outboard engine, and then your new boat will be ready for an adventure.

Adventures ready to begin in a 12' Garvey flex

Boat Building Master Course

3 Lofting Manual

Before you start lofting and cutting, it is recommended that you read the building instruction and this 'Boat Building Master Course' at least once from start to finish so you are familiar with the entire process. It is also advisable that you read these instructions before you purchase materials.

Basically you will meet two different types of elements when building one of our designs. There are the panels - bottom panels, side panels etc. - and the symmetric elements - frames, transom, thwarts etc.

The two different types of elements will be described separately in this manual, since they are from a lofting point of view very different to draw.

Another thing you will notice when going through the plans is that every time you need two elements, a side panel for both starboard and port side, only one of them is with dimensions.

The reason for this is simple. Instead of lofting two identical panels, it is far more rational to loft and cut one of the elements and then use this element as a template for the next one.

3.1 Tools

In order to perform the lofting these basic tools are needed:

Pencil - ink from a pen will soak into the wood grain and be harder to remove, so it is recommended you use a pencil.

Measuring tape - a tape measure will work, but drywall squares 48" long (found at any home improvement store) are inexpensive and make drawing very easy.

Lumber fillet - a piece of semi-flexible material (such as PVC tubing, woodworking trim or lumber fillet) to construct the curves and arcs. If you use wood, take care that it has long straight grains and doesn't have any knots.

Squares - a steel carpenter square is nice to have but not a must. You can manage to make the lofting without one, but it makes some of the work easier. Later in this section you will find how to make perpendicular lines without a square.

3.2 The boat plans

Your new boat plans consist of different drawings. The plans are labeled with different numbers. Below you will find a description of the different numbers and the content of the files.

Drawing 10000 and 10001-x is the line drawing and general arrangement. They are the most important drawings when designing the boat, but their importance for construction is limited.

Drawings 10002-x show all the different elements needed for the boat. Furthermore it gives you an overview of the nesting on the plywood sheets. Together with the drawing list it will give you the detailed information needed for cutting all the elements.

Drawings 10003-x give you the dimensions of all the elements. There is one drawing for each element. This way the plans can be kept simpler than when having dimensions for more panels on one paper sheet.

Drawings 10004-x are assembly details. The plans gives you dimensions for setting up the frames, and normally there is also a number of plans showing different kind of information related to the assembly.

Drawings 10005-x show some optional information. Not all designs contain plans in this category, so if you don't have any plans starting with 10005, don't worry. The plans can, for example, show dimensions for building jig, polycarbonate windshields, seats etc.

Boat Building Master Course

3.3 Lofting the panels

For a start let's look at part of a drawing showing the nesting. The part is not necessarily from the plans in this book, but consider it an example.

Here you can see plate 1. It shows that from that particular sheet of plywood you will cut two elements. Cut one element with the number 10003-01 and the other with number 10003-03. The number refers to the detailed plan with the same number.

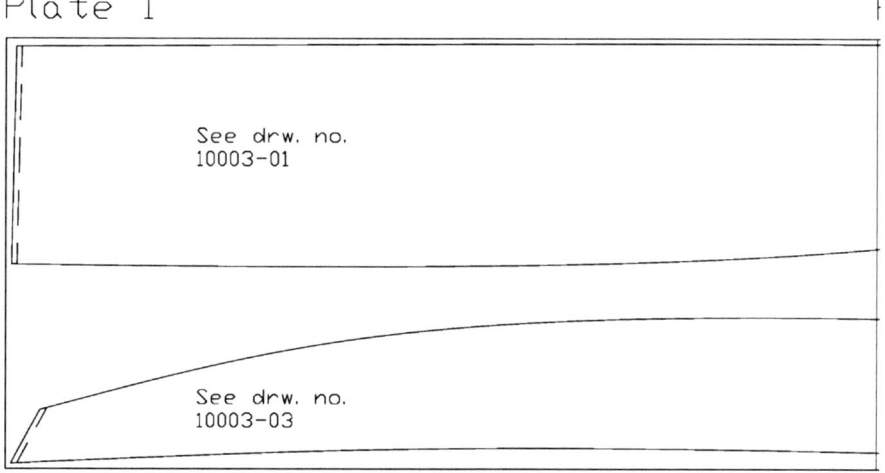

We will then continue finding the plan for 10003-03. A part of that plan is shown below.

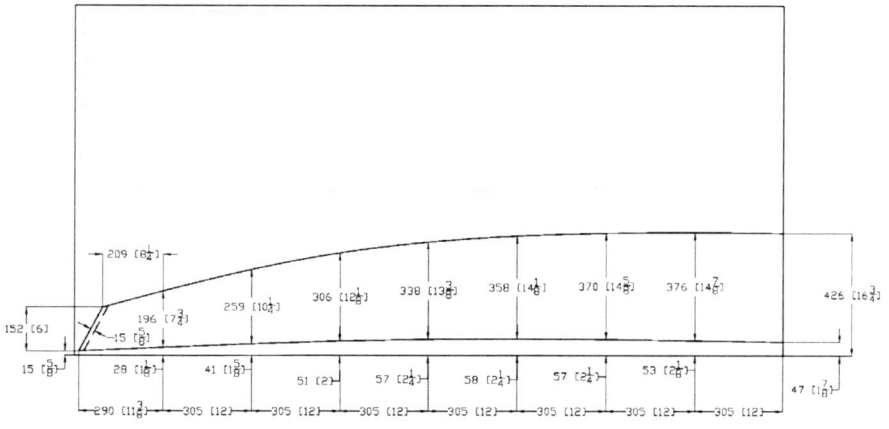

 **Boat Building Master Course**

Here you can find the dimensions that have to be drawn on the plywood. The dimensions are shown as both U.S. standard and metric units. The U.S. standard units are inside the [ ]. This is not always the case, for some designs the units are either metric or U.S. standard units. If only one set of dimensions is present in your plans, you have made your choice of dimension format when you ordered the plans.

As you might have noticed, the lofting of panels starts with a grid. The grid is drawn with vertical lines each 305 mm [12"]. The easiest way to draw the grid is to use a steel carpenter square.

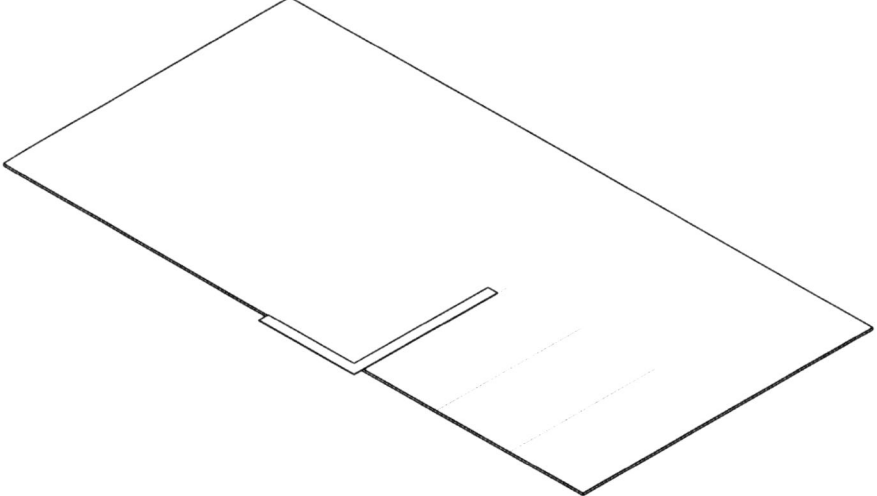

Another way could be to simply mark the grid distances from the short side of the plywood sheet and then mark the grid with a straightedge.

Boat Building Master Course

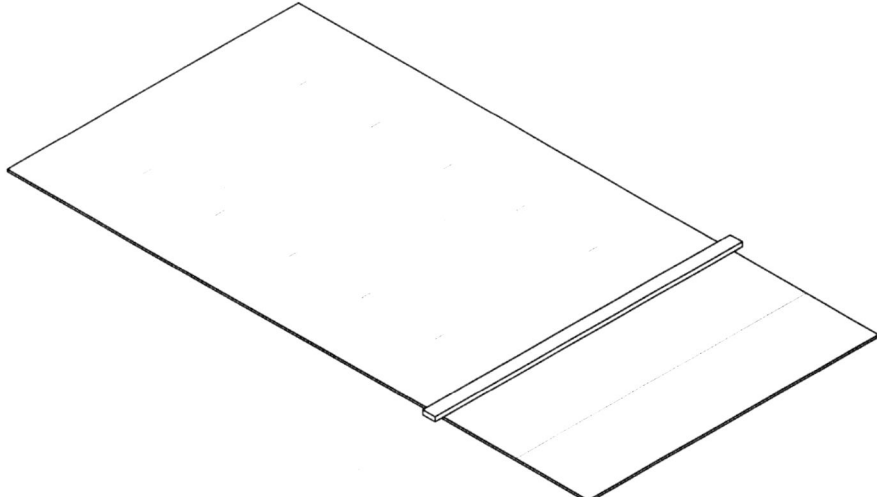

Once you finish marking the grid you will have a sheet of plywood that looks similar to the figure below.

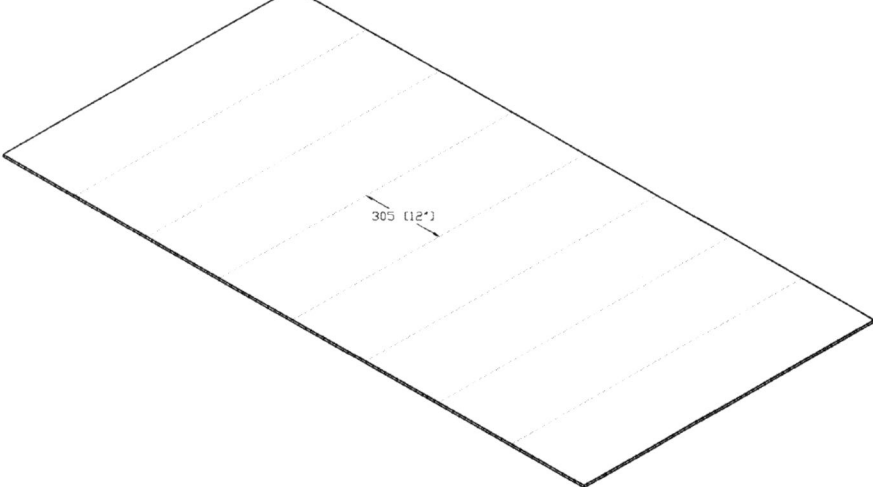

It is now time to set out the dimensions from the drawing. This is done from the long edge of the plywood sheet, and every distance set out is marked with a pencil. After the distances are set out your plywood sheet will look like this.

Boat Building Master Course

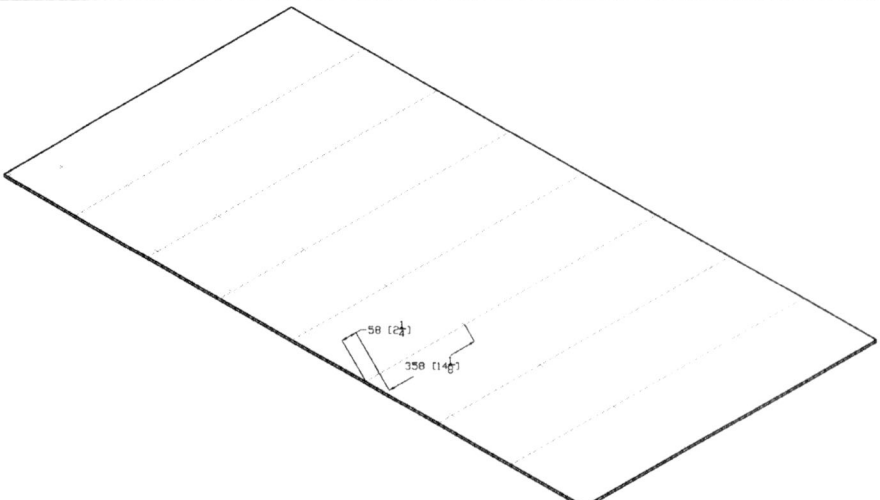

With the dimensions set out on the plywood sheet, it is time to make the curvature of the panel. This can be done in different ways. One way is to hold the lumber fillet in place with some weights. Another method is to hammer in some small nails [1"-5/4"] at the cross points. This method is used by professional boat builders and is recommended.

Simply start hammering in nails at every cross point you have marked on the plywood sheet.

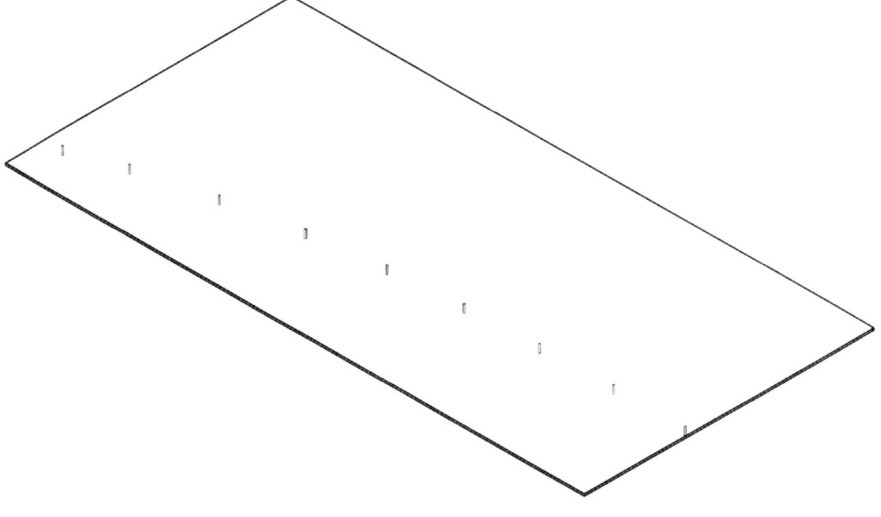

 **Boat Building Master Course**

Now fit the lumber fillet to the nails, making sure the fillet touches every nail, and hold the fillet in place with nails or weights on the outside.

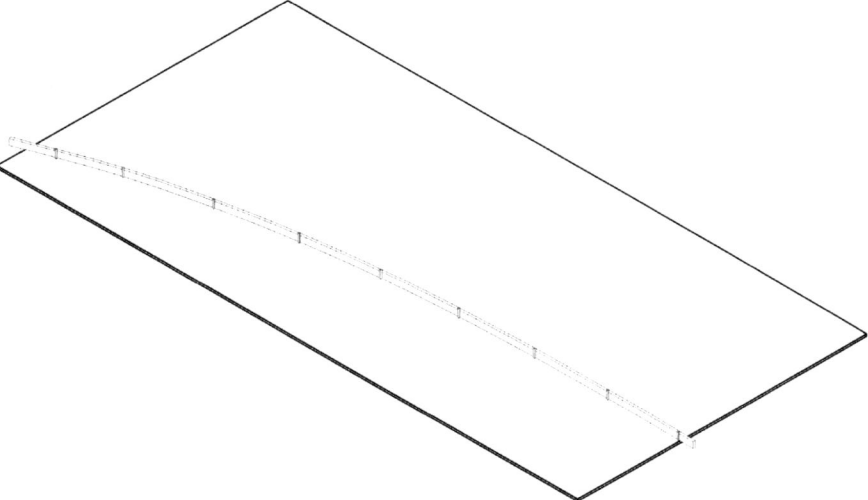

Before drawing up the curvature make sure the curve is fair. Pay special attention to the ends of the lumber fillet, since the free ends will have a tendency to sweep back, thus making the curvature wrong at the panel ends.

Continue using the same procedure lofting the other side of the panel. After making both curves you will have a plywood sheet looking like this.

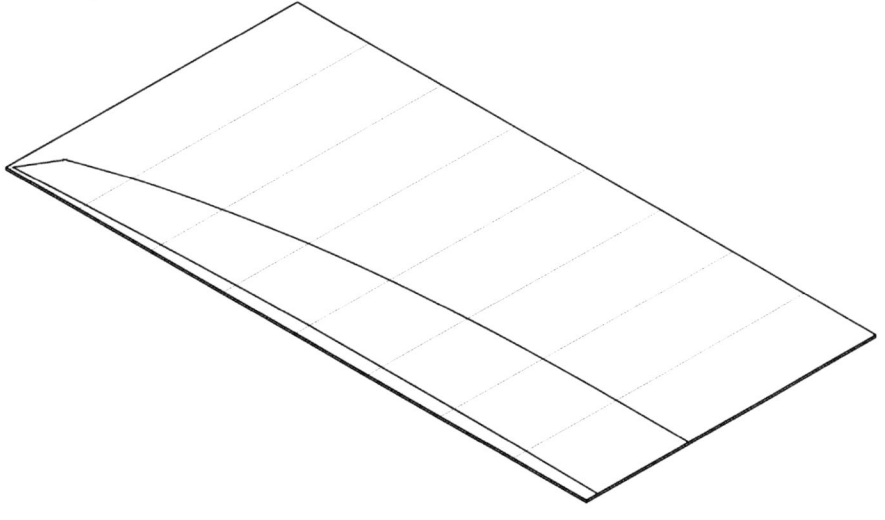

You can now cut out the panel using a circular saw or a saber saw. To minimize splintering, use a saw blade with a high tooth-per-inch count.

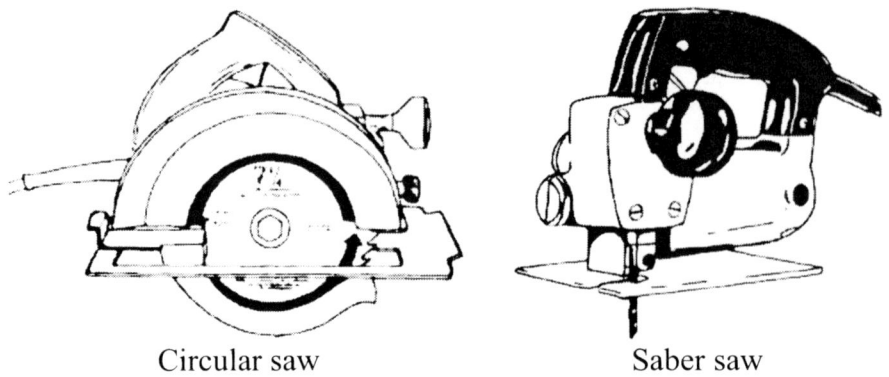

Circular saw   Saber saw

3.4 Lofting symmetric elements

Lofting symmetric elements are in many ways easier than lofting panels.

For a start let's look at a part of a drawing showing the nesting. This part is not necessarily from the plans in this book, but consider it an example.

Here you can see plate 5. It shows that from that particular sheet of plywood you will cut several elements, and the one we will use in this example is 10003-10. The number referees to the detailed plan with the same number.

Boat Building Master Course

Plate 5 F

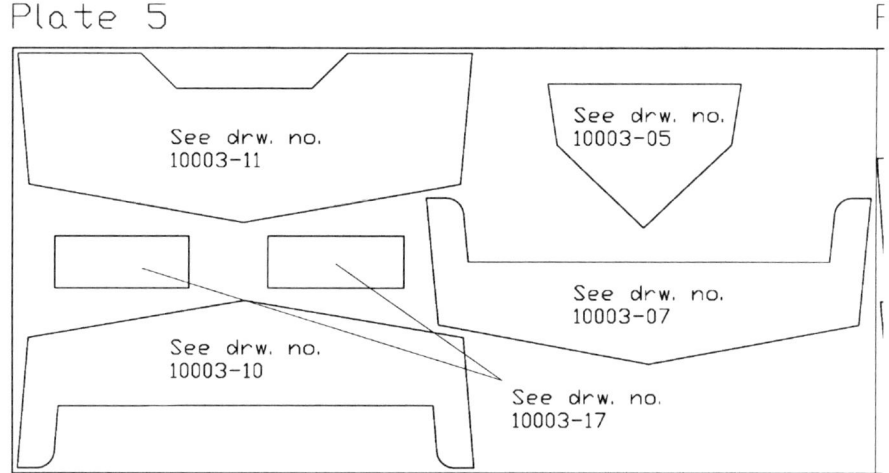

We will then continue finding the plan for 10003-10. A part of that plan is shown below.

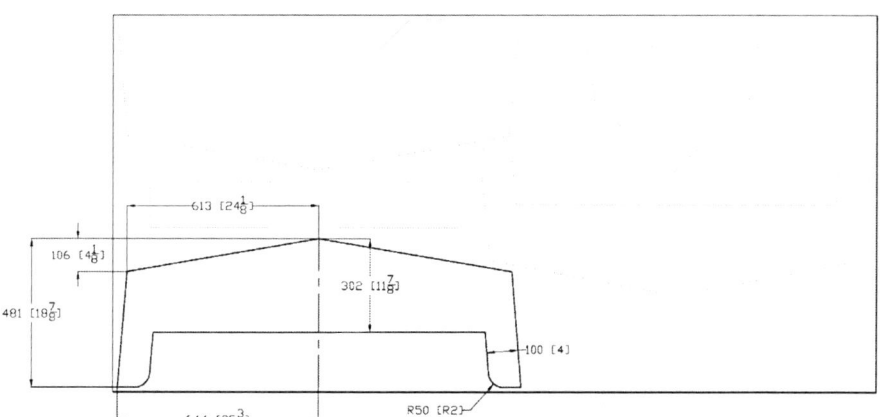

As you can see the element is a frame. Another thing to notice is that the element only has dimensions set out from the centerline (—— - ——). The centerline is therefore also the symmetry line.

Start by drawing the centerline on the plywood. Use a steel carpenter square.

 **Boat Building Master Course**

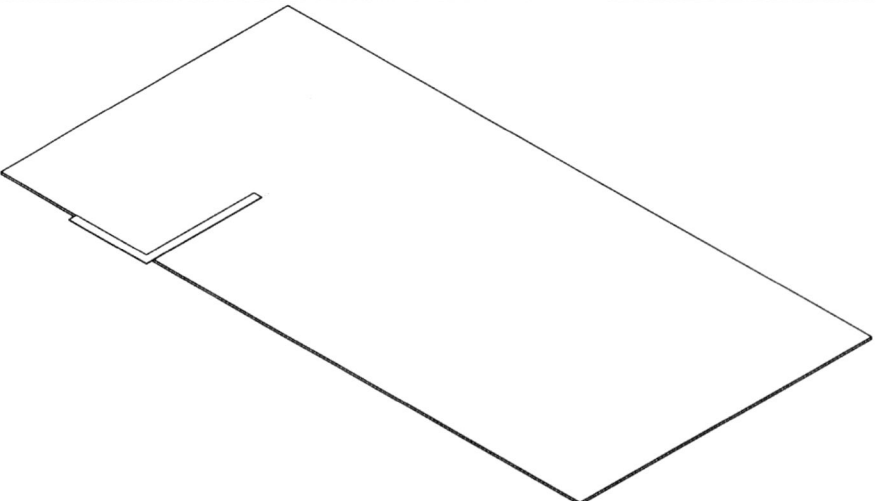

Then from the plan you can see that three dimensions are first needed for setting out the horizontal distances: 106 [4-1/8], 302 [11-7/8] and 481 [18-7/8]. Mark these dimensions on the centerline, giving you a plywood sheet looking similar to this.

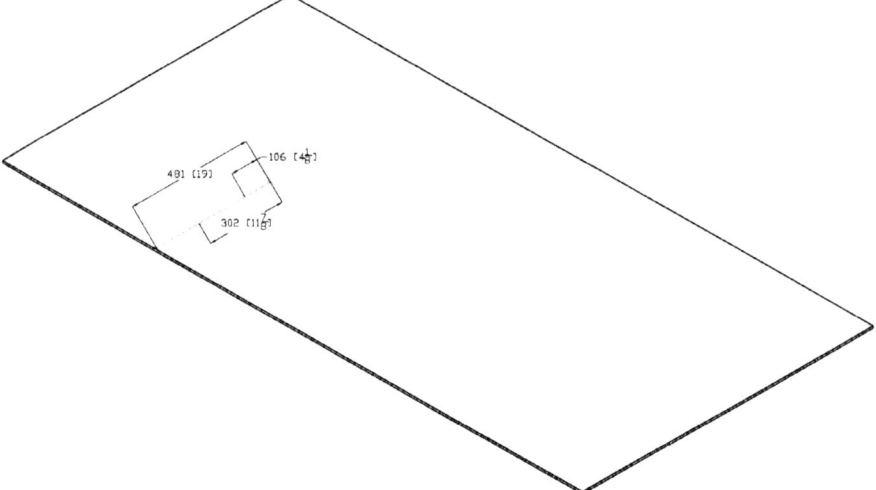

Now it is time to set out the horizontal distances. Once again, it is easiest to use the steel carpenter square. Your plywood sheet will then look like this.

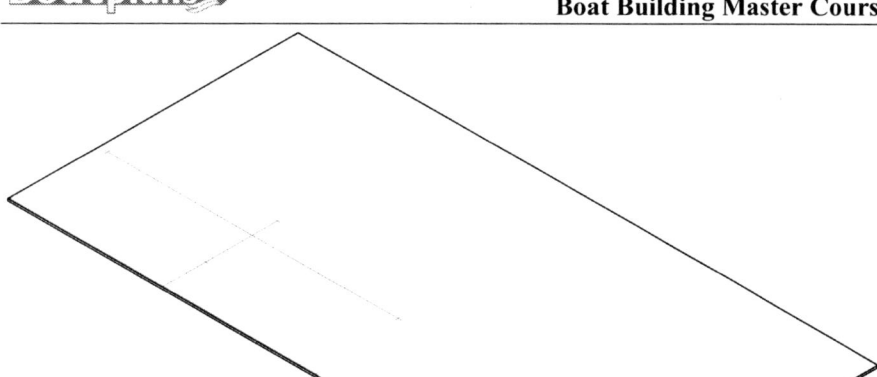

After setting out the horizontal distances it is possible to draw the outline of the element. Simply connect the points you have marked with straight lines. Your element will then look similar to this.

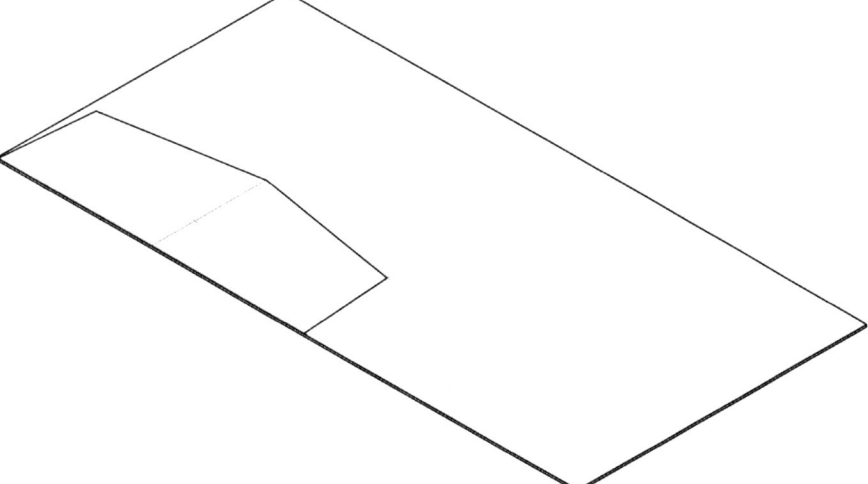

Now you can draw the inside of the element. From the plan you can see that the vertical sideline has to be displaced parallel 100 mm [4"]. So set the distance perpendicular to the sideline. Now use the last center mark to draw the horizontal line. After you have drawn the lines you will have a plywood sheet looking like this.

Boat Building Master Course

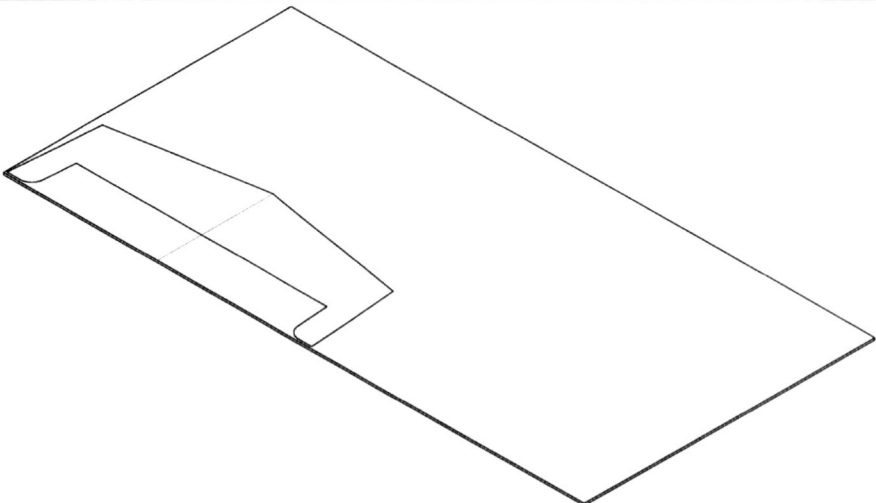

You might have noticed the R50 [2] fillets at the inside corners. The easiest way to construct them is by finding a saucer, paint can or another round item with approximately the same radius. It is not important that the radius is exactly the same.

You can now cut out the panel using a handsaw or a saber saw. To minimize splintering, use a saw blade with a high tooth-per-inch count.

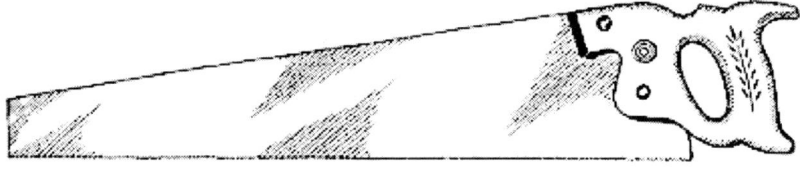

Handsaw

3.5 How to construct perpendicular lines

It is often necessary to construct perpendicular lines when building boats, and it is not always possible to have a square to use. You may not have one, or the one you have may be too small to use. You will need a way to construct two lines that you know for sure are perpendicular to each other.

The method is very simple, yet powerful and handy whenever you need to make perpendicular lines. You can also use this method to construct your own square from some pieces of plywood leftover.

We didn't invent the method. A Greek guy named Pythagoras did that some 2500 years ago ☺

So what do you do? First you make a straight line for instance 300 mm or 12" long. There are certain lengths that can be used, depending on the size of the perpendicular lines needed. We will come back to that later.

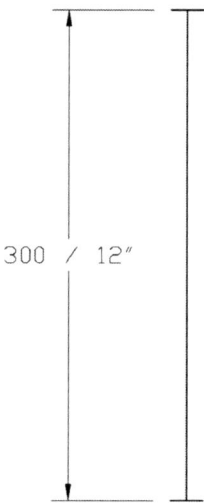

Then you take your measuring tape and make a mark approximately perpendicular to the first line. Make the mark at a distance of 400 mm or 16" from the first line. You will then have something similar to the figure below.

Boat Building Master Course

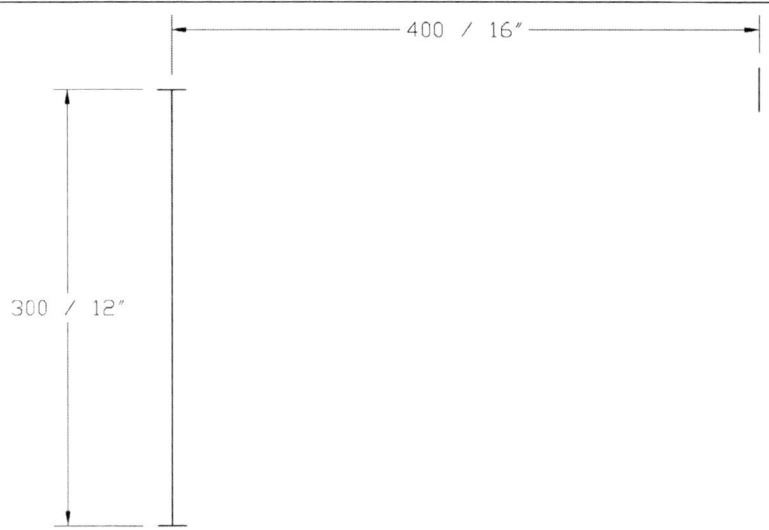

Now from the other end of the first line you set out 500 mm or 20" in the direction of the mark you made from the first end of the first line. You mark the distance where it crosses the first mark. Then you will have a figure looking like the one below.

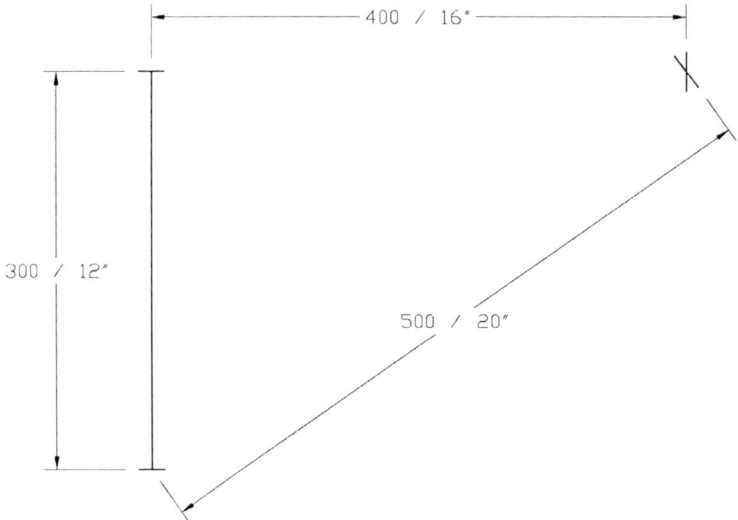

As you can see you have a cross to the right side of the first line. If you now connect the end of the first line with this cross point you will have two lines that are perfectly perpendicular to each other.

 **Boat Building Master Course**

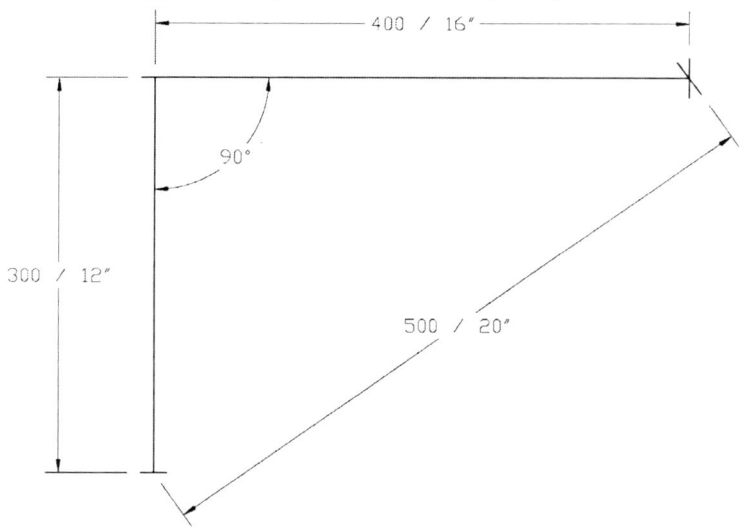

In principle, all numbers can be used for making the triangle, but some are more suitable than others, due to the fact that they are easier to remember and measure. Below you will find a table showing a set of numbers that is easy to remember. Different set of numbers can be used depending on the size of perpendicular lines you need to construct.

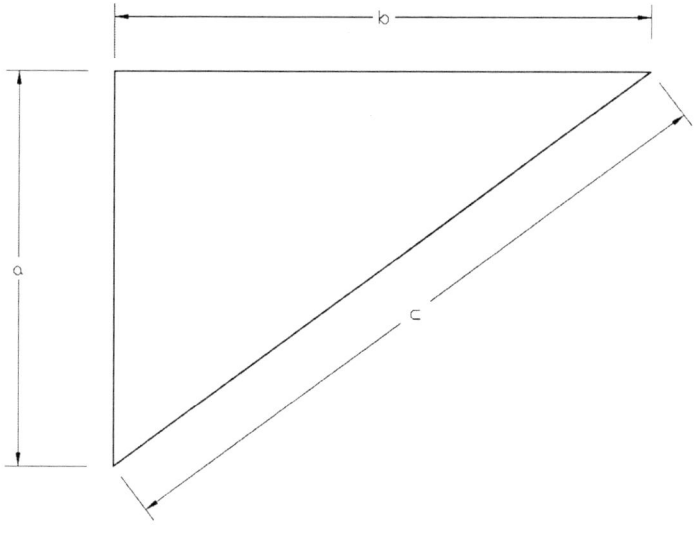

a (metric)	b (metric)	c (metric)	a (U.S.)	b (U.S.)	c (U.S.)
150 mm	200 mm	250 mm	6"	8"	10"
300 mm	400 mm	500 mm	12"	16"	20"
600 mm	800 mm	1000 mm	24"	32"	40"
900 mm	1200 mm	1500 mm	36"	48"	60"

4 Assembly Manual

After lofting and cutting the different panels needed to build your new boat, it is time to start assembling the hull.

There are many processes involved in assembling the hull and this section will describe the different steps.

Many panels are in more than one part. Side panels and bottom panels are long panels. Since the plywood sheet is only 2440 mm [96"] long, it is necessary to join the panels before the assembly of the hull can start.

4.1 Preparing the parts

After you have cut the parts it will be necessary to do some fairing of the edges. It is important that you sand or plane the edges so they are fair and smooth.

If you have more than one piece of each element it is advisable to stack the parts and sand or plane the edges simultaneously. By doing so you will ensure that the parts for both sides are the same size. This is the basis for a symmetric hull afterwards.

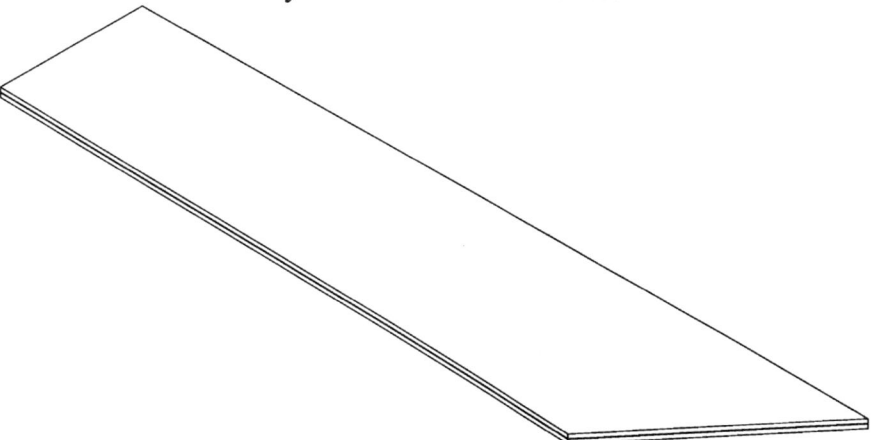

You can hold the elements together while sanding or planing by using some clamps, or you can apply some screws through all parts. If you choose the last option you will have to fill the holes with epoxy afterwards.

 **Boat Building Master Course**

4.2 Assembling the panels

In this section we will start looking at a panel in two parts. The panel might not be identical to the panels from the set of plans in this book, but consider it an example.

The first thing to do is align the panel pieces. You will get the best result if you have a flat and solid surface for that purpose. A concrete garage or workshop floor is fine for aligning the parts.

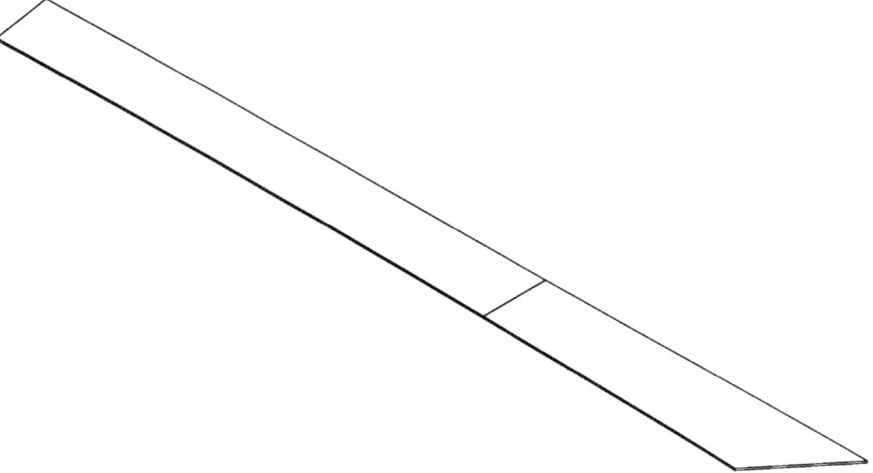

Remember to place some plastic underneath the seam so your panel doesn't get laminated to the floor.

Measure and cut a fiberglass patch that is a total of 200 mm [8"]. The patch will be centered over the panel seam. You may wish to cut the patch a little larger to allow for the woven fiberglass strands to unravel on the edges.

Apply resin to the splice area and place the fiberglass patch. Flatten out the fiberglass patch and allow 1-2 minutes for the fiberglass to soak up the resin. Apply additional resin where the fiberglass did not completely wet out. Remove all air bubbles and excess resin from the seam. Allow curing.

Boat Building Master Course

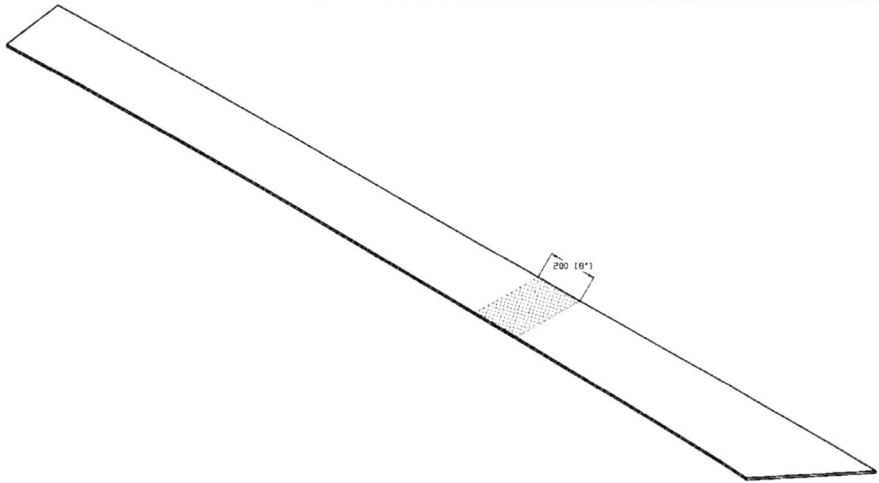

After the epoxy is cured, carefully turn over the panel and continue the process on the other side. Before applying epoxy and glass check the seam to ensure there are no voids in the seam. If there is, apply some thickened epoxy to fill the voids.

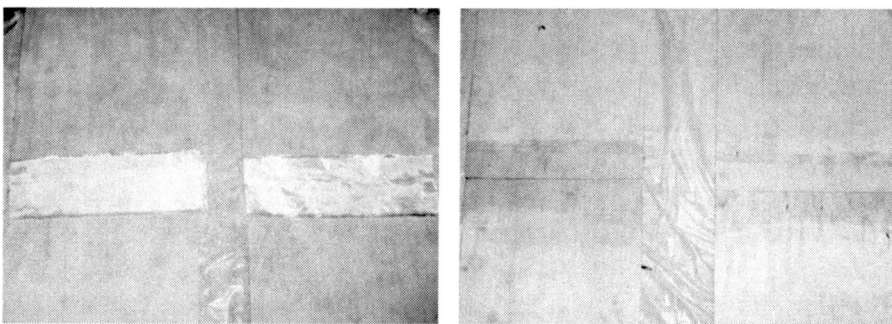

Now the panels are joined and the epoxy it dry. Sand the edges to remove any exceeding fiberglass, and sand the surface to make it smooth and fair.

4.3 Building jig

The easiest way to assemble the hull is to make a building jig. With a building jig you will have total control of the assembly and it will ensure that your frame spacing is accurate and your hull will be symmetric.

Some of our plans contain a plan for a building jig. But this section will describe how to build one for the assembly of the hull.

Boat Building Master Course

In the set of plans you will have a drawing number 10004-1. This is the main drawing for setting up the frames with the right distances. The drawing will look like the one below. Your drawing might not look exactly like this, but consider this an example.

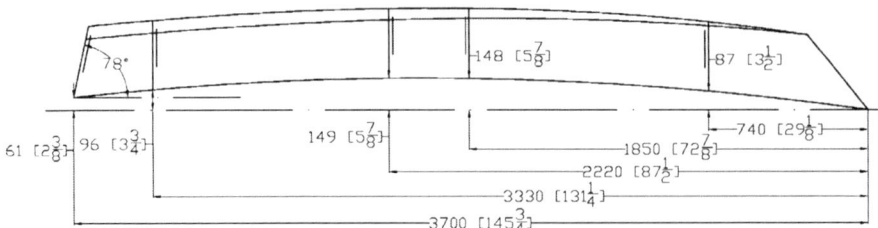

One thing to notice is the material offset of the frames. It is marked with a vertical line. For the two foremost frames the material has to be offset aft wards, and for the two next frames and the transom the material has to be offset forward.

Another thing to notice is the vertical offset of the frames. Here the dimensions are set out from a baseline, but it is recommended to offset the jig so the hull will have an appropriate working height. For instance, if you consider a working height of some +500 mm [+20"] to be appropriate for your workshop you simply add this distance to the vertical dimensions stated on the plan.

The first thing to do when building the jig is making the strongback. The strongback is made from some straight lumber. The dimension can be 100 mm x 50 mm [4" x 2"]. Other dimensions can also be used, but it is not advisable to use smaller dimensions. So if the lumberyard has a good deal on some other dimensions use that.

To start with, determine the dimensions of the strongback. If your plans don't contain plans for the building jig simply take the length from drawing 10004-1. In the example above the length should be approximately 3300 mm [131-1/4"]. The width can be determined by using the width to the chine from the smallest frame. In this example the width of the strongback will be 504 mm [20"] (2 x 252 mm [10"]).

Boat Building Master Course

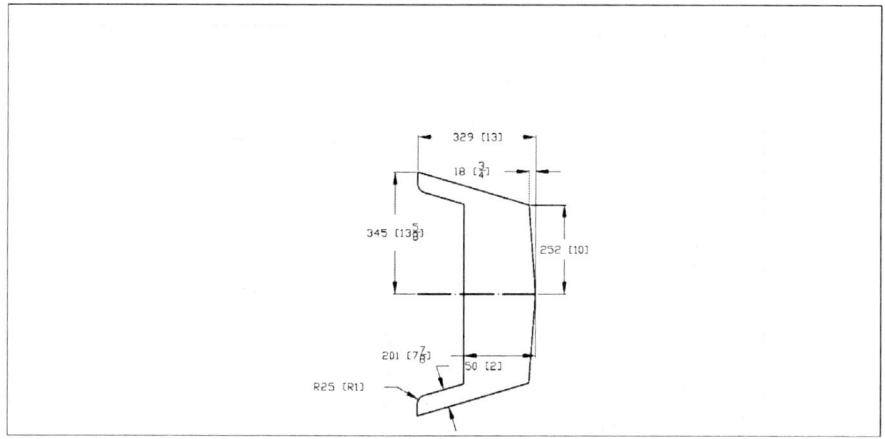

The strongback consist of a frame of lumber. Cut out the four pieces in the length determined before and assemble the frame. Remember to subtract two times the material thickness for the short pieces. This will ensure that the jig gets the right width after assembly. Use some long screws to assemble the frame.

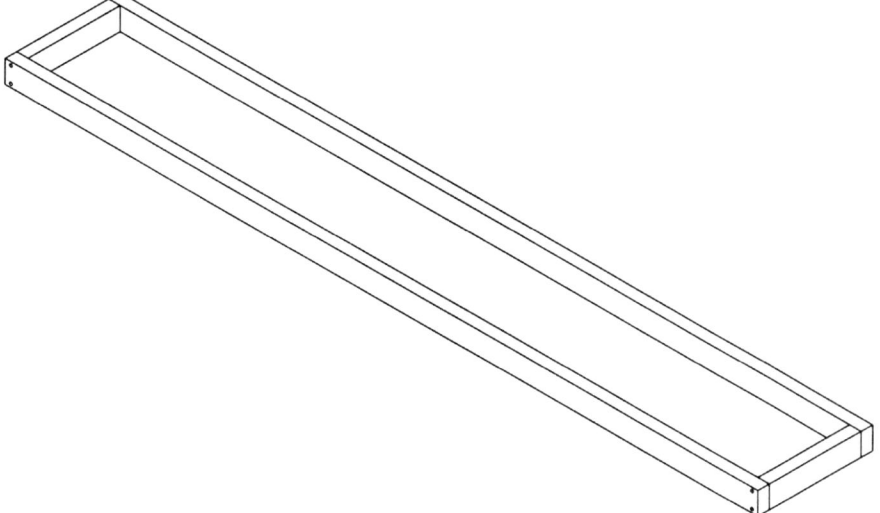

It is also possible to assemble the strongback with some nail brackets. Using nail brackets will make it easier to get the strongback square. It is important to make sure the strongback is leveled out. After the assembly, place the strongback at the right

 **Boat Building Master Course**

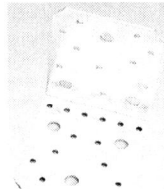

position on your shop floor and adjust the height so it is level and doesn't rock. Use some patches in different thicknesses to place under the strongback.

After the strongback is assembled and leveled out it is time to set up the frame supports. The frame supports have to be placed in accordance with drawing 10004-1. Remember to take the material side for the frames into consideration when positioning the supports.

The supports can be made from lumber 57 mm x 38 mm [2 ¼" x 1 ½"]. Other dimensions can also be used, but it is not recommended to use smaller dimensions. Cut the pieces in the length determined before, so the building height will be adequate. The support can be fastened to the strongback with screws.

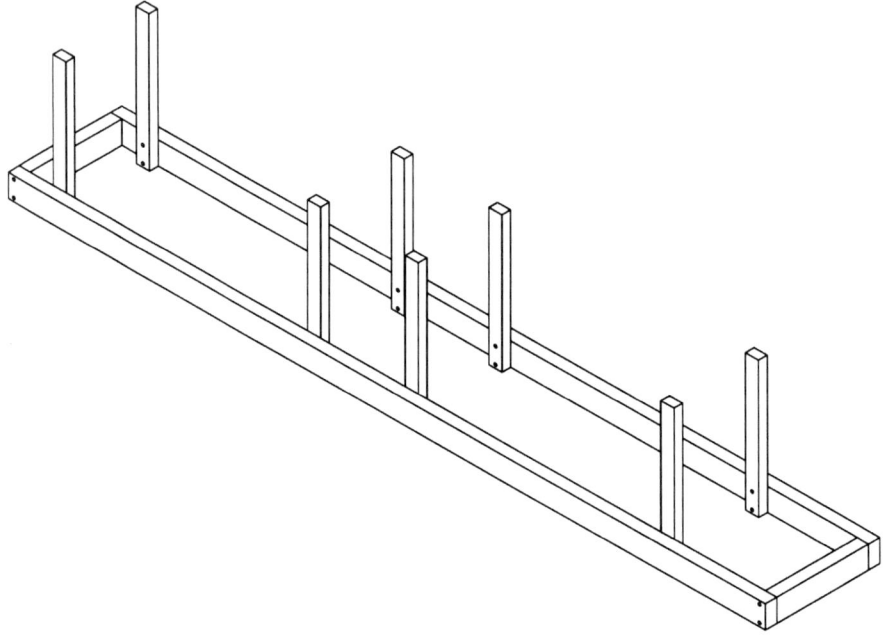

It is not always necessary to make a building jig. Lots of our designs are built without one, and with good results too. We do however recommend using a jig since it will make the assembly easier and more controllable.

4.4 Assembling the frames

Now the building jig is finished and you can assemble the frames with the jig. Before you assemble the frames it is important that they are faired and that the edges are smooth.

The easiest way to make sure the frames are aligned and vertical is to first mark the center on the building jig. Hammer in two nails, one on each end, and draw a thin line between the nails.

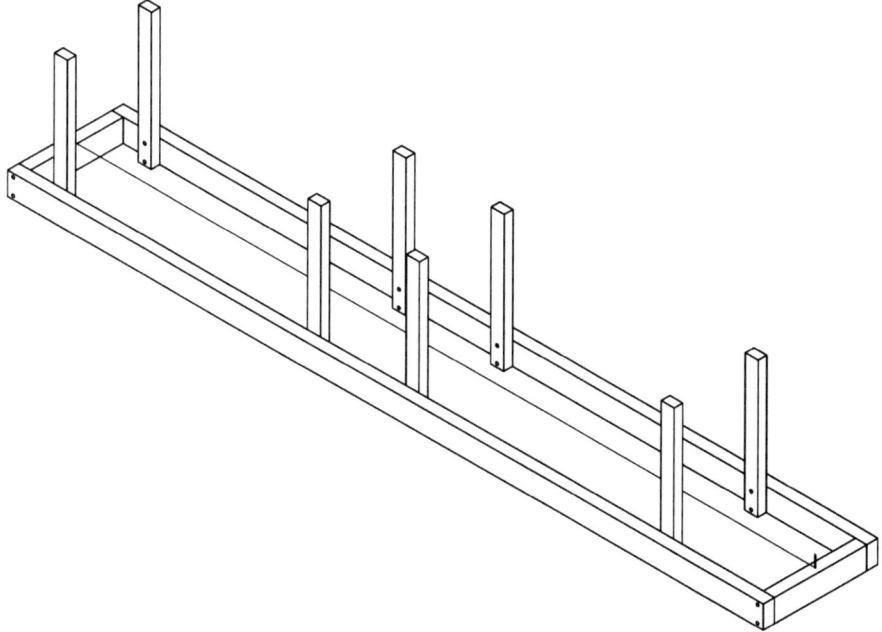

You can now mark the position for the frames on the vertical supports. Fasten the frames one at a time in the approximate position. Check and adjust the position with a plumb line to make sure the frames are exact, in case the jig is not precise. It is also possible to use a builder's level to adjust the frames, but it might be more difficult to do it that way.

Boat Building Master Course

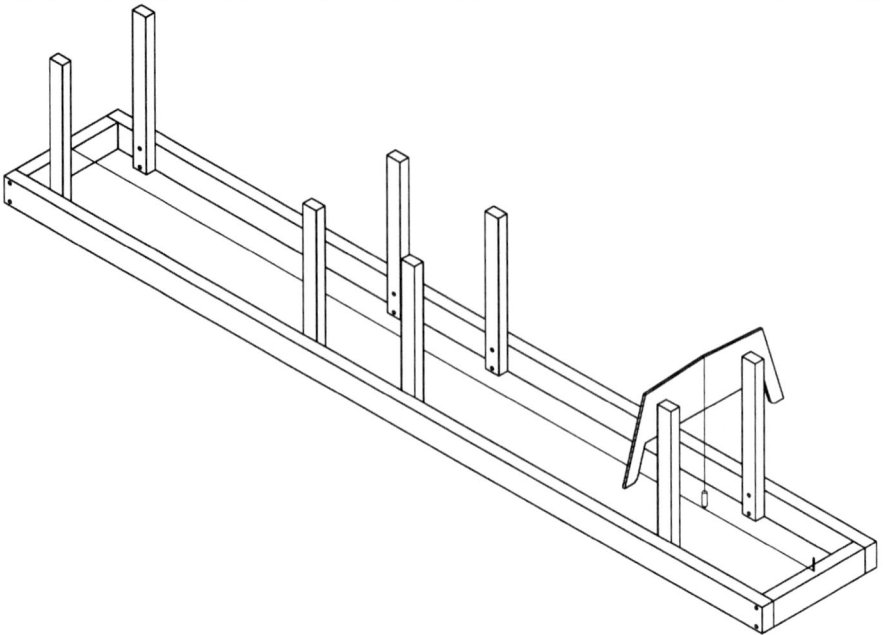

The frames can be fastened with screws. After assembling all the frames you will have a good foundation for the remaining work with the hull.

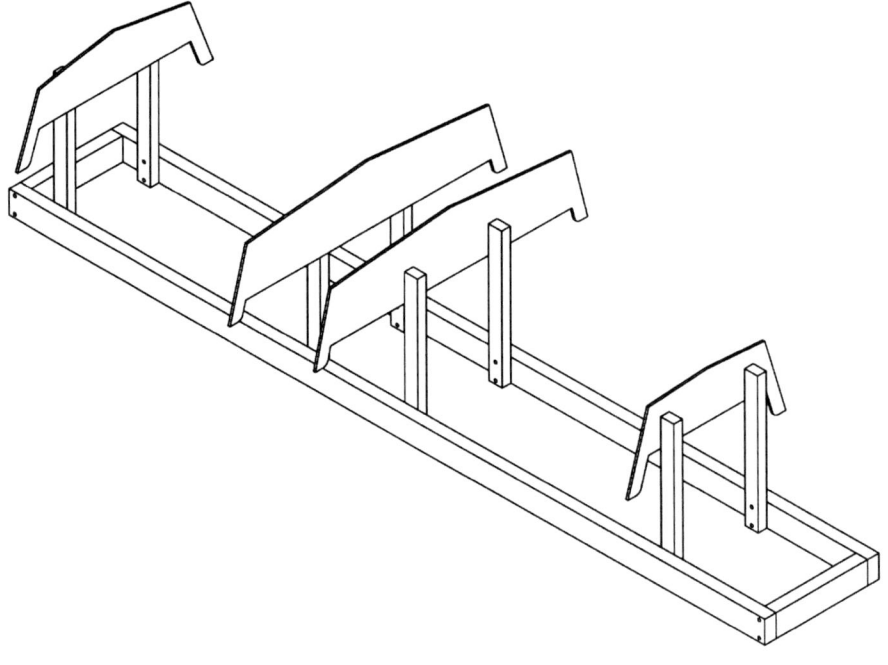

Boat Building Master Course

If the frames are very slender it might be necessary to add some temporary supports. Use some lumber board in adequate dimensions.

4.5 Assembling the panels

Now that the building jig and frames are assembled it is time to assemble the panels. Start with the first bottom panel. Position the panel, if the panels and frames are cut precise it should be easy to get the right longitudinal position for the panel. Temporarily fasten the panel to the frames with some small nails or screws.

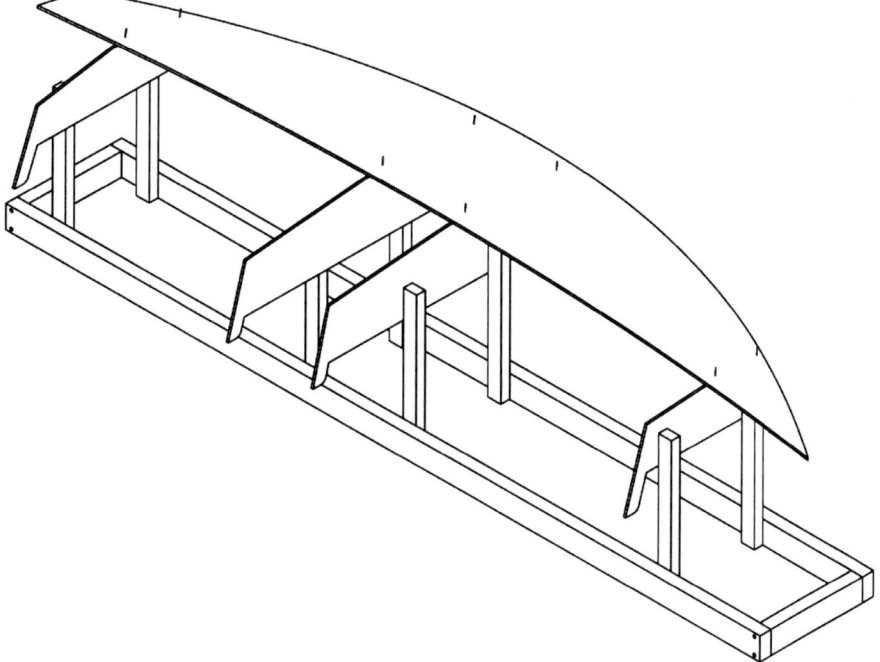

The building instruction for your design might specify a different sequence for the assembly of the panels. If it does, follow that sequence stated in the building instruction.

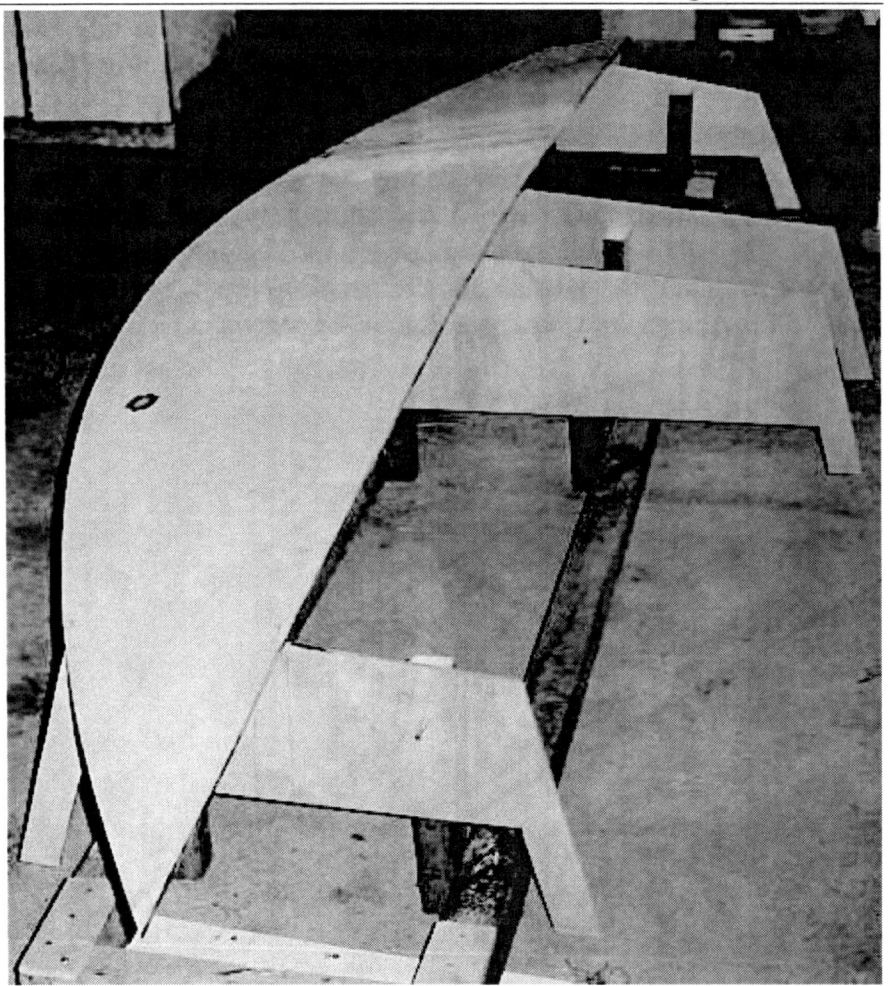

After assembling the first bottom panel continue to the second bottom panel. It is always important to assembly the different panels in a sequence such as the first panel on one side then the mirrored part on the other side. This will ensure the hull isn't asymmetric. Fasten the second bottom panel with small nails or screws.

Boat Building Master Course

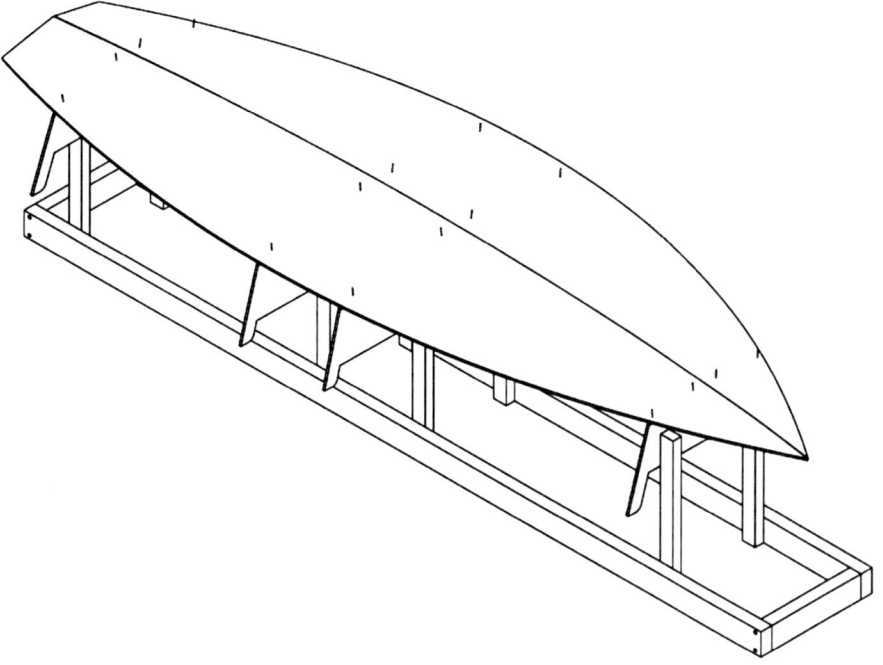

Now that you have the two bottom panels assembled it is time to do some stitching.

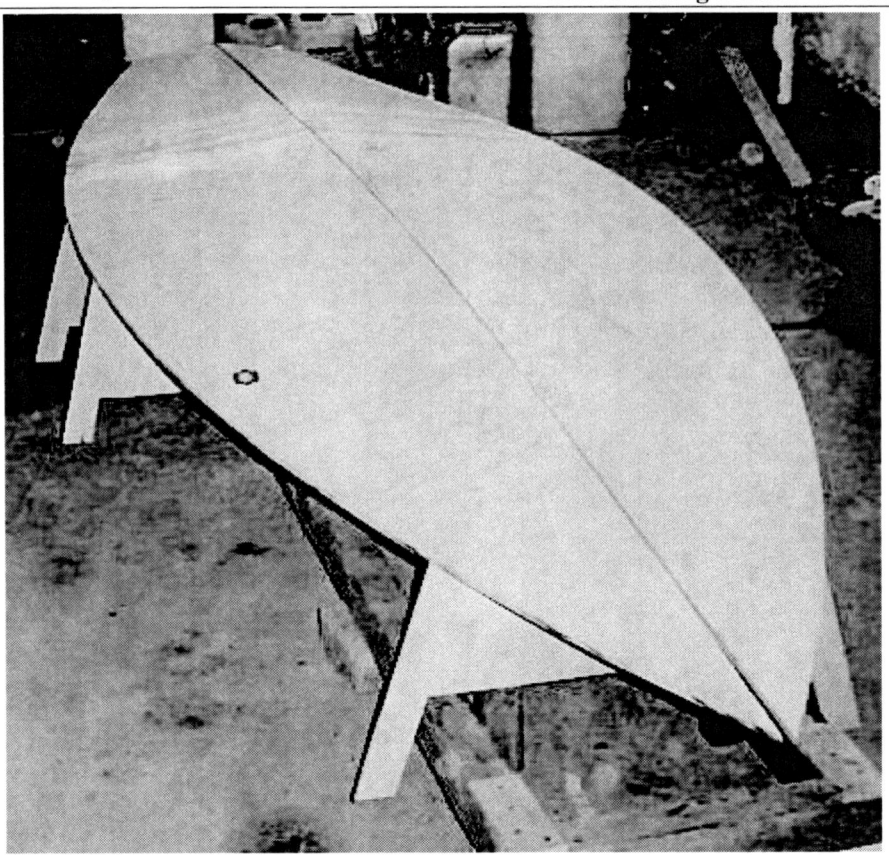

Drill some small holes near the center edge and stitch some cable ties or metal wire, then tighten them up. It is not always necessary to stitch the seam all the way. Depending on the curvature of the panels, stitching can be omitted where needed.

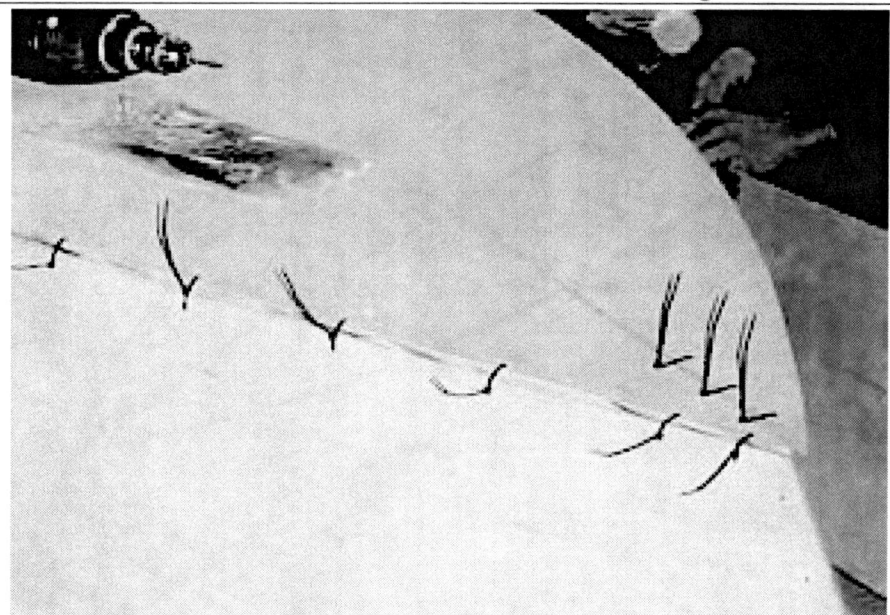

The next thing to do is assemble the side panels. Start with the side panel on one side and continue with the other side afterwards. Temporarily fix the side panels to the frame with small nails or screws.

 **Boat Building Master Course**

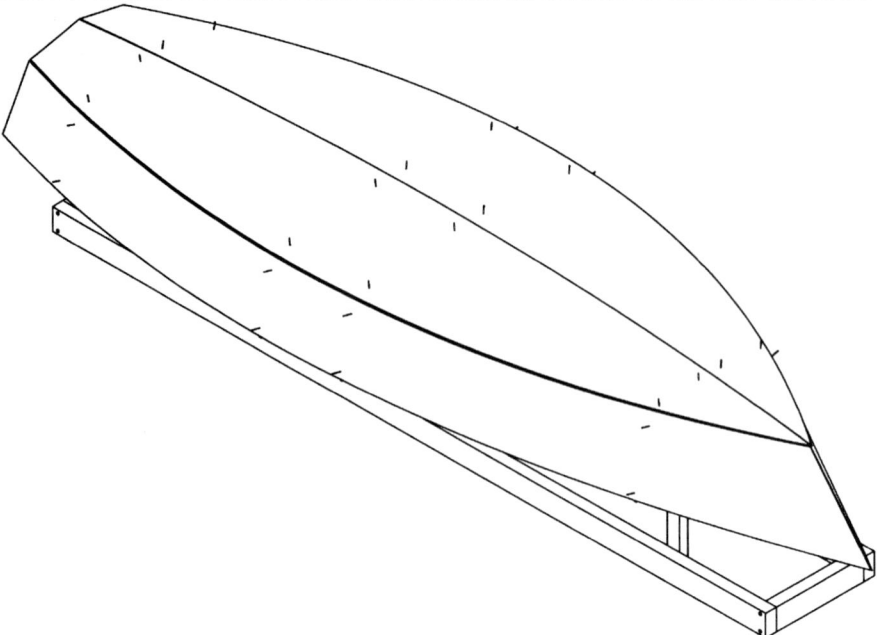

While assembling the side panels, stitch along the seam with cable ties or metal wire. You will get the best result if you do not tighten the stitches too much from the start. By not tightening the stitches too much, you will still have a chance to make small adjustments later on.

Once both side panels are assembled check the hull to make sure it is symmetric and not twisted. If the hull is fine tighten up the stitches.

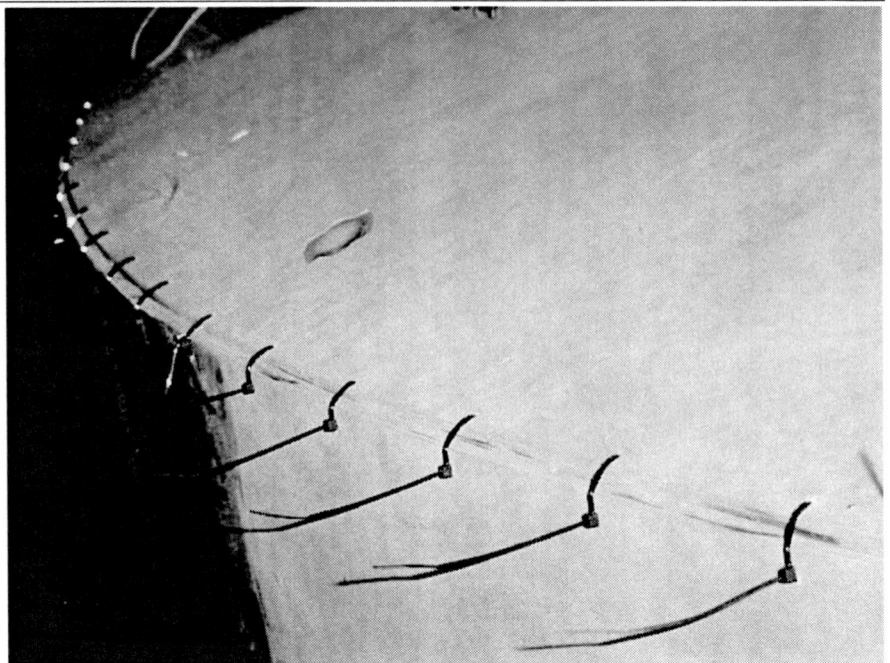

You may experience problems with the cable ties or metal wires if the panels have a large curvature. The cable ties or metal wires may break when forcing the panels in place. If that happens you can use some Ø2 mm [Ø1/12"] polyamide rope instead. The rope holds much better.

4.6 Assembling the transom

After stitching the sides and bottom it is time to assemble the transom. You should notice that the panels in most cases have some excess length. To assemble the transom simply offset and incline the transom until it fits between the sides and bottom. Fasten the transom with small screws, and remember to countersink, so it will be possible to fill on top later.

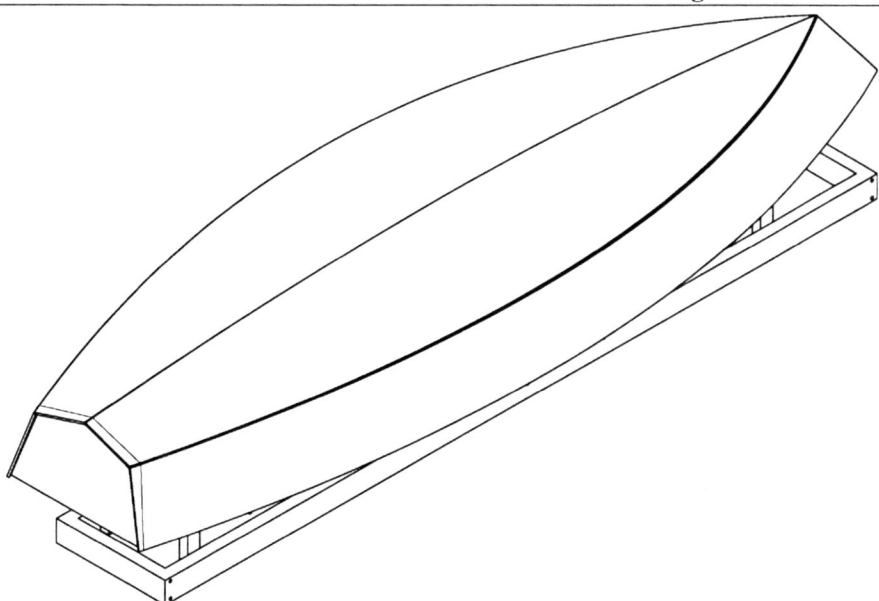

Make sure the transom is sufficiently fastened, but later on it will be secured with epoxy and glass tape.

Trim the side and bottom panels with a handsaw. It might be necessary to mark up the position of the transom on the outside of the side and bottom panels.

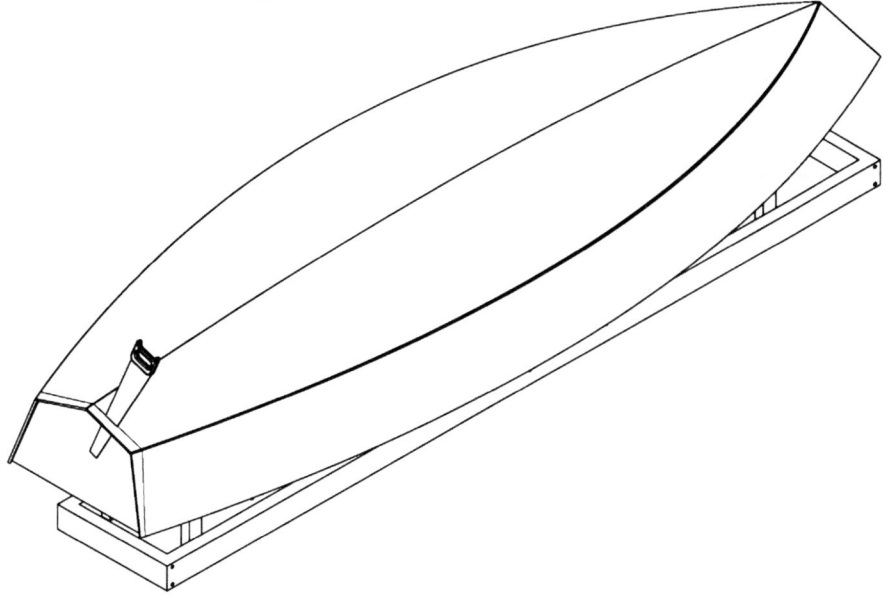

If your boat has a transom in both the fore and aft end, repeat the steps above to assemble both transoms.

4.7 Gluing the seams

Before the hull is turned upright it is recommended you finish the seams on the outside. For further details on gluing the seams see the section describing the laminating.

Start with gluing the seams between the stitches. Fill up the seams so you are sure there is enough material to make the fillet after the epoxy is dry.

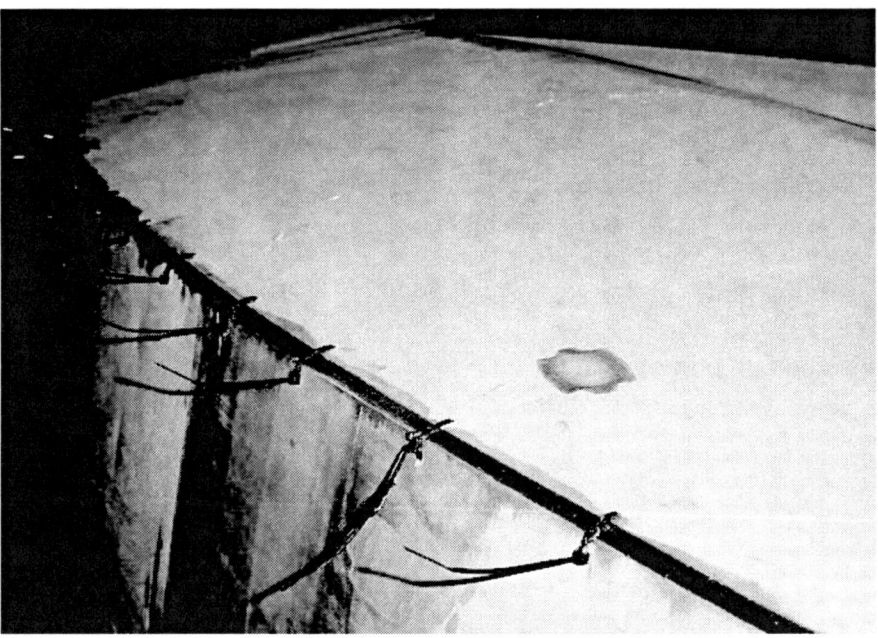

When the epoxy is dry remove the stitches and fill the seams where the stitches have been. Remember to fill the drilled holes in the plywood as well.

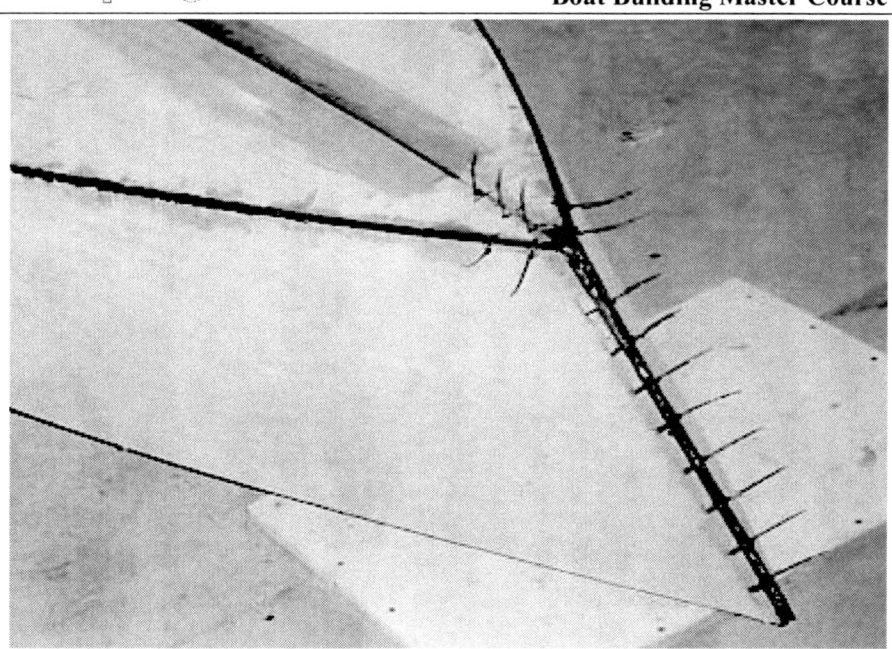

After the glue is dry, sand the seams and make sure the seams get a nice round curvature. Now apply the fiberglass tape and epoxy to finish the seams on the outside.

Your hull is now sufficiently stable to remove from the building jig and turn upright. In some cases it might be easier to completely finish the outside before turning the hull upright. If you wish to finish the outside first, fair and grind the hull as described in the laminating manual.

Once turned over, all the seams inside of the hull need to be glued. For making the fillets at the inside seams and at the frame, use the technique described in the laminating manual.

Finish the seams with fiberglass tape and epoxy before continuing to assemble the rest of the inside.

4.8 Assembling the inside

It is now time to assemble the rest of the inside construction. Depending on the design you are building, several things still need to be done. In this example we will continue assembling the thwarts.

The thwarts can have different arrangements, but mostly it is a question of a thwart in the bow, in the stern and one or more thwarts in between. Before assembling the thwarts there is some preparation that is recommended. After cutting and fairing the elements, some adjustment might be necessary.

The easiest way to install the thwarts is by applying some supports underneath. Cut out some pieces of plywood approximately 25 mm x 150 mm [1" x 6"]. Glue the pieces to the hull where the horizontal position of the thwarts will be.

Boat Building Master Course

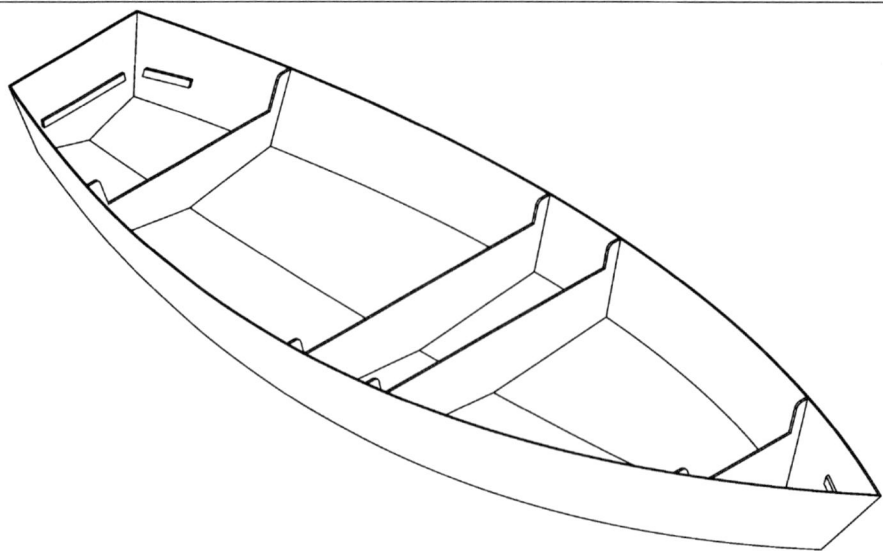

Before assembling the thwarts you will have to consider whether you will apply flotation material in the compartments underneath the thwarts. There are several materials that can be used; foam or expanded polystyrene are some of the widely used materials for flotation. Another possibility is to use some shipping peanuts. There are many places where the shipping peanuts are just thrown out, so it might be one of the cheapest possibilities.

It is, of course, also a possibility to use air for flotation. Just make sure your compartment is absolutely watertight and you will have world's cheapest and best flotation material.

Now adjust the plywood elements and assemble the thwarts. It is only possible to glue and glass the thwarts from the outside, which is fine as far as strength is concerned.

Some prefer to have the compartment underneath the thwarts for storage. This can also be achieved together with the flotation option by installing a watertight hatch in the frames.

 **Boat Building Master Course**

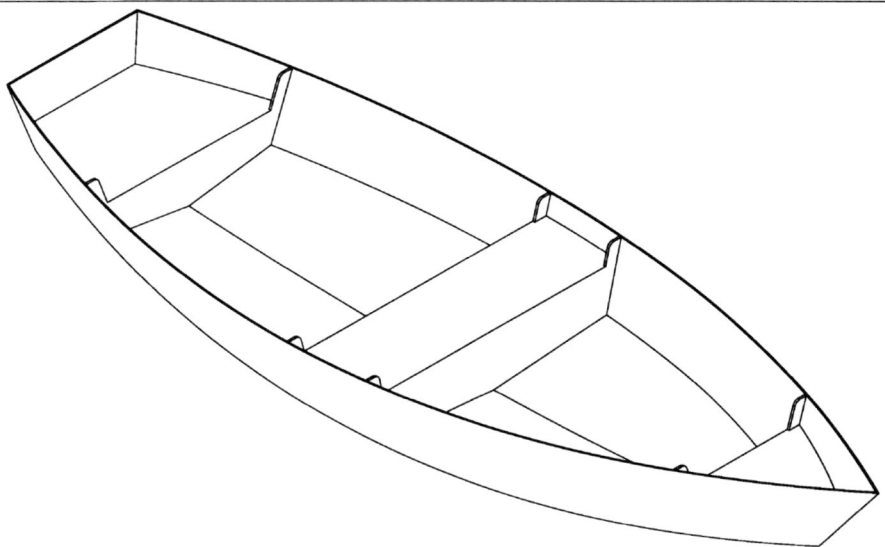

The only thing left to do is mount the rub rail. Your building instruction will contain the necessary information regarding the dimensions of the rub rail.

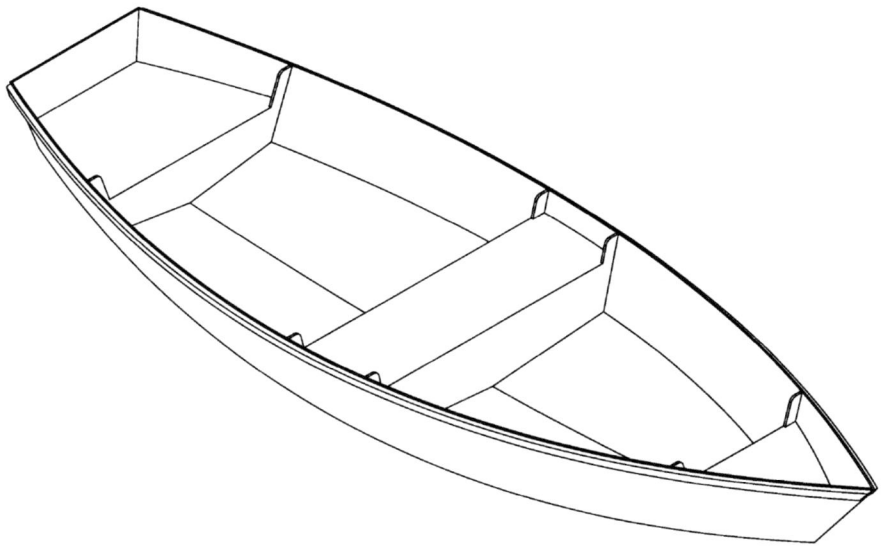

5 Laminating Manual

Epoxy resins are used and applied following one of four basic techniques. These are fiberglassing, filleting/fairing, gluing, and coating. Furthermore, the techniques are pretty much the same whether they involve new wooden boat construction, strip plank boat construction, stitch and glue boat construction or the repair of old boats. What might seem to be other techniques are usually just variations or combinations of the above.

This manual will describe the four basic techniques with basis in stitch and glue boat construction.

5.1 Composite theory

To fully appreciate the role and application of composite materials to a structure, an understanding is required of the component materials themselves and of the ways in which they can be processed. This guide looks at basic composite theory, properties of materials used, and then the various processing techniques commonly found for the conversion of materials into finished structures.

In its most basic form a composite material is one that is composed of at least two elements working together to produce material properties that are different than the properties of those elements on their own. In practice, most composites consist of a bulk material (the matrix), and a reinforcement of some kind, added primarily to increase the strength and stiffness of the matrix. This reinforcement is usually in fiber form. Today, the most common man-made composites can be divided into three main groups:
Polymer Matrix Composites (PMC's) – These are the most common and will be discussed here. Also known as FRP - Fiber Reinforced Polymers (or Plastics) - these materials use a polymer-based resin as the matrix, and a variety of fibers such as glass, carbon and aramid as the reinforcement.
Metal Matrix Composites (MMC's) - Increasingly found in the automotive industry, these materials use a metal such as aluminum as the matrix, and reinforce it with fibers such as silicon carbide.
Ceramic Matrix Composites (CMC's) - Used in very high temperature environments, these materials use a ceramic as the

matrix and reinforce it with short fibers, or whiskers such as those made from silicon carbide and boron nitride.

Resin systems such as epoxies and polyesters have limited use for the manufacture of structures on their own, since their mechanical properties are not very high when compared to most metals. However, they have desirable properties, most notably their ability to be easily formed into complex shapes.

Materials such as glass, aramid and boron have extremely high tensile and compressive strength, but in 'solid form' these properties are not readily apparent. This is due to the fact that when stressed, random surface flaws will cause each material to crack and fail well below its theoretical 'breaking point'. To overcome this problem, the material is produced in fiber form, so that, although the same number of random flaws will occur, they will be restricted to a small number of fibers with the remainder exhibiting the material's theoretical strength. Therefore, a bundle of fibers will reflect more accurately the optimum performance of the material. However, fibers alone can only exhibit tensile properties along the fiber's length, in the same way as fibers in a rope.

It is when the resin systems are combined with reinforcing fibers such as glass, carbon and aramid that exceptional properties can be obtained. The resin matrix spreads the load applied to the composite between each of the individual fibers and also protects the fibers from damage caused by abrasion and impact. High strengths and stiffness, ease of molding complex shapes, high environmental resistance all coupled with low densities, make the resultant composite superior to metals for many applications.

Since PMC's combine a resin system and reinforcing fibers, the properties of the resulting composite material will combine something of the properties of the resin on its own with that of the fibers on their own.

Overall, the properties of the composite are determined by:
1. The properties of the fiber
2. The properties of the resin

3. The ratio of fiber to resin in the composite (Fiber Volume Fraction)
4. The geometry and orientation of the fibers in the composite

5.2 General fiberglassing

The first place you will meet the general fiberglassing is when you assemble the panels. They are in two or more parts and in order to join them it is recommended you use fiberglass joints. It is possible to use wooden butt joints for the assembly, but by using fiberglass joints you will get a better joint that is easier to work with later on.

One thing that is important to understand before starting to apply fiberglass and epoxy is that the quality of the matrix is determined by a number of factors.

First of all, it is important to manufacture a matrix with no air bubbles. A laminate with air bubbles will not be as strong as one without, and the risk of getting osmosis or failure in the laminate is high when not manufactured carefully. Normally when we build boats, we would like a boat that is durable for many years, and the one single factor most important for having a good and durable laminate, is manufacturing it without air bubbles.

Fiber content is another important factor. The higher the relative fiber content you can get in your laminate, the better. This is, of course, an ideal situation where you will only use the amount of resin that is absolutely necessary. Then you will have the best laminate with the lowest weight possible.

It is very difficult to obtain this situation when using fiberglass and epoxy without being trained. But don't despair, laminate properties will be determined by the absolute content of fibers. This means that if you follow the building instruction and the fiber weights specified, your boat will be strong enough. You might, if not trained, use more resin than necessary, but that will not decrease your boat's strength. The only consequence is that your boat will be a few kilos/pounds heavier than absolutely necessary.

The first thing to do before starting the laminating is to determine which method you will use. As described in the Epoxy manual, you can use the dry or wet method. When building composite boats where wood is involved, the wet method is always recommended.

There are two reasons for using the wet method. The main reason is that because wood is a porous material and will soak up resin, you have the possibility that your fiberglass is not wetted out properly. You will get some dry spots in your laminate because the resin will soak into the wood. By priming the wood with resin before applying the fiberglass you will avoid this problem.

Another reason is that usually when laminating, the surface you work on is not horizontal. Therefore, it will be easier to position the fiberglass tape when the wood is primed with epoxy and the area in use is still sticky.

General fiberglassing is basically performed in four steps:
1. Prime the wood with epoxy resin
2. Apply the fiberglass
3. Apply additional resin
4. Remove all air bubbles and exceeding resin

First you prime the wood. Mix an amount of resin that corresponds to the job you are doing and the gel time for your resin. It can, if you are not trained, be a bit difficult to estimate the exact amount needed, but it will become easier when you get used to working with the resin.

Use a normal paint roller for applying the resin. It is our experience that a paint roller maximum 100 mm [4"] wide is best for the job. Also choose a paint roller with a relatively small diameter, 25 mm [1"], and with short hair. Whether the shaft is long or short doesn't really matter. However, if you are building a large boat or if the boat has places that are difficult to access, a long shaft is preferred.

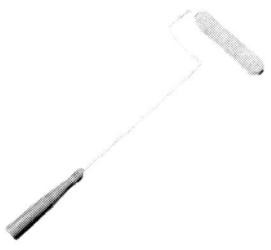

Remember to get some cheap rollers for the shaft since it is difficult to clean the rollers after the job is done. It is normally better and cheaper to throw away the roller afterwards. Solvent for cleaning the tools is not cheap, so it is more economical to throw away the roller.

A cheap paintbrush is also nice to have nearby. It can be used to make sure corners and other areas that are difficult to reach get coated with resin. The paintbrush is also excellent for removing excessive resin that might run out in corners and edges.

One thing that is important to remember when working with resin is that removing any unnecessary resin is always easier before the resin cures. You can clear up the resin before it cures with a putty knife, paintbrush or cloth. After the resin is cured, the only way to remove the excess resin is by grinding it away, and the amount of labor needed for that process is far greater than removing the resin before it cures.

After the wood is primed you can apply the fiberglass. It is recommended that you fit the fiberglass before you start laminating. That way, the only thing you have to do is lay the fiberglass in the right position on the plywood. By fitting the fiberglass before applying any resin you will ensure your cutting tools, scissors or knives, don't get covered with epoxy. Next, allow a minute or so for the fiberglass to soak up the resin.

Apply additional resin where the fiberglass did not completely wet out. Be careful not to apply more resin than necessary. Apply a little extra resin at a time and allow the fiberglass to soak it up.

When applying the extra resin use an air bleed roller or paddle roller to roll out any air in the laminate. Continue alternately applying resin where needed and rolling out air enclosure in the laminate.

When choosing the right air bleed roller or paddle roller it is important not to choose a roller that is too

wide. A roller width between 50 mm [2"] and 75 mm [3"] is recommended. A larger roller width will make it more difficult to access some parts of the hull, especially when working on the inside.

You can get air bleed rollers or paddle rollers in both aluminum and plastic. The plastic rollers are normally cheaper, but also more vulnerable to damage due to impacts. If the roller gets damaged you risk the chance that it will rub off the glass threads when used. If that happens you will have to discard the roller and get a new one. You can easily find replacement rollers for the shaft.

When you have mixed the resin and hardener in your mixing cup, you will find in some cases that it gels very fast. This is due to the amount of mass present in the cup. The more mass you have, the faster the exothermic reaction and the more heat it develops, thus speeding the process even more. A way to avoid that is by applying as much resin on the surface as fast as possible. If the mixed resin is spread in a thin layer, the chemical reaction is slowed down and it takes longer before it starts to gel. So with the mixed resin applied in a thin layer, there will be plenty of time to work with the laminate and get all the air bubbles out.

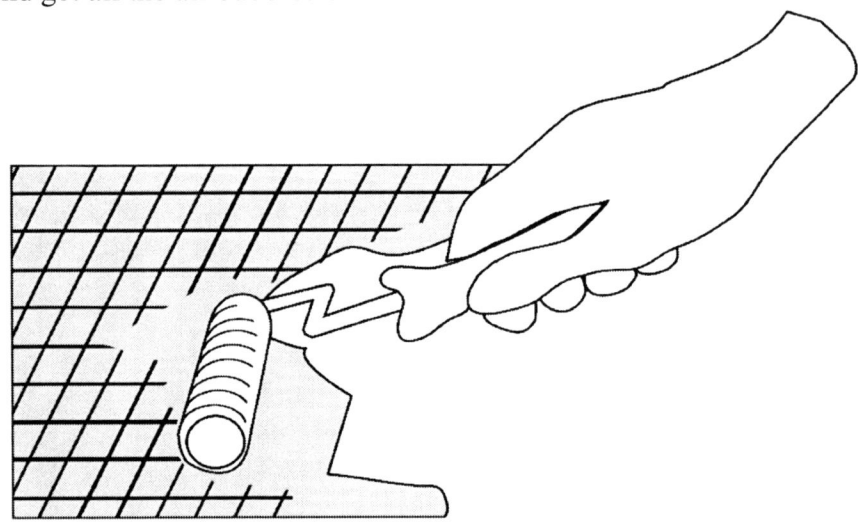

 Boat Building Master Course

5.3 Fillets at the chine

Before laminating fiberglass tape at the chine it is necessary to make rounding at the outside. It is not possible to apply fiberglass at a sharp corner, so in order to make a good durable laminate at the chine a rounding is necessary. A minimum radius of 4 mm [1/6"] is needed.

Start with mixing some thickened epoxy. Follow the guidelines described in the epoxy manual. Mix to a consistence somewhere between mayonnaise and peanut butter.

To thicken the epoxy it is possible to use wood flour. In a few of our plans Aerosil is specified due to the fact that a high quality bond is needed. Using Aerosil will create an excellent bond, but it also has the effect that the fillets get harder to fair after the epoxy is cured.

After mixing the epoxy with the filler, apply it to the gap between the panels with a putty knife. Try to get it as smooth as possible. It is much easier to shape before it cures than afterwards.

It is easiest to try and lay up the thickened epoxy as a quarter of an octagon. This way you will need less effort afterwards when you smooth the chine. The situation is illustrated below.

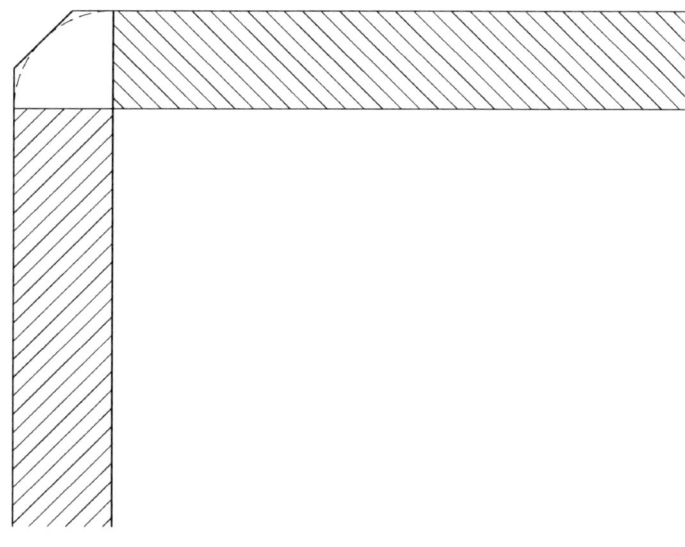

After the epoxy is cured you can smooth the chine. Use some medium grade abrasives (grade 60-80). It doesn't matter if there are grinding marks in the fillets after you finish. The epoxy and fiberglass tape will fill them in afterwards.

After the outside of the chine is filled and smooth, you will be ready to apply fiberglass tape to the outside. Follow the instructions in the section describing the taping of seams.

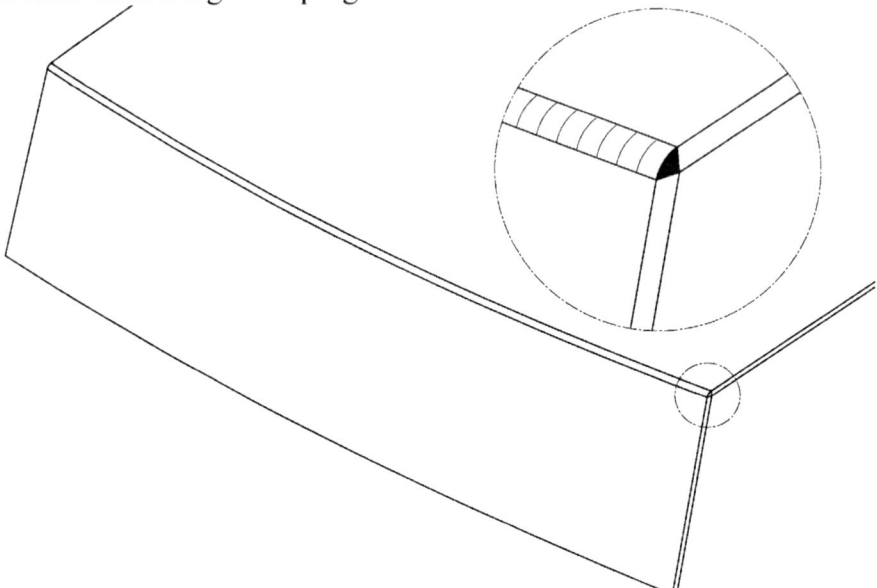

One thing you will notice when using thickened epoxy is that with some fillers you will experience a faster gel time. This is again due to the chemistry of the epoxy, and therefore you will need to take this into consideration when deciding on the amount you mix at a time. Often it is easier to mix some small portions instead of fewer larger portions.

5.4 Fillets at the inside

Making the inside fillets are in many ways similar to making the outside rounding at the chine. You will start with making some thickened epoxy in a consistency between mayonnaise and peanut butter.

 **Boat Building Master Course**

Before applying the epoxy, it is recommended to have some wooden tongue depressors, in an appropriate size for shaping the fillets. These cheap wooden sticks are ideal for making the fillets, and it is recommended you have some 'on stock' when working on the inside of the hull.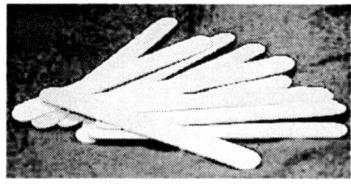

Another tool that can be used for shaping the fillets are plastic spoons. They are also cheap, but it can be a bit difficult getting an equal radius when using the spoons. However, since the price is so low it might be an alternative to the wood tongue depressors.

After you have mixed the thickened epoxy apply it in the corners. The best thing to use is a putty knife. It can be a bit difficult to apply the epoxy in the corners, but if you choose a plastic putty knife you can adjust the edge of the knife for easier access. Remember to fill between the frames and the hull so small openings aren't missed. That way you will get an even better bond between the frames and hull.

Now you take the wooden tongue depressors and shape the fillets. Be sure to fair the fillets. By keeping the same angle compared to the corner you will get a radius that is close to constant. Remember to clean up any excess epoxy before it cures. It is also much easier to clean before it cures than afterwards.

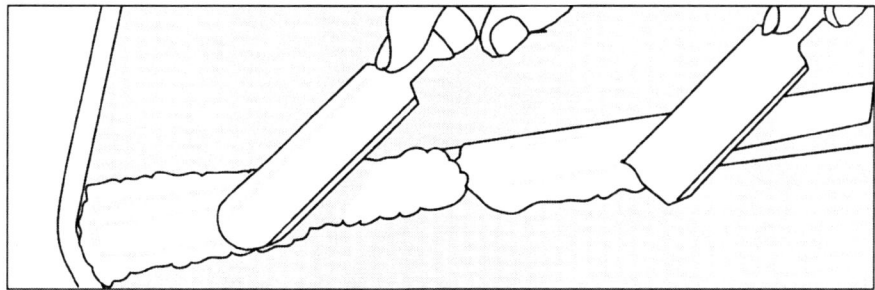

Some recommend making the fillets and applying the glass tape in one sequence. A sort of wet in wet method where the glass tape is laid in the not cured fillets. This technique can be more time efficient, but it also requires more skill. So, if you are not trained it is recommended you make the fillets and after they are cured smooth and fair them with sandpaper grade 60-80. Finally, apply the fiberglass tape.

After you have applied the tape, ground and faired the fillets, the inside of the hull will look like the figure below.

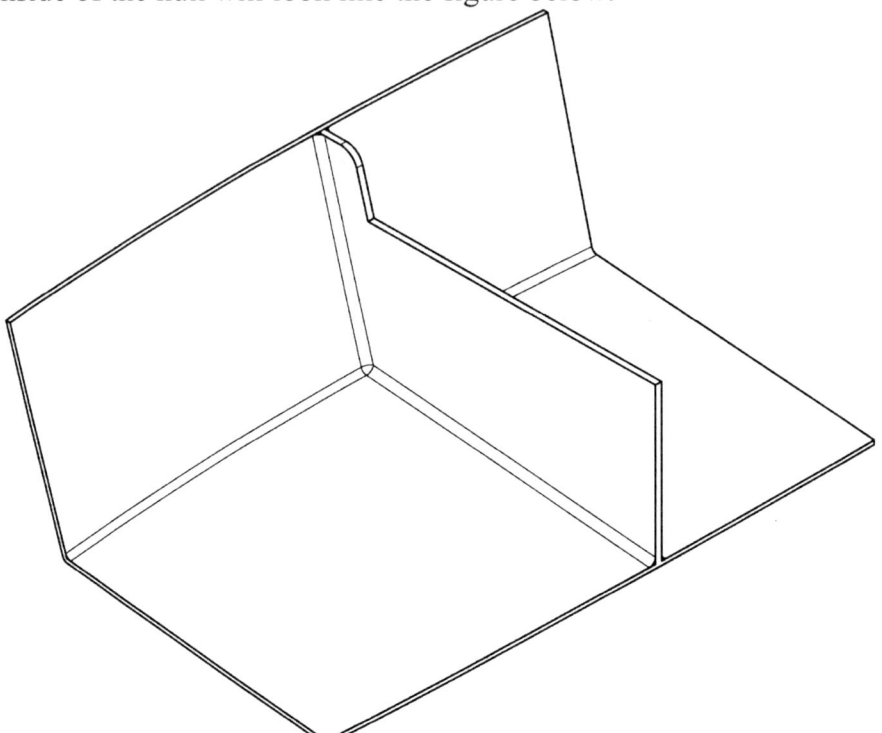

5.5 Applying fiberglass tape

There is not much difference between general fiberglassing and applying the fiberglass tape, so it is recommended that you read this section before you continue.

The purpose of applying fiberglass tape at the seams and frames is to ensure a good durable and efficient joint between the different plywood elements of the boat. The strength of the fiberglass tape is much higher than the plywood, so by combining the two materials you will make sure the hull can stand the loads it will be exposed to during the lifetime of the boat. Furthermore by bonding the fiberglass tape and the plywood with epoxy, you will ensure the elements can 'work' together.

The building instruction supplied with your boat plans will specify the fiberglass tape type and specific weight. It will also specify the amount of tape needed, but depending on the use of the tape this amount can be higher or lower. It depends very much on the builder's skills. Often it is cheaper to buy rolls of fiberglass tape, so it is recommended that you round up the amount and purchase whole rolls. The same aspect counts when purchasing epoxy. Check out the can size since it is often cheaper to buy one large can instead of two smaller cans.

The first thing you will do is apply fiberglass tape to the outside of the hull. It is always recommended to apply the tape in full length. This will in some situations mean that you will have to use more tape, but the advantages when fairing the hull is larger.

If, however, you need to join the tape pieces, you will have to overlap the two pieces with at least 50 mm [2"] to ensure sufficient strength at the seams.

Start with applying epoxy at the seam and the area where the tape will be applied. This step is important since the plywood soaks up some of the resin. In order to avoid dry spots at the finished laminate, be sure the plywood is primed with epoxy resin.

Now you place the fiberglass tape over the seam and smooth the tape so there is no crease. The fiberglass tape has to be laying flat on the plywood. Allow a few minutes for the fiberglass to soak up the resin. Apply additional resin where needed, and follow the procedure described in the section 'General fiberglassing'. Be sure to roll out all air bubbles in the laminate.

 **Boat Building Master Course**

It is important to place the fiberglass tape over the seams so there is an equal amount of tape at each side of the seam. That way you will be sure that there are no weak spots at the seam where the hull can delaminate, with the result of a leaking boat.

Also make sure the tape is following the contour of the seams rounding. This is especially important when using the air bleed roller, since you can displace the tape pieces with it and this may cause air enclosures in the laminate. If that happens and you discover it after the epoxy resin is cured, you will have to grind down the area and repair by applying extra fiberglass and resin where the air enclosure has been.

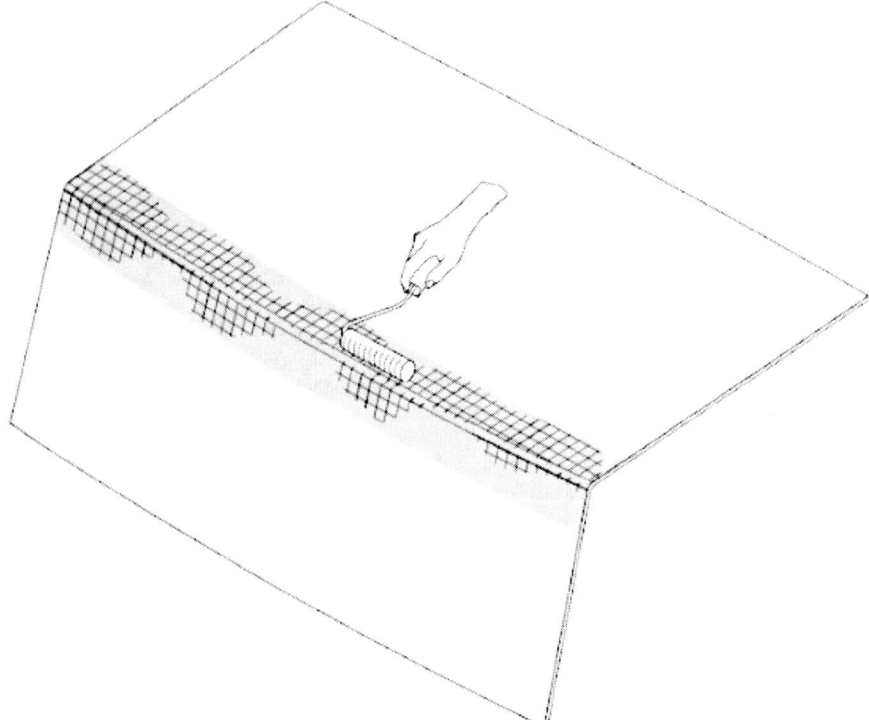

After the epoxy resin is cured you can fair and grind smooth the seams.

When the outside of the hull is finished it is time to do the inside. Follow the same procedure as described for the outside. One thing to pay special attention to is the corner. Here you will experience up to three layers of fiberglass tape running together, and the corner can get pretty crowded. The best thing to do is have the different layers run to the center of the corner, and then the layers will overlap on half the tape width. After the epoxy is cured you can grind smooth and fair the corners for a nice look.

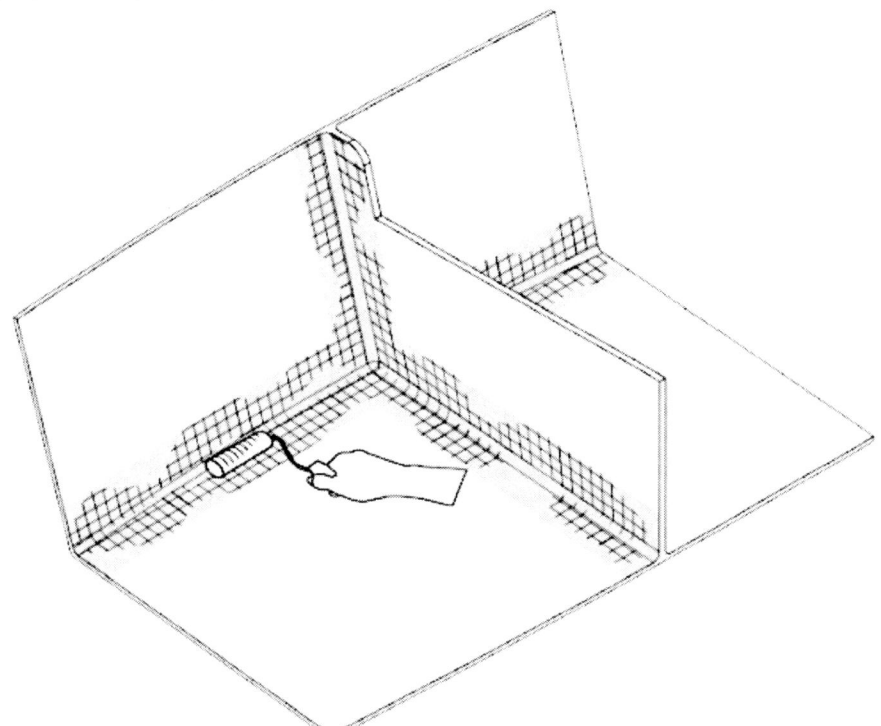

5.6 Fairing and epoxy coating

An important issue for the look of your new boat is the fairing. Depending on the plywood quality and the assembly, there can be a smaller or larger amount of fairing on your hull.

Fairing takes time and requires patience. But the time invested in this process will give you a result that will make people's heads turn when you arrive in harbors and slipways.

When working with fairing it is important to remember that you will achieve the best result with a minimum of labor by making the fairing as accurate and fair as possible before the epoxy cures. It is, like stated elsewhere in this manual, easier to shape the not cured epoxy instead of grinding the cured epoxy. So by being careful you can save yourself a lot of work. It is not an easy task, but the more experienced you get the easier it gets.

You can read further on the subject of fairing in the Epoxy manual.

The hull has to be coated with epoxy before it is finished. The purpose of the coating is to encapsulate the plywood and making it water resistant. By coating all parts of the plywood you will ensure the plywood doesn't delaminate and that the fiberglass continues to bond to the plywood.

You can read further about epoxy coating in the Epoxy manual.

We often get the question about glass fabric covering of the hull. Unless your building instruction states that your boat should be covered with glass fabric it is not necessary. Of course you could choose to cover the hull with fabric, but for normal use it is not necessary. One thing you must keep in mind if you choose to cover the hull with glass fabric is that your boat will gain weight. Even if you choose to decrease the plywood thickness, it cannot compensate for the extra weight of glass and epoxy.

We make every effort to give you a design that is as easy to build and as light as possible, without compromising the seaworthiness, safety and durability of the finished boat. It is, of course, your choice whether or not to use glass fabric. We only want to make sure you know the consequences of your choice. One of them is that your boat will be heavier, another is that the fairing will be more difficult, since grinding in glass is not easy and, therefore, the amount of labor needed will be higher.

We will of course support you in the building process no matter what you choose.

6 Epoxy Manual

This epoxy manual explains the different techniques and methods of using epoxy. This section is distributed with permission of West System®. It's recommended to use quality epoxy system like the West System® epoxy.

Please pay special attention to the section describing the health and safety issue of using epoxy. It's important to your health and safety to read and follow these guidelines.

6.1 Handling epoxy

This section explains the fundamentals of epoxy safety, curing and the steps for proper dispensing, mixing and adding fillers to ensure that every batch cures to a high strength solid.

6.2 Epoxy safety

Epoxies are safe when handled properly but it is essential to understand the hazards and take precautions to avoid them.

Hazards
The primary hazard associated with epoxy involves skin contact. WEST SYSTEM Resin may cause moderate skin irritation; WEST SYSTEM Hardeners may cause severe skin irritation. Resins and hardeners are also sensitisers and may cause an allergic reaction but, from our experience, most people are not sensitive to WEST SYSTEM Resin and Hardeners. These hazards decrease as resin/hardener mixes reach full cure but it is important to appreciate that the hazards also apply to the sanding dust from partially cured epoxy. Please refer to the Material Safety Data Sheets for specific product warnings and safety information.

Precautions
Avoid contact with resin, hardeners, mixed epoxy and sanding dust. Wear protective gloves and clothing when handling WEST SYSTEM materials. WEST SYSTEM Barrier Cream provides additional protection for sensitive skin and allergies. DO NOT use solvents to remove epoxy from the skin. Immediately after skin contact with resin, hardeners, sanding dust from epoxy and/or

solvents, use WEST SYSTEM Resin Removing Cream for the initial clean-up, followed by a wash with soap and warm water. If a skin rash develops while working with epoxy, stop using the product until the rash completely disappears. If problems persist when work is resumed, discontinue use and consult a doctor.

Protect your eyes from contact with resin, hardeners, mixed epoxy, and sanding dust by wearing appropriate eye protection. If contact occurs, immediately flush the eyes with water for 15 minutes. If discomfort persists, seek medical attention.

Avoid breathing concentrated vapors and sanding dust. WEST SYSTEM epoxy vapors can build up in unvented spaces and ample ventilation must be provided when working with epoxy in confined areas such as boat interiors. When adequate ventilation is not possible, wear an approved respirator.

Avoid ingestion. Wash thoroughly after handling epoxy, especially before eating. If epoxy is swallowed, drink large quantities of water - DO NOT induce vomiting. Call a doctor immediately. Refer to First Aid procedures on the Material Safety Data Sheet.

KEEP RESINS, HARDENERS, FILLERS AND SOLVENTS OUT OF THE REACH OF CHILDREN.

6.3 Clean Up

Contain spills with sand, clay or other inert absorbent materials and use a scraper to collect as much material as possible. Follow up with absorbent towels.

DO NOT use either sawdust or other fine cellulose materials to absorb hardeners and/or dispose of hardener in waste containing sawdust or other fine cellulose materials - spontaneous combustion may occur.

Clean resin, or mixed epoxy residue or uncured epoxy with WEST SYSTEM Cleaning Solvent. Clean hardener residue with warm soapy water.

Dispose of resin, hardener and empty containers safely in accord with local disposal regulations.

DO NOT dispose of resin or hardener in a liquid state. Waste resin and hardener should be mixed and cured (in small quantities) to a non-hazardous inert solid.

CAUTION! Large volumes of curing epoxy can become hot enough to ignite surrounding combustible materials and produce hazardous fumes. Place containers of mixed epoxy in a safe and ventilated area away from Dispose of the solid mass when the cure is complete and the mass has cooled. Comply with the local disposal regulations.

6.4 Epoxy Chemistry

Understanding cure time. Open time and cure time determine the build and repair operations. Open time dictates the time available for mixing, application, smoothing, shaping, assembly and clamping. Cure time dictates the time before removing clamps, abrading or proceeding to the next step in the project. Three factors determine the open time and cure time of an epoxy mix – *hardener cure speed, epoxy temperature and volume of mix.*

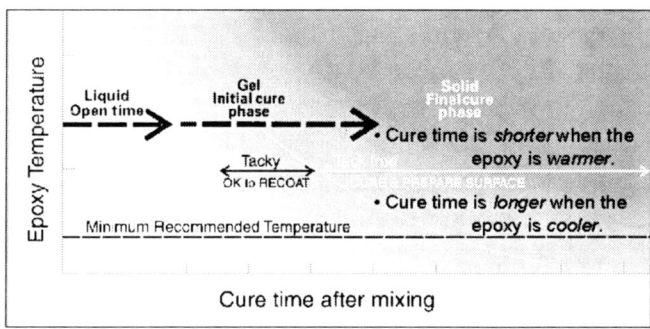

As it cures, mixed epoxy passes from a liquid state, through a gel state, to a solid state.

a) Hardener speed
Each hardener has an ideal temperature cure range. At any given temperature each resin/hardener combination will go through the

same cure stages but at different rates. Select the hardener that gives adequate working time for the job in hand at the temperature and conditions under which the work is to be completed. The Product Guide describes hardener pot lives and cure times.

Pot life is a term used to compare the cure speeds of different hardeners. It is the period of time a specific mass of mixed resin and hardener remains a liquid at a particular temperature e.g. a 100g mass of an epoxy mix in a standard container at 25°C is a routine quality control test procedure.

Because pot life is a measure of the speed of cure of a specific mass (volume) of epoxy rather than a thin film, the pot life of a resin/hardener mix is much shorter than its open time.

b) Epoxy temperature

The warmer the temperature the faster an epoxy mix will cure. The temperature at which epoxy cures is determined by the ambient temperature plus the exothermic heat generated by the reaction. Ambient temperature is the temperature of the air and/or the material in contact with the epoxy. Epoxy cures faster when the ambient temperature is warmer.

c) The volume of mixed epoxy

Mixing resin and hardener together creates an exothermic (heat producing) reaction. Always mix small batches of epoxy because the greater the quantity, the more heat generated, the shorter the pot life and cure time. In a larger volume, more heat is retained, causing a faster reaction and yet more heat e.g. a plastic mixing cup containing, say, a 200g mix can generate enough heat to melt the cup. However, if the same quantity is spread into a thin layer, the exothermic heat is not produced as quickly and the cure time of the epoxy is determined by the ambient temperature.

6.5 Controlling cure time

In warm conditions use a slower hardener to increase the open time. Mix smaller batches that can be used quickly or pour the epoxy mix into a container with greater surface area e.g. a roller pan, thereby spreading out the epoxy into a thin film and extending the open time. After thorough mixing, the sooner the epoxy is transferred or

applied, the more open time is available for coating, lay-up or assembly.

In cool conditions use a faster hardener and employ a hot air gun, a heat lamp or other heat source to warm the resin and hardener before mixing and/or after the epoxy is applied. At room temperature, additional heat is useful when a quicker cure is desired. NOTE! Unvented kerosene or propane heaters can inhibit the cure of epoxy and contaminate epoxy surfaces with unburned hydrocarbons.

CAUTION! Warming a resin/hardener mix will lower its viscosity, allowing the epoxy to run or sag more easily on vertical surfaces. In addition, heating epoxy applied to a porous substrate (soft wood or low density core material) may cause the substrate to "out-gas" and form bubbles in the epoxy coating. To avoid out-gassing, wait until the epoxy coating has gelled before warming it. Never heat mixed epoxy in a liquid state over 50°C.

Regardless of the steps taken to control the cure time, thorough planning of the application and assembly will allow maximum use of the open time and cure time of the epoxy mix.

6.6 Cure stages of epoxy

Mixing epoxy resin and hardener begins a chemical reaction that transforms the combined liquid components into a solid. As it cures, the epoxy passes from the liquid state, through a gel stage before it reaches a solid state.

1. Liquid – Open time
Open time (also working time) is the period, after mixing, that the resin/hardener mix remains a liquid and is workable and suitable for application. All assembly and clamping should take place during this period to ensure a dependable bond is achieved.

2. Gel – Initial cure phase
The mix passes into an initial cure phase (also known as the "Green Stage") when it begins to gel. The epoxy is no longer workable and will progress from a tacky consistency to the firmness of hard rubber. An indent can be made with the thumb nail and it is too soft

to dry sand. While the epoxy is tacky, a new application of epoxy will chemically link with it, so the surface may be bonded or recoated without sanding. This ability diminishes as the mix approaches the final cure phase.

3. Solid – Final cure phase
The epoxy mix has cured to a solid state and can be dry sanded and shaped. It is no longer possible to indent the surface with the thumb nail. At this stage, the epoxy has reached 90% of its ultimate strength, so clamps can be removed. The mix will continue to cure over the next few days at room temperature. A new application of epoxy will no longer chemically link to it, so the surface must be thoroughly washed and sanded before recoating to achieve a good mechanical, secondary bond.

6.7 Dispensing and Mixing

Careful measuring of resin and hardener and thorough mixing of the two components are essential for a proper cure. Whether the resin/hardener mix is applied as a coating or modified with fillers or additives, observing the following procedures will ensure a controlled and thorough chemical transition to a high strength epoxy solid.

Dispense the correct proportions of resin and hardener into a clean plastic, metal or wax-free paper container. Do not use glass or foam containers because of the potential hazard from exothermic heat build-up. DO NOT attempt to adjust the cure time by altering the mix ratio. An accurate ratio is essential for a proper cure and full development of physical properties.

Most problems related to the curing of epoxy can be traced to the wrong ratio of resin and hardener. To simplify metering, use calibrated WEST SYSTEM Mini Pumps to dispense the correct working ratio of resin and hardener. (*For one full pump stroke of resin use one full pump stroke*

of hardener.) Depress each pump head fully and allow the head to return completely before beginning the next stroke. Partial strokes will give an incorrect ratio. Read the pump instructions before using the pumps and verify the correct ratio before using the first mix on a project. Recheck the ratio whenever curing problems are experienced. One full depression of each pump will give approximately 30g of mixed epoxy. With Mini Pumps - One full pump stroke of resin for one full pump stroke of hardener will give the correct ratio

First time users

If using WEST SYSTEM epoxy for the first time, begin with a small test batch to get the feel for the mixing and curing process before applying a mix to the job in hand. This will demonstrate the open time for the resin/hardener mix at the present ambient temperature and give assurance that the mix ratio is correctly metered. Mix small batches until confident of the handling characteristics of the epoxy.

Thoroughly blend the two ingredients for 2 minutes - longer in cooler temperatures. Scrape the sides and bottom of the pot when mixing. If using the mix for coating, after mixing, quickly pour into a roller pan to extend the open time.

scrape corners

WARNING! Curing epoxy generates heat. Do not fill or cast layers of epoxy thicker than 10 to 12mm – thinner if enclosed by foam or other insulating material. If left to stand for the full pot life in a plastic mixing cup, the mixed epoxy will generate enough heat to melt the plastic. If a pot of mixed epoxy begins to exotherm (heat up), quickly move it outdoors. Avoid breathing the fumes. Do not dispose of the mixture until the reaction is complete and the material has cooled.

6.8 Adding Fillers and Additives
Fillers

Throughout this section, reference to epoxy or resin/hardener mixes is defined as mixed resin and hardener without fillers added; thickened mixes or thickened epoxy will mean mixed resin and hardener with fillers added. Fillers are used to thicken epoxy for specific applications such as bonding or fairing.

After selecting an appropriate filler for the job in hand, use it to thicken the epoxy to the desired consistency. The viscosity or thickness of a mix required for a specific job is controlled by the amount of filler added. There is no strict formula or measuring involved - visually judge the consistency which is best suited for the task in hand. The table below gives a general guide to the differences between unthickened epoxy and the three other consistencies referred to in this manual.

Always add fillers in a two-step process:
1. Mix the desired quantity of resin and hardener thoroughly before adding fillers. Begin with a small batch - allow room for the filler.
2. Blend in small quantities of the appropriate filler until the desired consistency is reached. Ensure the filler is thoroughly blended before the mix is applied.

For maximum strength, add only enough filler to completely bridge gaps between surfaces without sagging or running out of the joint or gap. A small amount should squeeze out of joints when clamped. When making fairing compounds, add as much as can be blended in smoothly - for easy sanding, the thicker the viscosity, the better. Spread the mix into a thinner layer, either around the inside of the mixing cup or onto a flat non-porous surface or palette, to extend the working life.

Epoxy can be thickened to the ideal consistency needed for a particular job. The procedures in this manual refer to four common consistencies: syrup, ketchup, mayonnaise and peanut butter.

Additives

Although additives are blended with mixed epoxy in a similar two-step process, they are not designed to thicken the epoxy. Additives give the epoxy additional physical properties when used as a coating and pigments provide a color base for future overcoating with quality marine paint.

CONSISTENCY	Unthickened	Slightly thickened	Moderately thickened	Maximum thickness
	"SYRUP"	"KETCHUP"	"MAYONNAISE"	"PEANUT BUTTER"
GENERAL APPEARANCE				
CHARACTERISTICS	Drips off vertical surfaces.	Sags down vertical surfaces.	Clings to vertical surfaces. Peaks fall over.	Clings to vertical surfaces. Peaks stand up.
USES	Coating, "wetting-out" before bonding, applying fibreglass, graphite and other fabrics.	Laminating/ bonding flat panels with large surface areas, injecting with syringe.	General bonding, filleting, hardware bonding.	Gap filling, filleting, fairing, bonding uneven surfaces.

6.9 Basic techniques

The following procedures are common to the majority of repair or building projects – on the boat or in the home and regardless of the type of structure or material on which work is being carried out.

Surface preparation

Whether bonding, fairing or applying fabrics, the success of the application depends not only on the strength of the epoxy but also on how well the epoxy adheres to the surface to which it is being applied. Unless bonding to partially cured epoxy, the strength of the bond relies on the ability of the epoxy to mechanically "key" into the surface. Thus, the following three steps of surface preparation are a critical part of any secondary bonding operation.

For good adhesion, bonding surfaces must be:

Boat Building Master Course

1. Clean

Bonding surfaces must be free of any contaminants such as grease, oil, wax or mould release. Clean contaminated surfaces with WEST SYSTEM Solvent. Wipe the surface with fresh paper towels before the solvent dries. Clean surfaces before sanding to avoid abrading the contaminant into the surface. Follow all safety precautions when working with solvents.

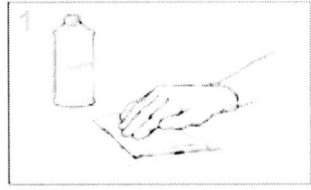

2. Dry

All bonding surfaces must be as dry as possible for good adhesion. If necessary, accelerate drying by warming the bonding surface with a hot air gun, hair dryer or heat lamp. Use fans to move the air in confined or enclosed spaces. Be careful of condensation when working outdoors or whenever the temperature of the work environment changes.

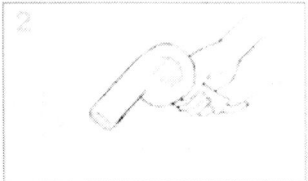

3. Sanded

Thoroughly abrade hardwoods and non-porous surfaces with 80-grit aluminium oxide paper to provide a good mechanical "key" for the epoxy. Ensure the surface to be bonded is solid. Remove any flaking, chalking, blistering or old coating before sanding. Remove all dust after sanding.

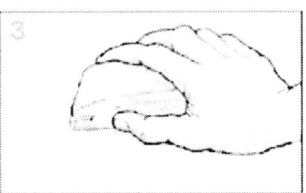

The importance of the three operations detailed above cannot be stressed too strongly – for high strength, durable bonds, surfaces must be clean, dry and thoroughly abraded after removing previous surface coatings.

Primary/Secondary bonding

Primary bonding relies on chemical linking of adhesive layers such as the wet lay-up of fibreglass laminate in a mould. All the layers of adhesive cure together in a single fused layer. Epoxy applied over

partially cured epoxy will chemically link with it to form a primary bond. The ability to chemically link diminishes as the previous layer of epoxy cures and the bond becomes a secondary bond.

Secondary bonding requires a mechanical, rather than chemical linking of an adhesive to a material or cured epoxy surface. The adhesive must "key" into pores or scratches in the surface -a microscopic version of a dovetail joint. Correct surface preparation provides a texture that will help link the cured epoxy to the surface

6.10 Special preparation for various materials
Cured epoxy
Amine blush can appear as a wax like film on cured epoxy surfaces. It is a by-product of the curing process and is more noticeable in cool, moist conditions. Amine blush can clog sandpaper and inhibit subsequent bonding but it is water soluble and can easily be removed. It is not unreasonable to assume it has formed on any cured epoxy surface.

To remove the blush, thoroughly wash the surface with clean water and an abrasive pad. Dry the surface with fresh paper towels to remove the dissolved blush before it dries on the surface. Sand any remaining glossy areas with 80-grit sandpaper and clean.

Wet-sanding will also remove the amine blush. If a release fabric (peel ply) is applied over the surface of fresh epoxy, amine blush will be removed when the release fabric is peeled from the cured epoxy and no additional sanding is required.

Epoxy surfaces that are still tacky i.e. not fully cured, may be bonded to or coated with epoxy without washing or sanding. Before applying coatings other than epoxy (paints, bottom paints, varnishes, gelcoats, etc.), allow epoxy surfaces to cure fully, then wash, sand, clean and follow coating manufacturer's instructions.

Removing uncured or non-curing epoxy. Scrape as much material as possible from the surface using a stiff metal or plastic scraper warm the epoxy to lower its viscosity. Clean the residue with WEST

SYSTEM Cleaning Solvent. Allow solvents to dry before recoating. After recoating wood surfaces with epoxy, brush the wet epoxy (in the direction of the grain) with a wire brush to improve adhesion.

Removing fibreglass cloth applied with epoxy. Use a heat gun to warm and soften the epoxy. Begin in a small area near a corner or edge. Apply heat until a putty knife or chisel can be slipped under the cloth (about 50°C). Grab the edge with a pair of pliers and slowly pull up the cloth while heating just ahead of the separation. On large areas, use a utility knife to score/cut the glass and remove in narrower strips. Resulting surface texture may be coated or remaining epoxy may be removed as follows.

Removing cured epoxy coating. Use a heat gun to soften the epoxy (about 50°C). Heat a small area and use a paint or cabinet scraper to remove the bulk of the coating. Sand the surface to remove the remaining material. Provide ventilation when heating epoxy.

Hardwoods/Plywood
Thoroughly abrade with 80-grit paper and remove dust before coating.

Teak/oily woods
Wipe the surface with WEST SYSTEM solvent or pure acetone and when the solvent has evaporated, abrade with 80-grit paper. Clean the sanding dust away and then wipe the abraded surface with solvent – the solvent dries the oil at the surface and allows the epoxy to penetrate. Ensure the solvent has evaporated before coating but apply the epoxy within 15 minutes of the solvent wipe.

Porous woods
No special preparation needed but it is advisable to abrade with a medium grit paper to open pores. Remove dust.

Metals
Metals must have all previous surface pre-treatments and contaminants

e.g. rust removed, taking the surface back to the bare metal by thoroughly degreasing then abrading with a coarse paper such as 80-grit or grit blasting and then degreasing again. The use of an adhesion promoter is advised on non-ferrous metal substrates. Given below is the preparation for the more common metals used in boat building:

Mild Steel
Degrease and then thoroughly abrade (ideally, grit blast), removing all contamination to expose bright metal. Apply epoxy as soon as possible and certainly within 4 hours after surface has been prepared.

Stainless Steel
Degrease and then thoroughly abrade (ideally, grit blast), removing all contamination and the stainless coating to expose bright metal. Apply epoxy as soon as possible and certainly within 4 hours after surface has been prepared.

Aluminium
Non-anodised material must be degreased and either thoroughly abraded or chemically etched, (sulphuric acid/sodium dichromate solution or branded aluminium etch compound).

Anodised aluminium and anodised aluminium alloys
Must be bonded as quickly as possible after degreasing and abrading and certainly within 30 minutes.

Hard anodised aluminium alloy
Must be stripped by abrasive blasting or by etching in sulphuric acid/sodium dichromate solution or branded aluminium etch compound. Unstripped metal is not suitable for bonding.

Polyester/GRP
Remove contamination with WEST SYSTEM 850 Solvent. Thoroughly abrade with 80-grit paper to a dull finish and remove dust.

Ferrocement
Remove all previous paints and coatings by wet sand blasting - this is less aggressive than using dry sand and should not damage the sound surface. If after blasting, laitance is visible on the surface or rust from the reinforcing wires can be seen, then it is necessary to wash with dilute solution of hydrochloric acid, this should be fresh water with a 4% to 5% addition of hydrochloric acid. Wash thoroughly with water and allow to dry completely before coating.

Concrete
Remove all previous coatings and abrade with a stiff wire brush. Remove all dust and debris before coating.

6.11 Bonding (gluing)
This section refers to two types of structural bonding. Two step bonding is the preferred method for most situations because it promotes maximum epoxy penetration into the bonding surface and prevents resin starved joints. Single step bonding is occasionally used when joints have minimal loads and excess absorption into porous surfaces is not a problem. In both cases, to achieve the ultimate bond strength, work the epoxy into the surface with a roller or brush.

Before mixing epoxy, ensure all parts to be bonded fit properly and that surface preparation has been completed. Clamps and tools necessary for the operation and cover any areas that need protection from spills.

Bonding
Joint strength -the ability to adequately transfer a load from one part to another depends on the combined effects of three factors.

GLUE STRENGTH - Careful metering and thorough mixing will ensure the epoxy mixture cures to full strength.

SURFACE PREPARATION - For the best adhesion and load transfer, the surface must be correctly prepared.

JOINT AREA - The bonding or adhesive area of the joint must be adequate for the load on the joint. Increased overlap, scarf joints, fillets and reinforcing fibres across the joint can be used to increase bonding area.

Two-step bonding
1. Apply a resin/hardener mix to the surfaces to be joined. This is called "wetting-out" or "priming" the bonding surfaces. The epoxy is applied with a disposable brush in small or tight areas; wet-out larger areas with foam roller or by spreading resin/hardener mix evenly surface with a plastic squeegee/spreader. Proceed with step two immediately or any time before the wet-out coat becomes tack free.

2. Modify the resin/hardener mix by stirring in the appropriate filler until it becomes thick enough to bridge any gaps between the mating surfaces and to prevent "resin-starved" joints. Apply an even coat of the thickened epoxy to one of the bonding surfaces, sufficient so that a small amount will squeeze out when the surfaces are joined together.

As already stated, the thickened epoxy can be applied immediately over the wet out surface or any time before the epoxy becomes tack free. For most small bonding operations, add the filler to the resin/hardener mix remaining in the batch that was used for the wet-out. Mix enough resin/hardener for both steps. Add the filler quickly after the surface is wet out and allow for a shorter working life of the mix.

1. Clamp components. Attach clamps as necessary to hold the components in place. Use only enough clamping pressure to

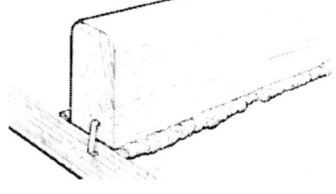

squeeze a small amount of the thickened mix from the joint, indicating that the epoxy is making good contact with both mating surfaces. Do not squeeze all the thickened mix from the joint by using too much clamping pressure.

2. Remove or shape excess adhesive that squeezes out of the joint as soon as the joint is secured with clamps. A mixing stick with one end sanded to a chisel edge is an ideal tool for removing the excess.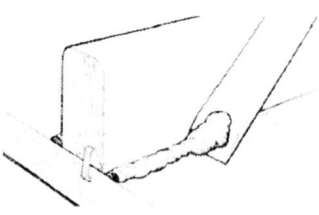
Allow to cure thoroughly before removing clamps.

Single-step bonding
Single-step bonding is applying a thickened epoxy mix directly to both bonding surfaces without first wetting out the surfaces with a resin/hardener mix. However, it is strongly recommended that the epoxy is thickened no more than is necessary to bridge gaps in the joint (the thinner the mix, the more it can penetrate the surface) and this method is not used for highly-loaded joints or for bonding either end grain or other porous surfaces.

Bonding with fillets
A fillet is a cove-shaped application of thickened epoxy that bridges an inside corner joint. It is an excellent technique for bonding components because the surface area of the bond is increased and serves as a structural brace. All joints that will be covered with glasscloth will require a fillet to support the cloth at the inside corner of the joint.

The procedure for bonding with fillets is the same as normal bonding but, instead of removing the squeezed-out thickened epoxy after the components are clamped in position, the epoxy/filler blend is shaped into a fillet. For larger fillets, as soon as the bonding operation is complete and before the squeezed-out epoxy becomes tack free, add more thickened mix to the joint and shape into a fillet.

1. Bond components as described above.

2. Shape and smooth the squeezed-out thickened epoxy into a fillet by drawing a rounded filleting tool (a mixing stick is ideal) along the joint, dragging excess material ahead of the tool and leaving a 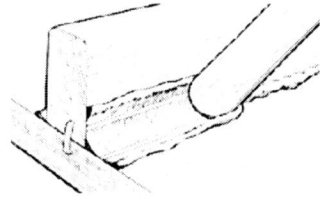 smooth cove-shaped fillet bordered on each side by a clean margin. Some excess filleting material will remain outside the margin which can be used to refill any voids. Smooth the fillet until you are satisfied with the appearance. A mixing stick will leave a fillet with about a 10mm radius. For larger fillets, a plastic squeegee is recommended, cut to shape or bent to the desired radius.

Apply additional thickened epoxy to fill voids or make larger fillets. Add sufficient mix along the joint line with the rounded mixing stick to create the desired size of fillet. For longer or multiple fillets, empty caulking gun cartridges or disposable cake decorating bags can be used. Cut the plastic tip to lay a bead of thickened epoxy large enough for the desired fillet size. Heavy duty, sealable food storage bags with one corner cut off may also be used.

3. Clean up the remaining excess material outside the margin by using a mixing stick or a putty knife. Glasscloth or tape may be applied over the fillet area before the fillet has cured (or after the fillet is cured and sanded).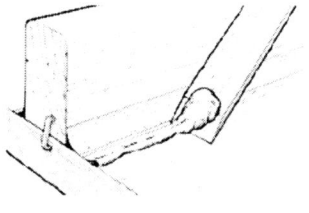

4. When the fillet has fully cured, sand smooth with 80-grit sandpaper. Wipe the surface clean of dust and apply two or three coats of resin/hardener over the entire fillet area before final finishing.

6.12 Laminating

The term "laminating" refers to the process of bonding together a number of relatively thin sheets, like plywood, veneers, fabrics or core material, to create a composite. A composite may be any number of layers of the same material or combinations of different materials. Methods of epoxy application and clamping will differ depending on the materials being laminated.

A quick method to apply epoxy for laminating is to use a foam roller. An even faster method for large flat surfaces is to simply pour the resin/hardener mix onto the middle of the panel/veneer/ fabric and spread the epoxy evenly over the surface with a plastic spreader. Apply thickened mixes with an notched spreader.

Using staples or screws is the most common method of clamping when there is a solid material on which to fasten. An even distribution of weights will suffice when laminating over a base that will not hold mechanical fixings, such as a foam or honeycomb core material.

Vacuum bagging is a specialized clamping method for laminating a wide range of materials. Using a vacuum pump and plastic sheeting, the atmosphere is used to apply perfectly even clamping pressure over all areas of a panel regardless of the size, shape or number of layers.

6.13 Clamping

Any method of clamping is suitable to prevent movement between the parts being joined. Methods of clamping include spring clamps, "C" clamps and adjustable bar clamps, rubber bands cut from inner tubes, packaging tape, applying weights, and vacuum bagging. When placing clamps near epoxy covered areas use polyethylene sheeting or peel ply under the clamps so they do not inadvertently bond to the surface. Staples, nails or drywall screws are often used where conventional clamps are unsuitable. Any fasteners that need to remain should be of a non-corroding alloy such as bronze. In some cases, the thickened epoxy or gravity will hold parts in position without clamps.

6.14 Fairing

Fairing refers to the filling and shaping of low or uneven areas so they blend with the surrounding surfaces and appear "fair" to the eye and touch. After major structural assembly has been completed, final fairing can be accomplished easily with WEST SYSTEM epoxy and fillers.

1. Prepare the surface as detailed for bonding. Sand smooth any bumps or ridges on the surface and remove all dust from the area to be faired.
2. Wet out porous surfaces with resin/hardener mix.
3. Mix resin/hardener and filler to a peanut butter consistency. The thicker the mix, the easier it will be to sand when cured.

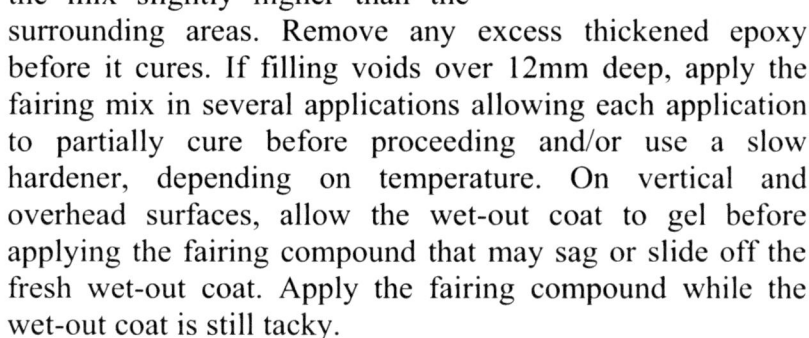

4. Trowel the thickened epoxy mix onto the wetted surface with a plastic spreader, working it into all voids and depressions. Smooth the epoxy to the desired shape, leaving the mix slightly higher than the surrounding areas. Remove any excess thickened epoxy before it cures. If filling voids over 12mm deep, apply the fairing mix in several applications allowing each application to partially cure before proceeding and/or use a slow hardener, depending on temperature. On vertical and overhead surfaces, allow the wet-out coat to gel before applying the fairing compound that may sag or slide off the fresh wet-out coat. Apply the fairing compound while the wet-out coat is still tacky.
5. Allow the final application of thickened epoxy to cure thoroughly.
6. Sand the fairing material to blend with the surrounding contour. Begin with 50-grit sandpaper if it is necessary to remove a lot of fairing material. Use 80-grit paper

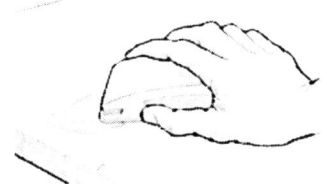

when close to the final contour.

7. When satisfied with the fairness, apply two or three coats of resin/hardener mix to the area with a disposable brush or roller. Allow the final coat to cure thoroughly before final sanding and finishing.

6.15 Applying woven cloth and tape

Glass cloth may be applied to surfaces by two methods to provide reinforcement and/or abrasion resistance. It is usually applied after fairing and shaping are completed and before the final coating operation. It is also applied in multiple layers i.e. laminated and in combination with other materials to build composite parts.

The "wet" method refers to the cloth being applied to an epoxy-coated surface before the coating reaches final cure. The "dry" method is to apply the cloth over a dry surface and then impregnate the glass with epoxy. The wet method is preferred whenever possible.

Wet method
By working with small quantities of epoxy, it is possible to work at a comfortable pace over quite large areas to be reinforced.

1. Prepare the surface for bonding as discussed in surface preparation.

2. Pre-fit and trim the cloth to size. Roll the cloth neatly so that it may be conveniently rolled back into position later.

3. Roll a heavy coat of epoxy on the surface.

4. Unroll the glass cloth into position over the wet epoxy. Surface tension will hold most cloths in position. (If applying the cloth vertically or overhead, it is possible to wait until the epoxy becomes a little tacky). Work out wrinkles by lifting the edge of the cloth and smoothing from the center with a gloved hand or a squeegee/spreader. If cutting a pleat or

notch in the cloth, lay it flat on a curve or corner, make the cut with sharp scissors and temporarily overlap the edges.

5. Any areas of cloth that appear to be dry, (white in appearance) apply more epoxy with a foam roller.

6. Remove the excess epoxy with a squeegee, using long overlapping strokes of uniform pressure. The object is to remove the excess epoxy that may allow the cloth to "float off" the surface but avoid creating dry spots by exerting too much pressure on the squeegee. Excess epoxy appears as a shiny area while a properly wet out surface appears evenly transparent with a smooth cloth texture. Subsequent coats of epoxy will fill the weave of the cloth.

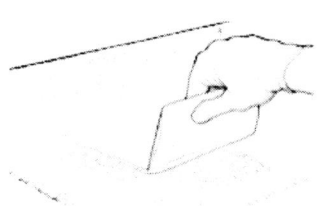

7. Further layers of cloth may be applied immediately by repeating the steps above.

8. Trim the excess and overlapped cloth after the epoxy has reached its initial cure. The cloth will cut easily with a sharp utility knife as long as the epoxy is not fully cured. If required, trim overlapped cloth as follows.

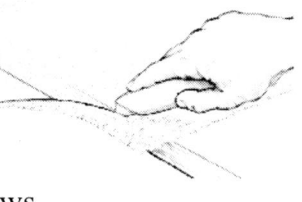

a) Place a metal straightedge on top of and midway between the two overlapped edges.

b) Cut through both layers of cloth with a sharp utility knife, being very careful not to cut too deeply.

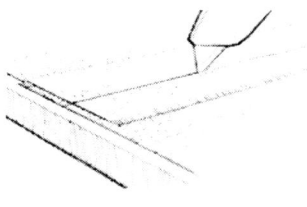

c) Remove the top-most trimming and then lift the opposite cut edge to remove the overlapped trimming.

d) Re-wet the underside of the raised edge with epoxy and smooth into place.

e) The result should be a near perfect butt joint, eliminating double cloth thickness. However, a lapped joint is stronger than a butt joint, so if appearance is not important, it may be advisable to leave the overlap and fair in the unevenness after coating.

f) Any remaining irregularities or transitions between cloth and substrate can be faired by using an epoxy/filler fairing compound if the surface is to be painted. Any fairing completed after the final glass cloth layer should receive several additional coats of epoxy over the faired area.

9. Coat the surface to fill the weave before the wet-out becomes tack free. Follow the procedures for final coating in the next section. It will take two or three coats to completely fill the weave of the cloth and to allow for a final sanding that will not damage the cloth.

Dry method

1. Prepare the surface for bonding.

2. Position the cloth over the surface and cut it 30 mm larger on all sides. If the surface area to be covered is larger than the cloth size, allow multiple pieces to overlap by approximately 5 mm. On sloped or vertical surfaces, hold the cloth in place with masking or duct tape, or with staples.

3. Mix a small quantity of epoxy.

4. On horizontal surfaces, pour a small pool of resin/hardener near the center of the cloth but it is essential to use a roller or brush for wetting cloth on vertical surfaces.

5. Spread the epoxy over the cloth surface with a plastic squeegee, working the epoxy gently from the pool into the dry areas. As the fabric is wet out it becomes transparent, indicating the cloth has absorbed sufficient epoxy. 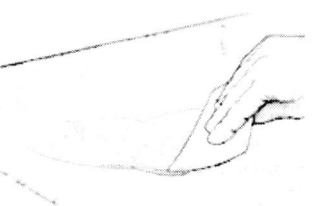 If applying cloth over a porous surface, ensure that sufficient epoxy is left to absorb into both the cloth and the surface below. Try to limit the amount of squeegeeing as excessive "work" on the wet surface produces minute air bubbles that are placed in suspension in the epoxy. This is especially important if a clear finish is required.

6. Continue pouring and spreading (or rolling) small batches of epoxy from the center towards the edges, smoothing wrinkles and positioning the cloth. Check for dry areas (especially over porous surfaces) and re-wet as necessary before proceeding to the next step. If cutting a pleat or notch in the cloth, lay it flat on a compound curve or corner, make the cut with a pair of sharp scissors and temporarily overlap the edges.

7. Now refer to Steps 5, 6, 7, 8 and 9 detailed above in the "wet method" to complete the procedure.

6.16 Epoxy barrier coating

The object of barrier coating is to build up an epoxy thickness that provides an effective moisture barrier and a smooth base for final finishing.

Apply a minimum of two coats of WEST SYSTEM epoxy for an effective moisture barrier. Apply three coats if sanding is to be carried out. Moisture protection will increase with additional coats and, in the case of osmosis repair and protection, six coats or about a thickness of 600 microns must be applied. Six coats, with Barrier Coat Additive in the final five coats, provides maximum moisture protection. Additives or pigments should not be added to the first coat.

Disposable, thin urethane foam rollers, such as WEST SYSTEM Roller Covers, allow greater control over film thickness, are less likely to cause the epoxy to exotherm and leave less stipple than thicker roller covers. Cut the covers into narrower widths to reach difficult areas or for long narrow surfaces like stringers. A paintbrush can be used for smaller areas, if the bristles are stiff enough to spread the epoxy to an even film.

Complete all fairing and cloth application before beginning the final coating. Allow the temperature of porous surfaces to stabilise before coating otherwise, as the material warms up, air within the porous material may expand and pass from the material (out-gassing) through the coating and leave bubbles in the cured coating.

1. Prepare the surface for bonding.

2. Mix only as much resin/hardener as can be applied during the open time of the mix. Pour the epoxy into a roller pan as soon as it is mixed thoroughly.

3. Load the roller with a moderate amount of the epoxy. Roll out the excess on the raised section of the roller pan to obtain a uniform coating on the roller.

4. Roll lightly and randomly over an area approximately 600mm x 600mm to transfer the epoxy evenly over the area.

5. As the roller dries out, increase pressure to spread the epoxy into a thin even film. Increase the coverage area if necessary to spread the film more thinly and evenly. The thinner the

film, the easier it is to keep it even and avoid runs or sags in each coat.

6. Finish the area with long, light, even strokes to reduce roller marks. Overlap the previously coated area to blend both areas together.

7. Coat as many of these small working areas as possible with each batch. If a batch begins to thicken before it can be applied, discard it and mix a fresh, smaller batch.

8. "Tip off" the coating by dragging a foam roller brush lightly over the fresh epoxy in long, even, overlapping strokes after each batch is applied. Use enough pressure to smooth the stipple, but not enough to remove any of the coating. Alternate the direction in which each coat is tipped off, 1st coat vertical, 2nd coat horizontal, 3rd coat vertical, etc. A roller cover can be cut into segments to make an excellent "tipping" brush.

Recoating
Apply second and subsequent coats of epoxy following the same procedures. Ensure the previous coat is still tacky, but has cured firmly enough to support the weight of the next coat. To avoid sanding between coats, apply all coats in the same day.

6.17 *Final surface preparation*
After the final coat has cured overnight, wash with clean water and abrade the surface to prepare for the final finish.

Correct finishing techniques will not only add beauty, but will also protect surfaces from ultraviolet light which will break down the epoxy over a long period of time. The most common methods of finishing are painting or varnishing. These coating systems protect the epoxy from ultraviolet light and require proper preparation of the surface before application.

Preparation for the final finish is just as important as it is for recoating with epoxy. The surface must be clean, dry and sanded and free of amine blush.

1. Allow the final epoxy coat to cure thoroughly.

2. Wash the surface with a Scotch-brite pad and water to remove the amine blush. Dry with paper towels.

3. Sand to a smooth finish. If there are runs or sags, begin sanding with 80-grit paper to remove the highest areas. Sand until the surface feels and looks fair. Complete sanding with the  appropriate grit for the type of coating to be applied - check coating instructions. Paint adhesion partly relies on the mechanical grip of the paint keying into the sanding scratches in the surface of the epoxy. If a high-build or filling primer is to be applied, 80-100 grit is usually sufficient. For primers and high-solids coatings, 120-180 grit may be adequate. Finishing with 180 grit paper is often recommended for coatings with high-gloss finishes. Grits finer than this may not provide enough "tooth" for good adhesion and may promote sags and runs. Always follow the paint manufacturer's recommendations for surface preparation. Many people prefer wet sanding because it reduces sanding dust and in addition, Steps 2 and 3 above become one operation.

4. When satisfied with the texture and fairness of the surface, rinse the surface with fresh water that should flow evenly without beading or fisheyeing. If the rinse water forms into droplets or beads (a sign of contamination), wipe the area dry with a paper

towel, then wet sand again until all water droplets are eliminated.

Proceed with the final coating after the surface has dried thoroughly. To reduce the possibility of contamination, it is advisable to begin coating within 24 hours of the final sanding. Follow the paint manufacturer's instructions but we suggest making a test panel to evaluate the degree of surface preparation required and the compatibility of the finish system.

6.18 Finish coatings

Coating function

Paint or varnish applied over an epoxy barrier coat is intended to decorate the surface and protect the epoxy from sunlight. In so doing, the finish coating extends the life of the epoxy moisture barrier that, in turn, provides a stable base that extends the life of the finish coating. Together, the two form a protective system far more durable than either coating by itself.

Protection from sunlight is a primary consideration in the selection of a final coating. Long term UV (ultraviolet) protection of the barrier coat depends on the effectiveness with which the finish coating resists UV and retains its pigmentation and/or shield of UV filters on the surface of the epoxy barrier coat. A high gloss finish reflects a higher proportion of the light from the surface than a dull finish. Therefore, a white - especially a high gloss white – coating is much more durable.

Most types of coatings are compatible with cured epoxy that is an almost completely inert, hard plastic. Thus, most paint solvents will not soften, swell or react with an epoxy surface. However, it is advisable to build a test panel to assure coating compatibility. It is always recommended to check manufacturer's instructions to verify compatibility and suitability.

Coating types

Latex paints are compatible with epoxy and they do an adequate job of protecting the epoxy barrier from UV radiation. In many

architectural applications latex paint may be the most suitable coating to use. Their durability is limited.

Alkyd finishes - enamel, alkyd enamel, marine enamel, acrylic enamel, alkyd modified epoxy, traditional varnish and spar varnish - offer ease of application, low cost, low toxicity, and easy availability. Their disadvantages are low UV resistance and low abrasion resistance.

One-part polyurethanes offer easy application, cleanup and better properties than alkyds. They are also more expensive and some may be incompatible with amine cured epoxy systems such as WEST SYSTEM epoxy. Test first.

Two-part linear polyurethane (LP) paints offer the most durable protection available. LP's are available as pigmented or clear coatings and offer excellent UV protection, gloss retention, abrasion resistance and complete compatibility with epoxy. However, compared to other types of coatings, they are expensive, require more skill to apply and present a greater health hazard, especially when sprayed.

Epoxy paints are available in one-part and two-part versions. Two-part epoxies offer many characteristics similar to the higher performance polyurethanes. They are durable and chemically resistant, but offer limited UV protection compared to the linear polyurethanes.

Antifouling paints are available in a variety of formulations. Most antifouling paint systems are compatible with epoxy and can be applied directly over a prepared epoxy barrier coat. If unsure of compatibility or having curing or adhesion problems with a specific paint, use the primer recommended for that antifouling paint over the barrier coat. Follow the recommendations given for preparation of GRP surfaces. Other paints, including marine LP's and primers, are not recommended for use below the waterline.

Primers are usually not needed to bond a paint film to epoxy, although interfacing primers may be required with some specialized bottom paints and high-build primers are useful for hiding scratches or flaws in the substrate. If the instructions on the selected paint or varnish recommend a specially primed surface, follow the recommendations given for fibreglass preparation. Self-etching primers are not effective on an epoxy coating because of the chemical resistance of the epoxy.

Polyester gelcoat is a pigmented version of polyester resin used to build GRP boats and many other products. Gelcoat provides a smooth pre-finished surface and is applied during the production process of the boat or component part. It is not often used as a post-production finish coating, but it can be applied over epoxy and is useful in some repair situations. Unreacted epoxy will interfere with gelcoat cure.

Always follow the instructions from the manufacturer of the coating systems. Nevertheless, as previously stated, it is recommended to make a test panel to evaluate the degree of surface preparation required and the compatibility and handling characteristics of the finish system.

About the author

Master boat builder and Naval Architect Morten Olesen is the owner of the company Boatplans.dk, which for decades has delivered boat plans for home and back yard boat builders all over the world. Morten's company Boatplans.dk is devoted to deliver innovative boat plans that are simple to understand. Or as Morten puts it:

"Boat building can seem like an overwhelming task. How can someone take a boat design, follow the boat plans and turn it into a gorgeous sailing vessel he can be proud of? It's easy when you are under my direction."

Morten was born and raised on the waters of Denmark/Scandinavia where wooden boat building is a life-long tradition. He learned about boat design first-hand from generations of experts that came before him. His idea was to create a line of exclusive, quality boat designs as well as detailed instruction and support materials that would allow boat builders of every skill level to create the wooden boat of their dreams. Incorporating innovative features, his line of boat plans gives you more than just ordinary boat designs.

Boat Building Master Course

Appendix A, Boat plans for the 10' Rowboat

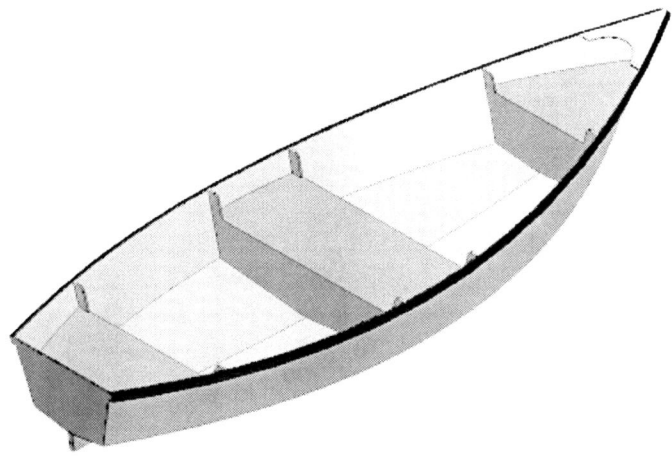

The 10' Rowboat is a real car topper, you can cruise everywhere with this nice little boat. It will easy load 2 adults and a large picnic basket.

The shallow v-bottom gives this boat some really nice rowing qualities and you can be sure this boat will make your days on the water worth remembering.

With only 3 sheets of plywood this rowboat is very affordable to build. So no matter if you are new to boatbuilding this is a project you can be sure to finish and that you can be proud of rowing on the water.

 Boat Building Master Course

Drawing list

Drawing no.	Title	File
10000	Line drawing	10000.pdf
10001	General arrangement	10001.pdf
10002-1	Overview 6 mm [1/4"] plates	10002-1.pdf
10002-2	Overview 9 mm [3/8"] plate	10002-2.pdf
10003-01	Bottom panel rear part	10003-01.pdf
10003-02	Bottom panel front part	10003-02.pdf
10003-03	Side panel front part	10003-03.pdf
10003-04	Side panel rear part	10003-04.pdf
10003-05	Frame A	10003-05.pdf
10003-06	Frame B	10003-06.pdf
10003-07	Frame C	10003-07.pdf
10003-08	Frame D	10003-08.pdf
10003-09	Transom	10003-09.pdf
10003-10	Front seat	10003-10.pdf
10003-11	Middle Seat	10003-11.pdf
10003-12	Rear seat	10003-12.pdf
10003-13	Bow bracket	10003-13.pdf
10003-14	Skeg (optional)	10003-14.pdf
10004-1	Assembly details, frame spacing	10004-1.pdf
10004-2	Assembly details, frame C	10004-2.pdf
10004-3	Assembly details	10004-3.pdf
10004-4	Assembly details, skeg (optional)	10004-4.pdf

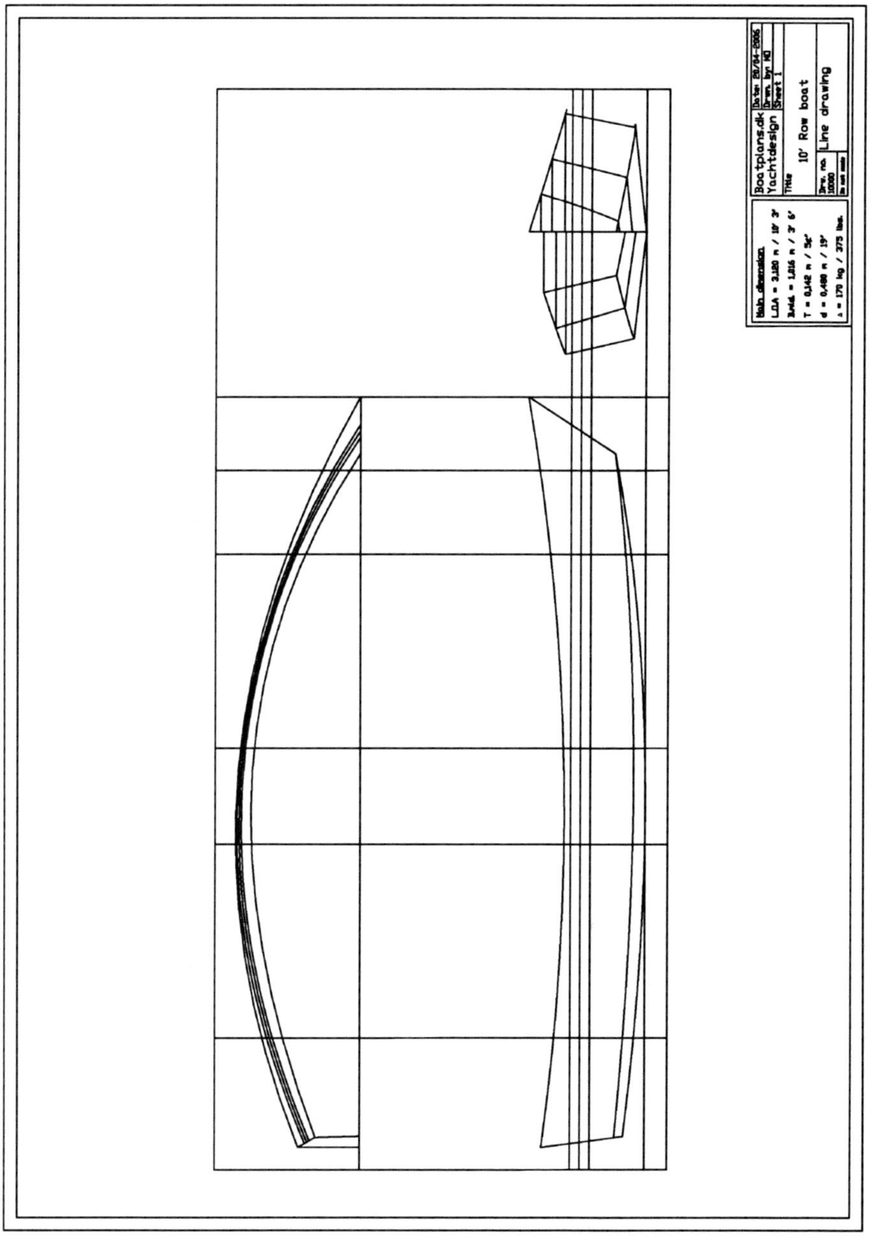

Boat Building Master Course

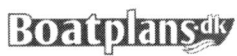

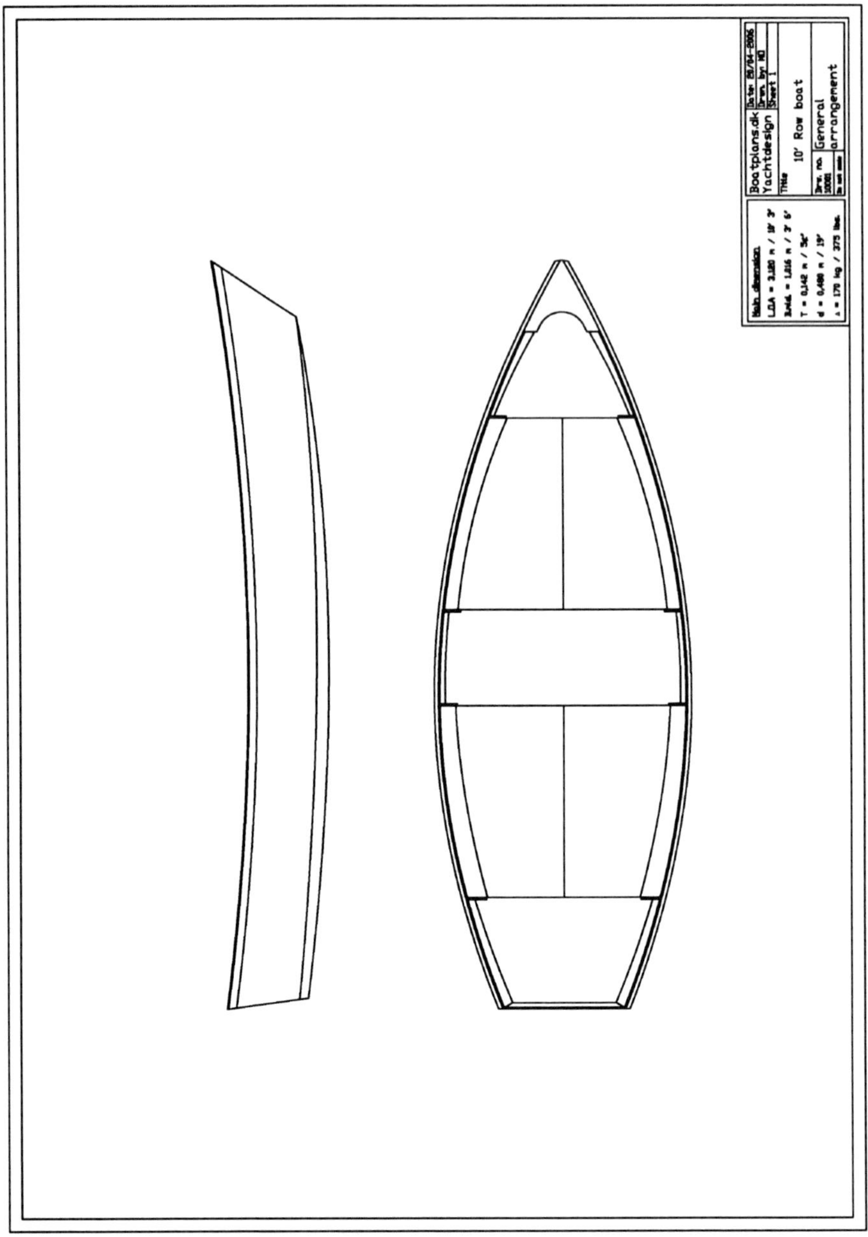
Boatplans.dk
Yachtdesign
10' Row boat
General
arrangement

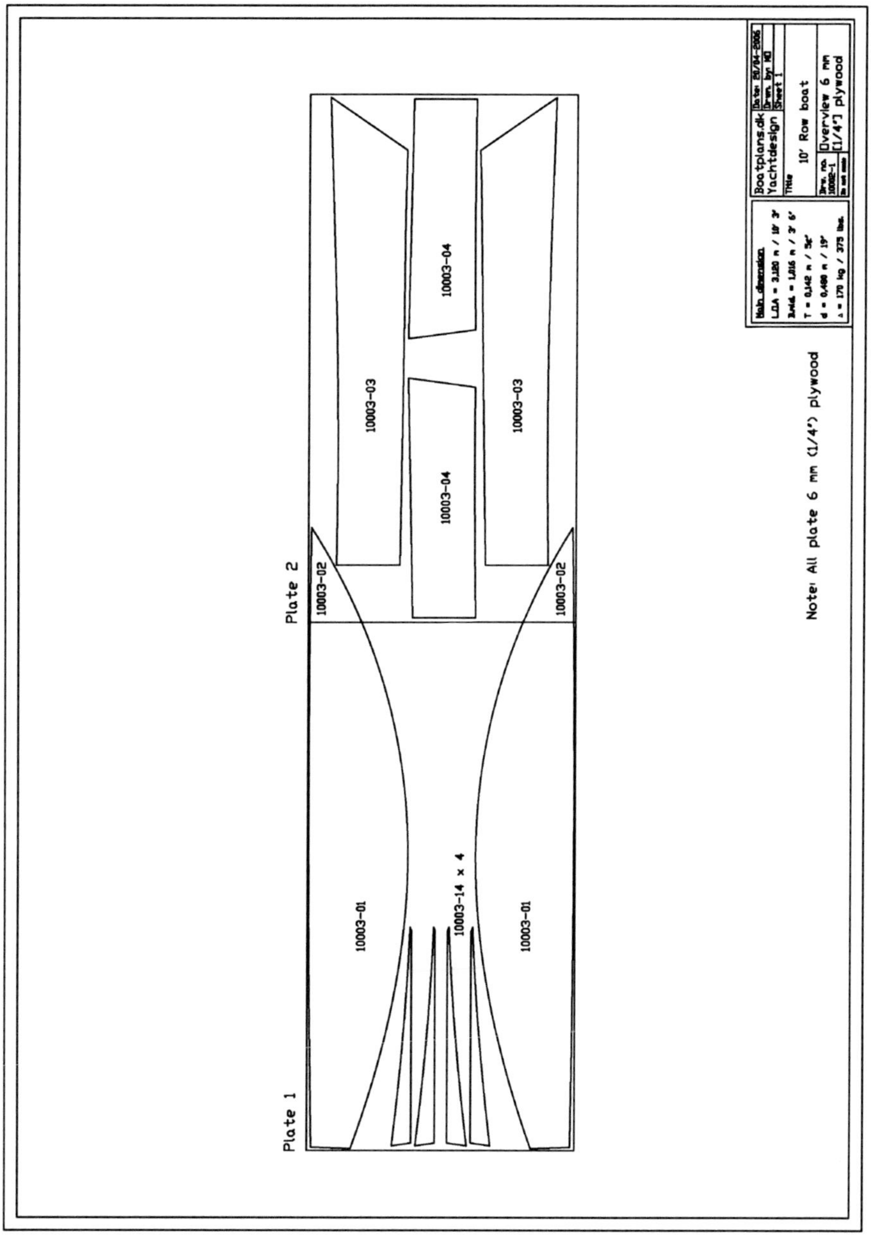

Boat Building Master Course

# Boat Building Master Course

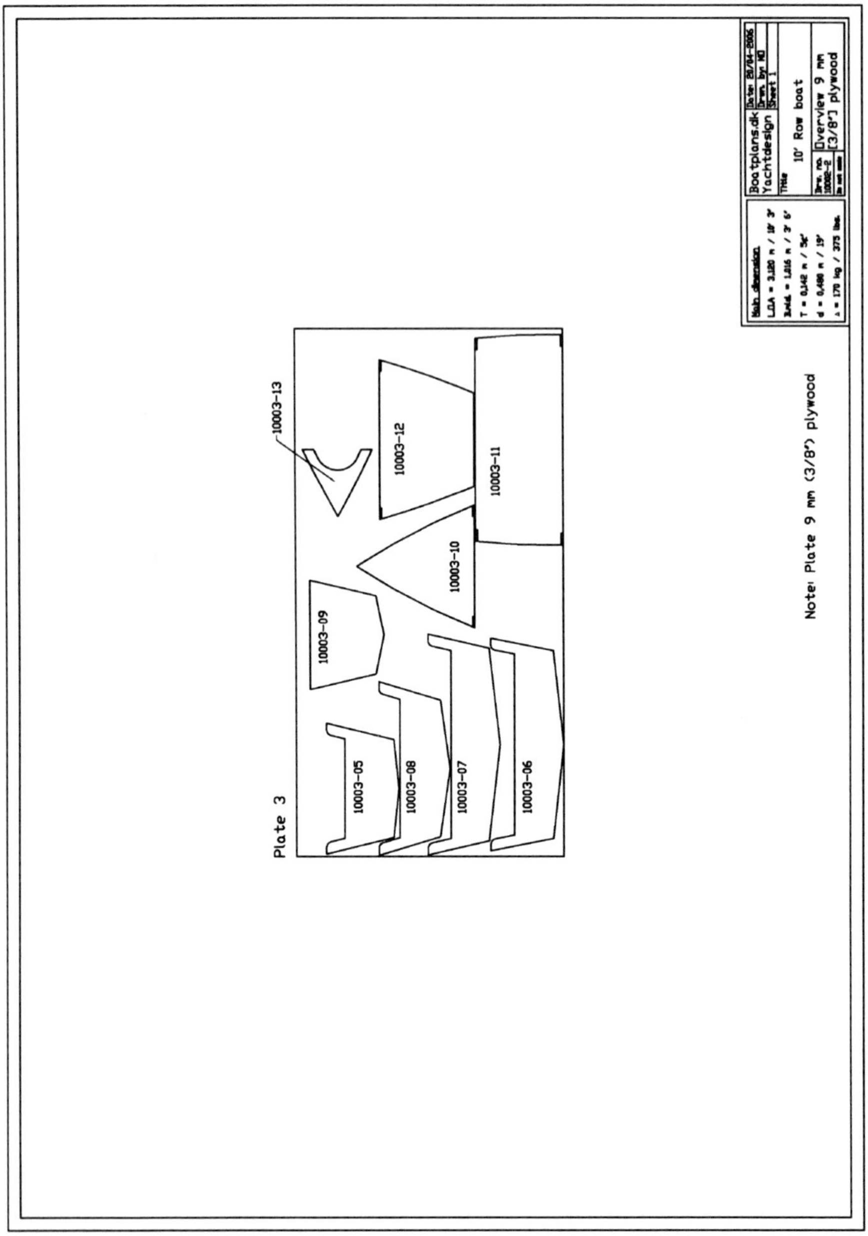

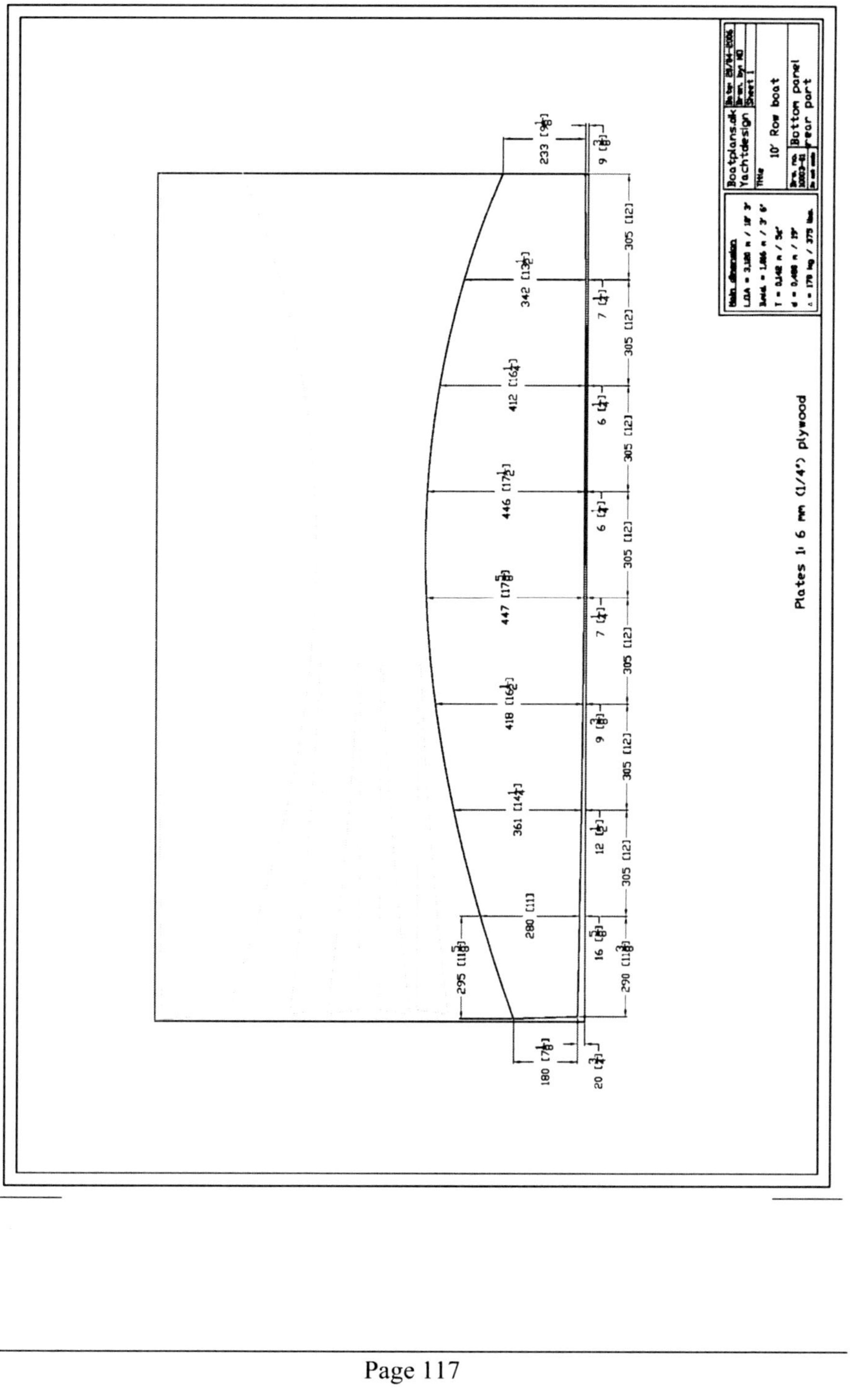

Boat Building Master Course

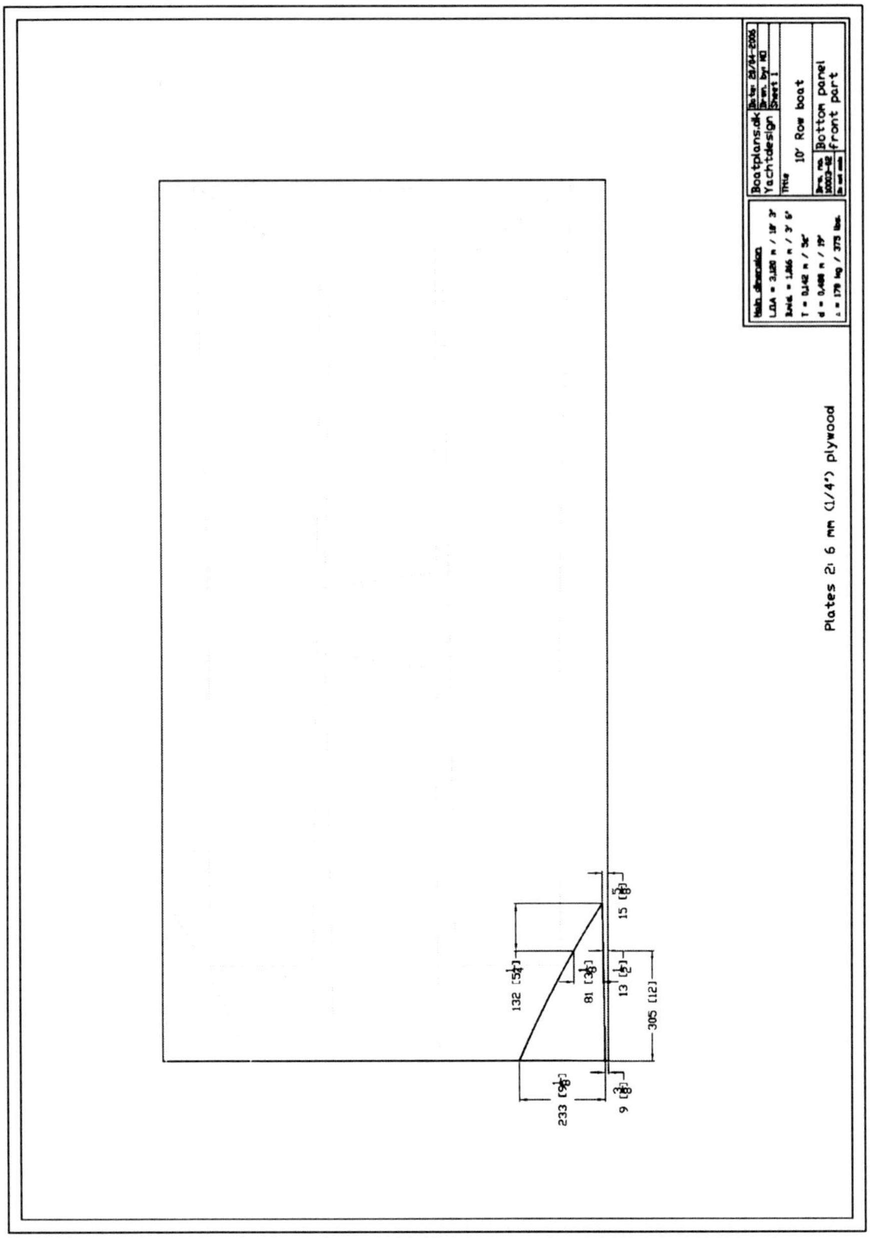

Boat Building Master Course

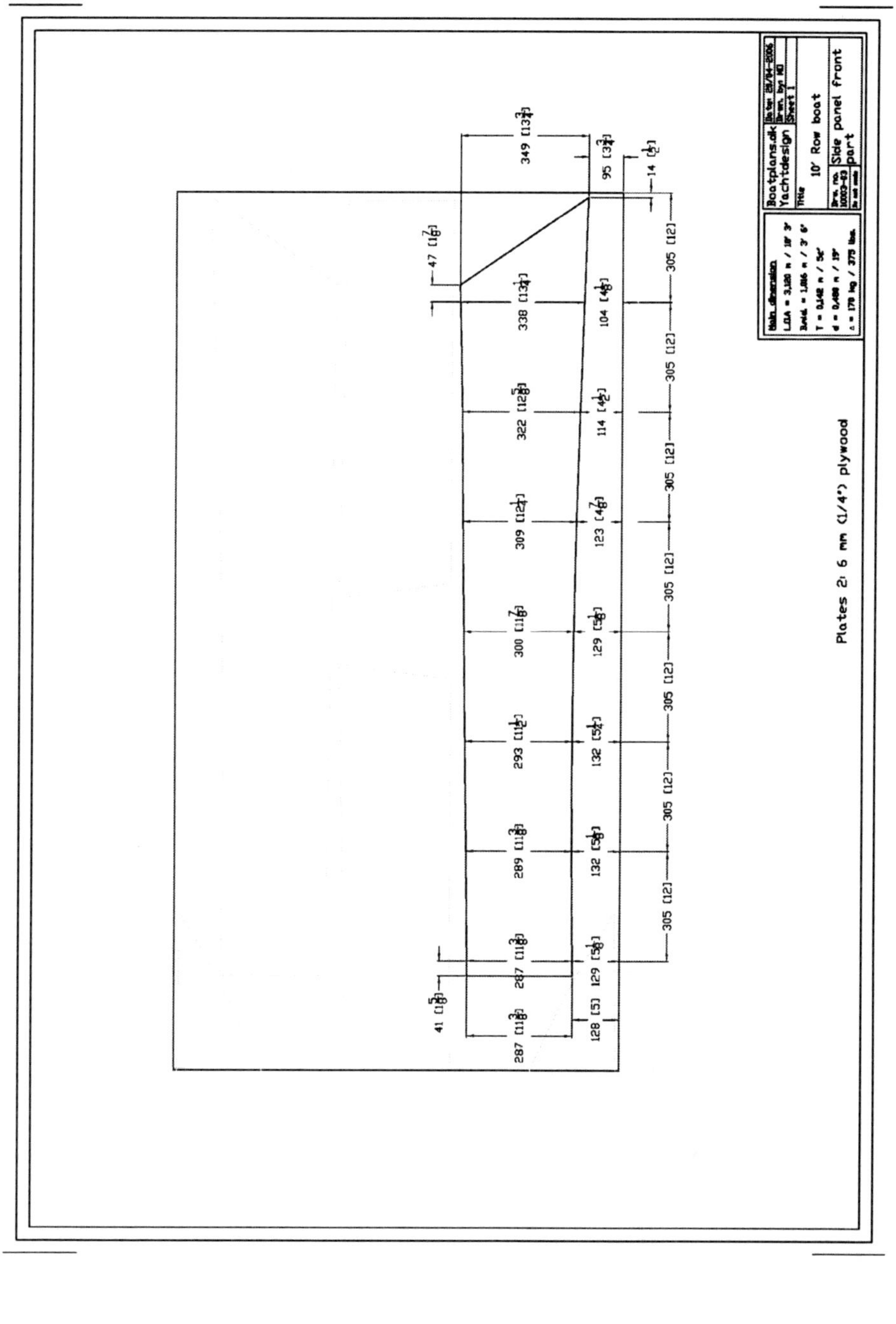

Boat Building Master Course

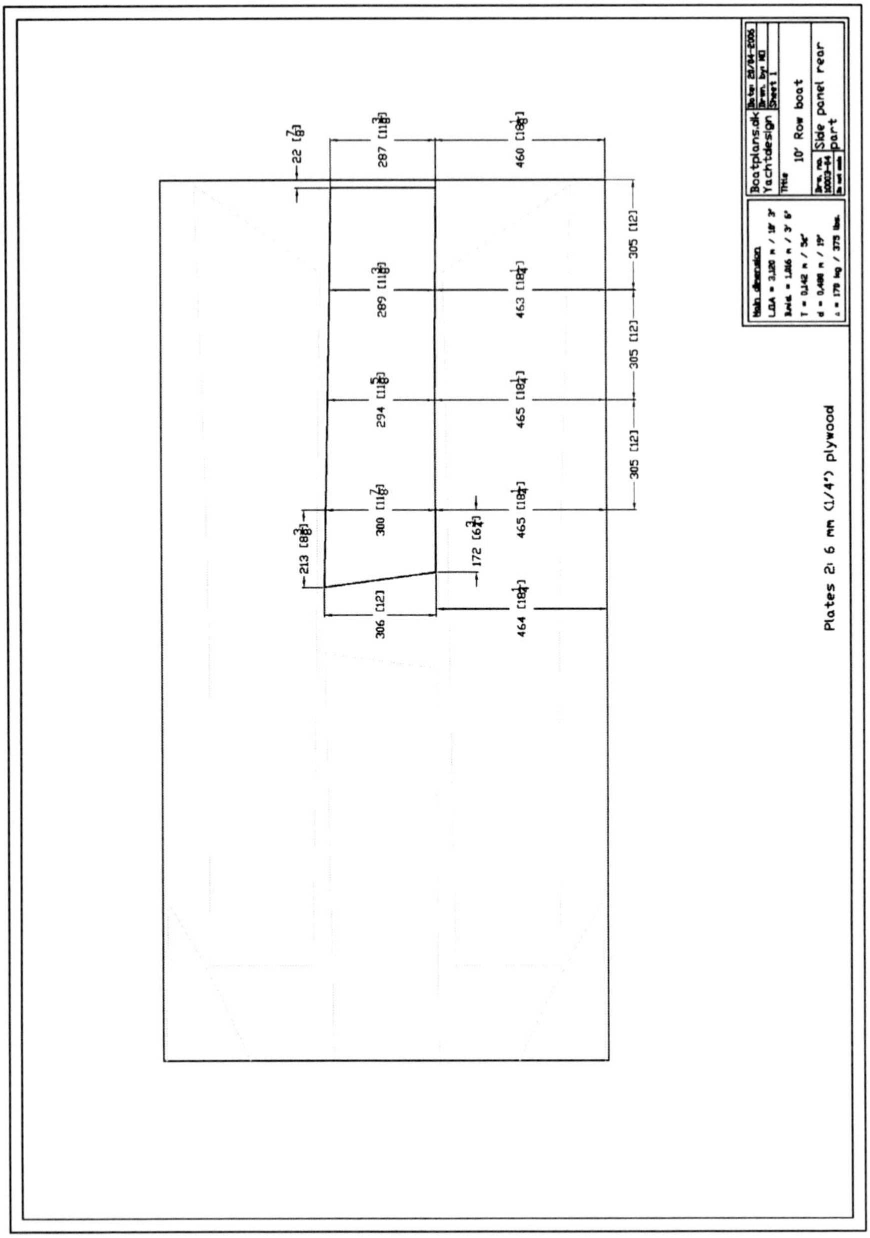

Boat Building Master Course

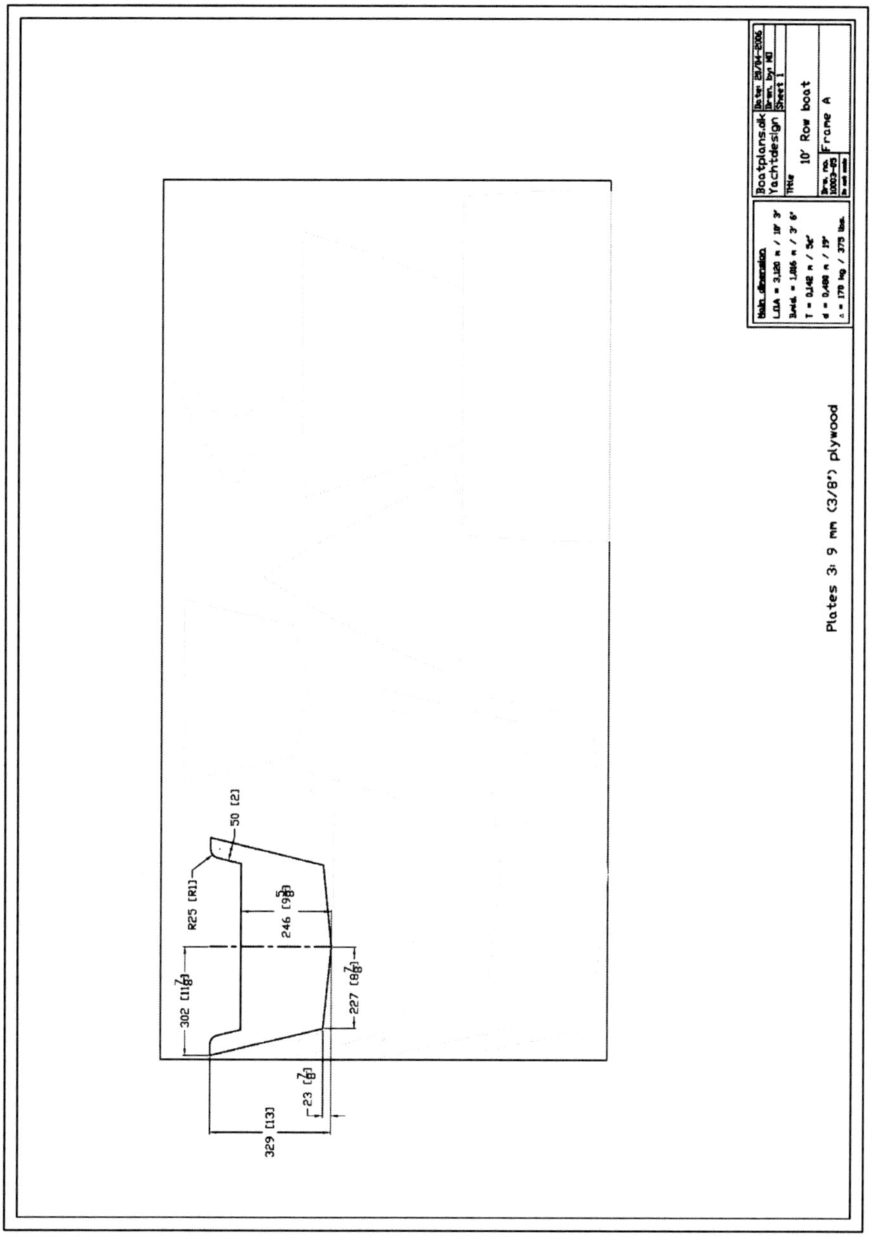

Boat Building Master Course

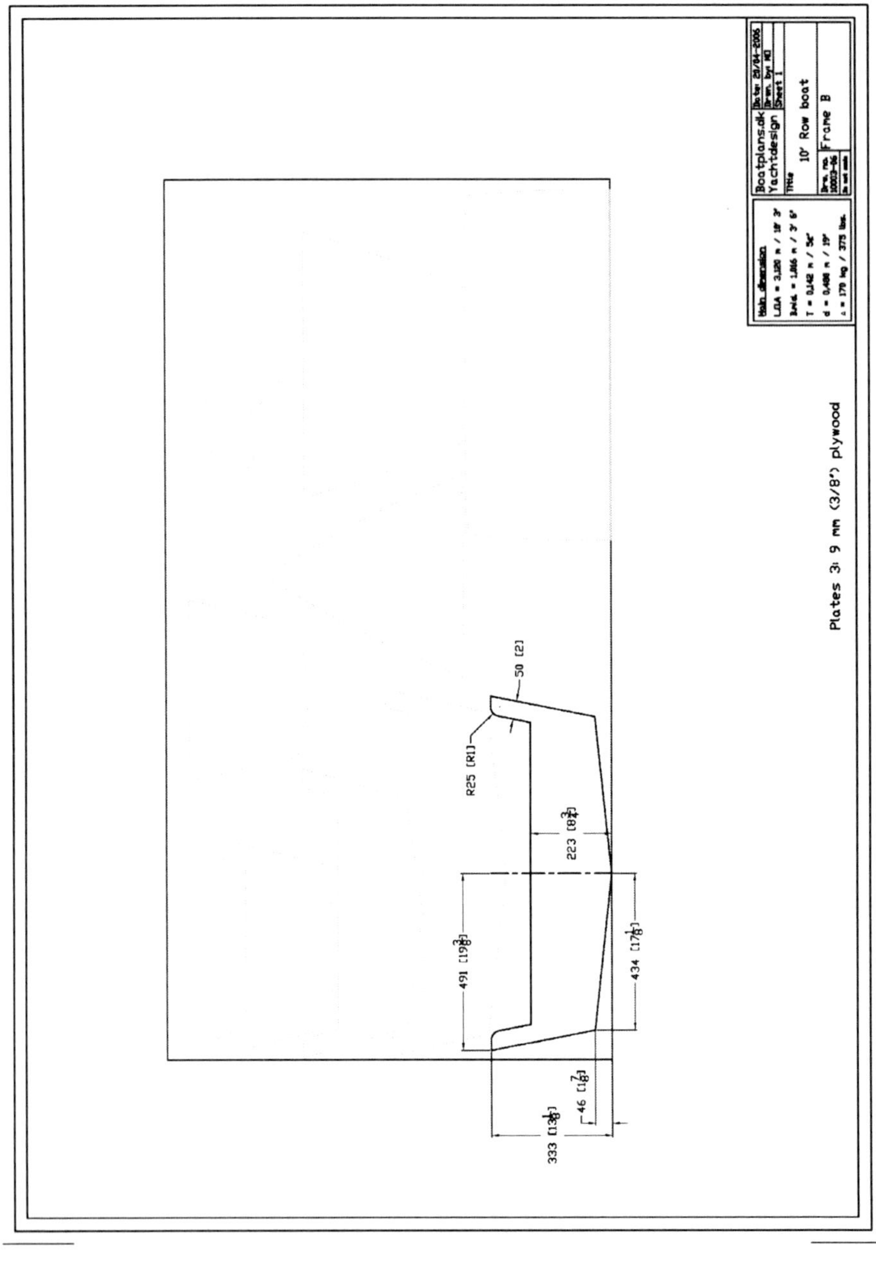

Boat Building Master Course

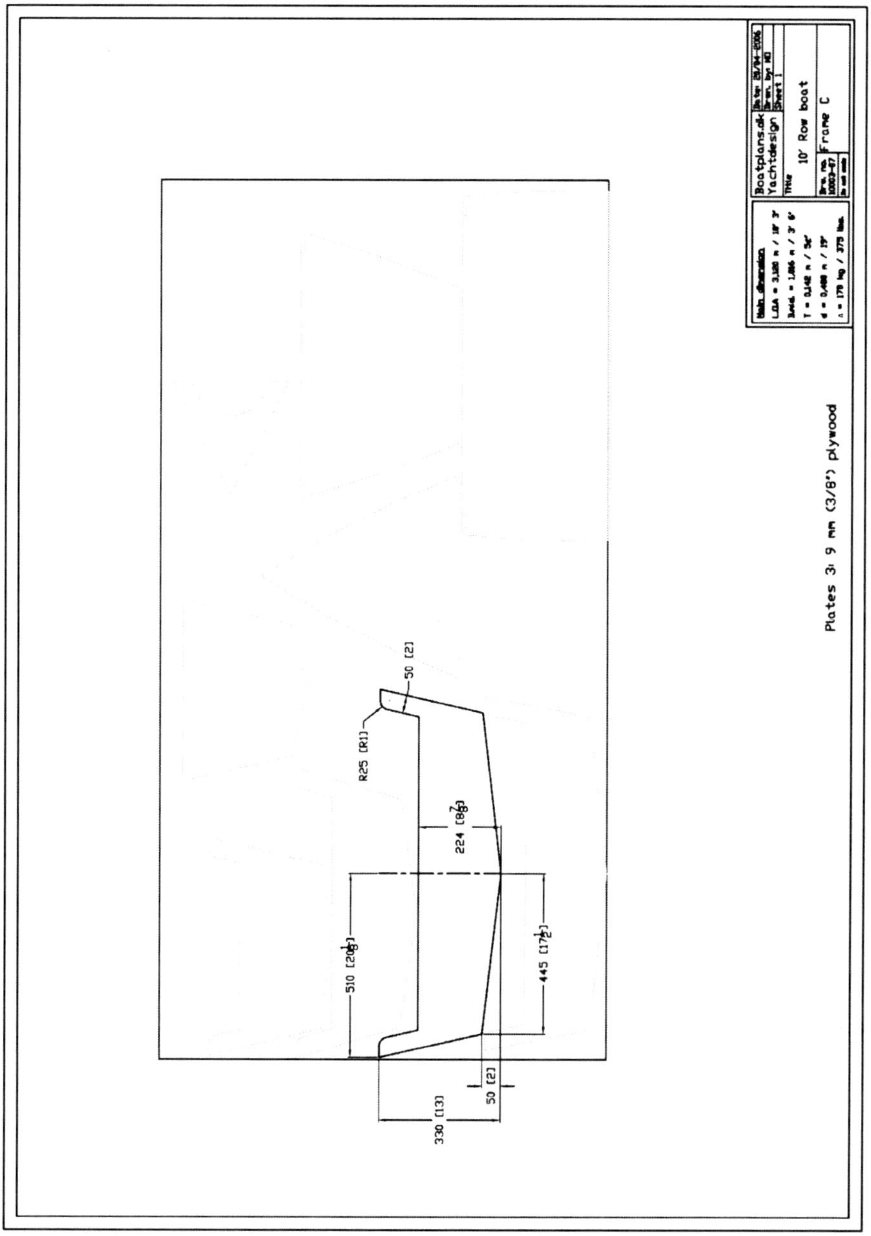

Boat Building Master Course

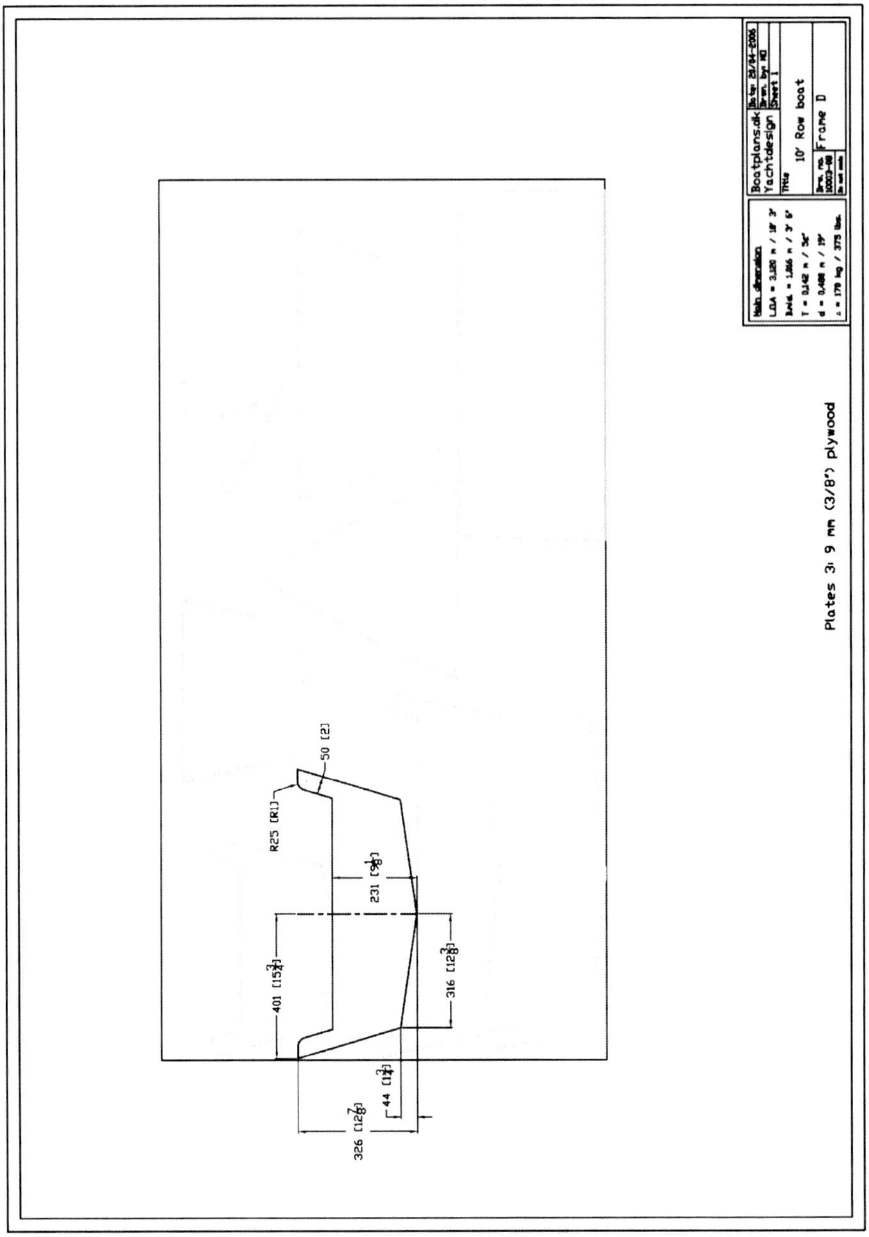

Boat Building Master Course

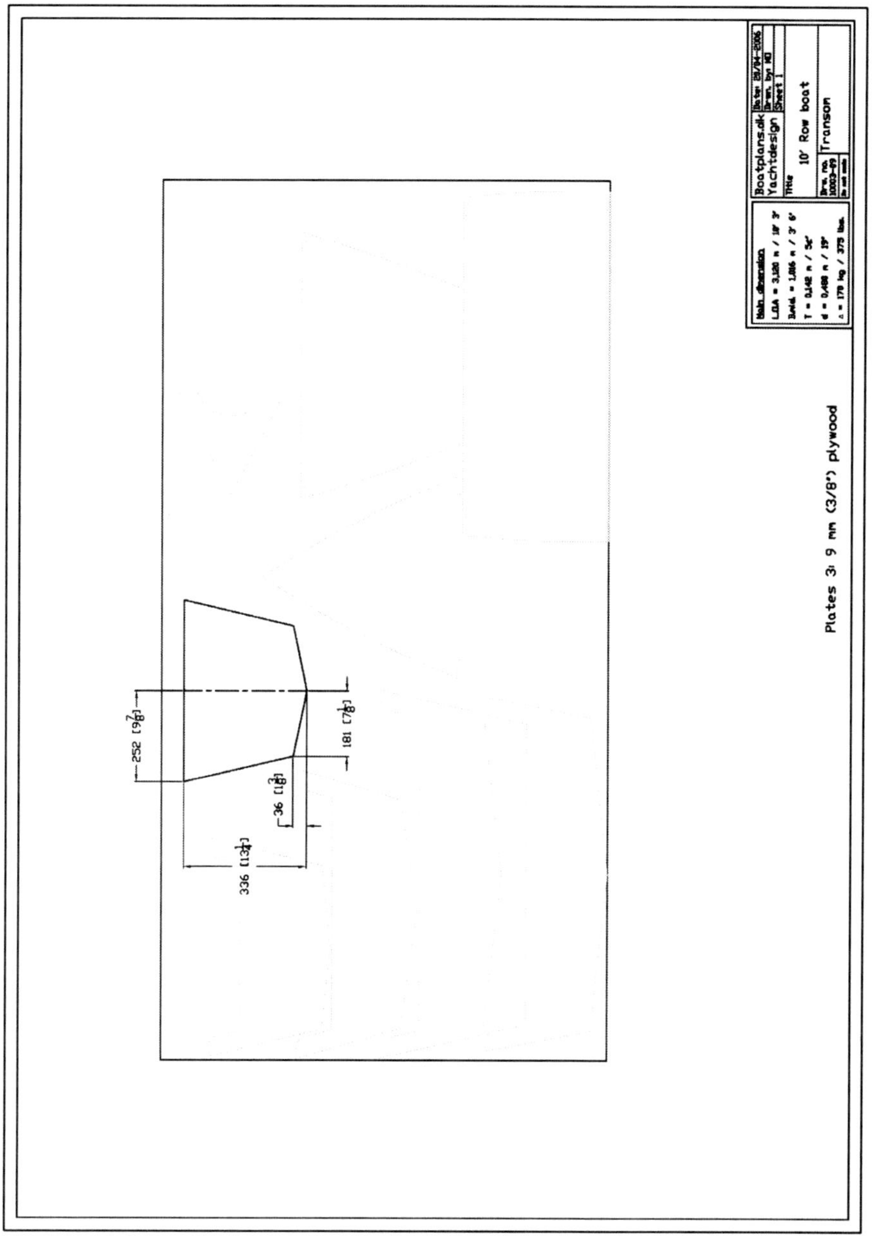

Boat Building Master Course

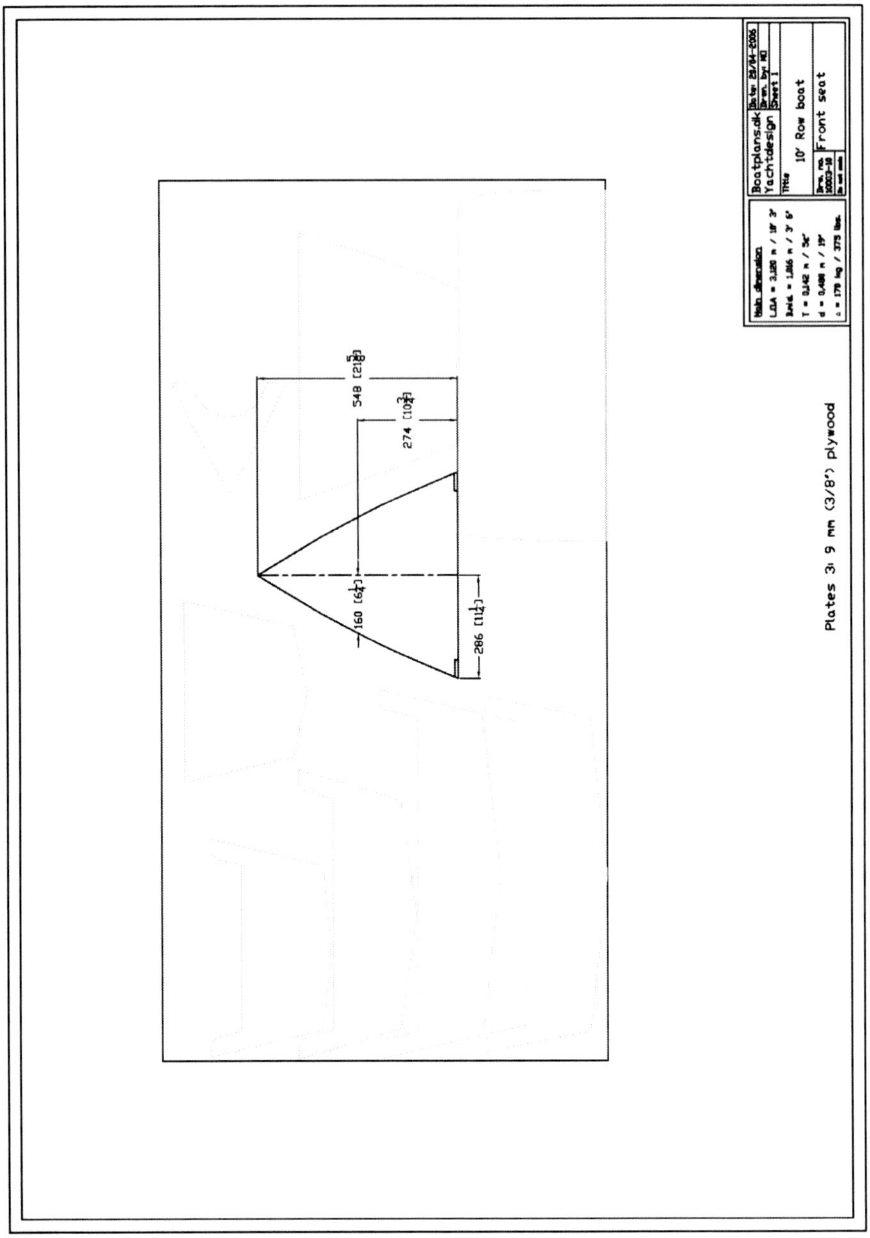

Boat Building Master Course

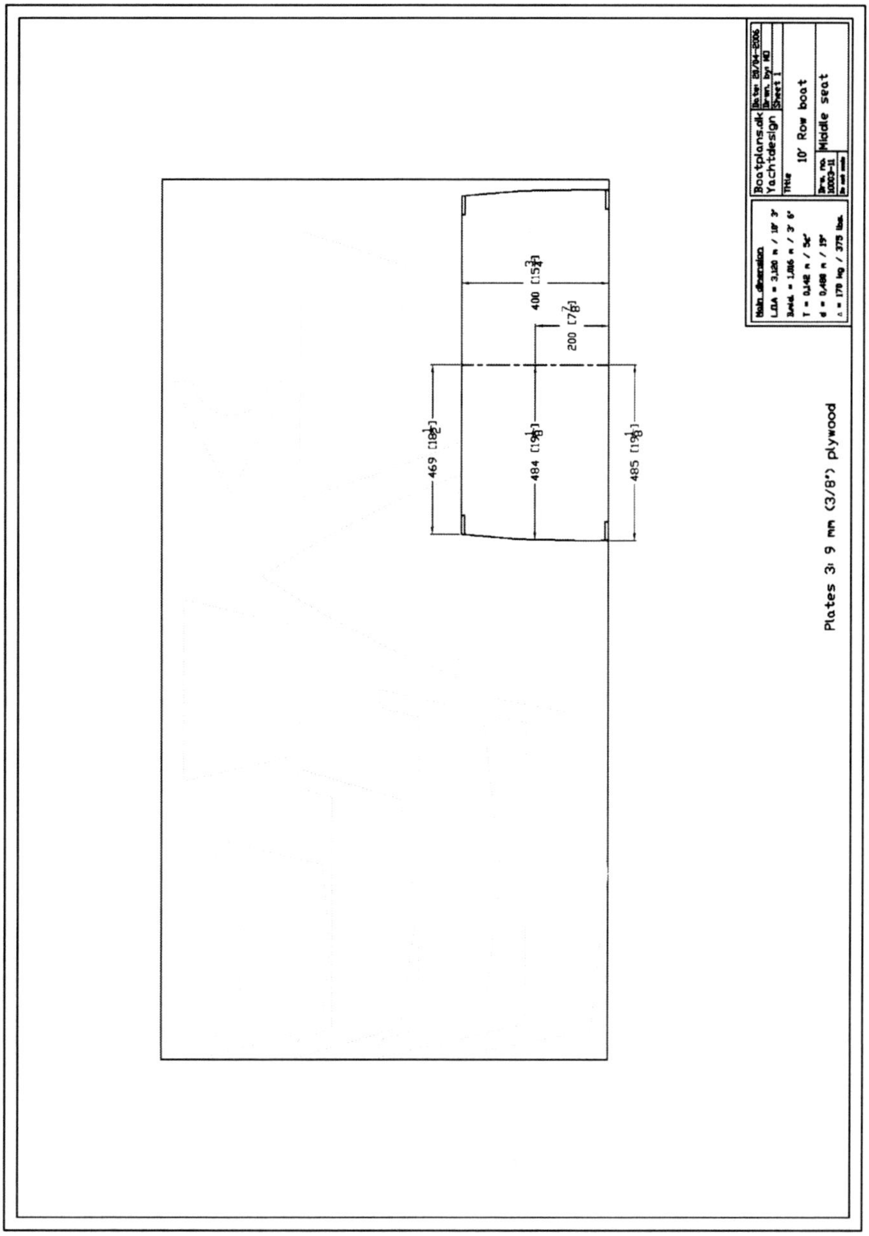

Boat Building Master Course

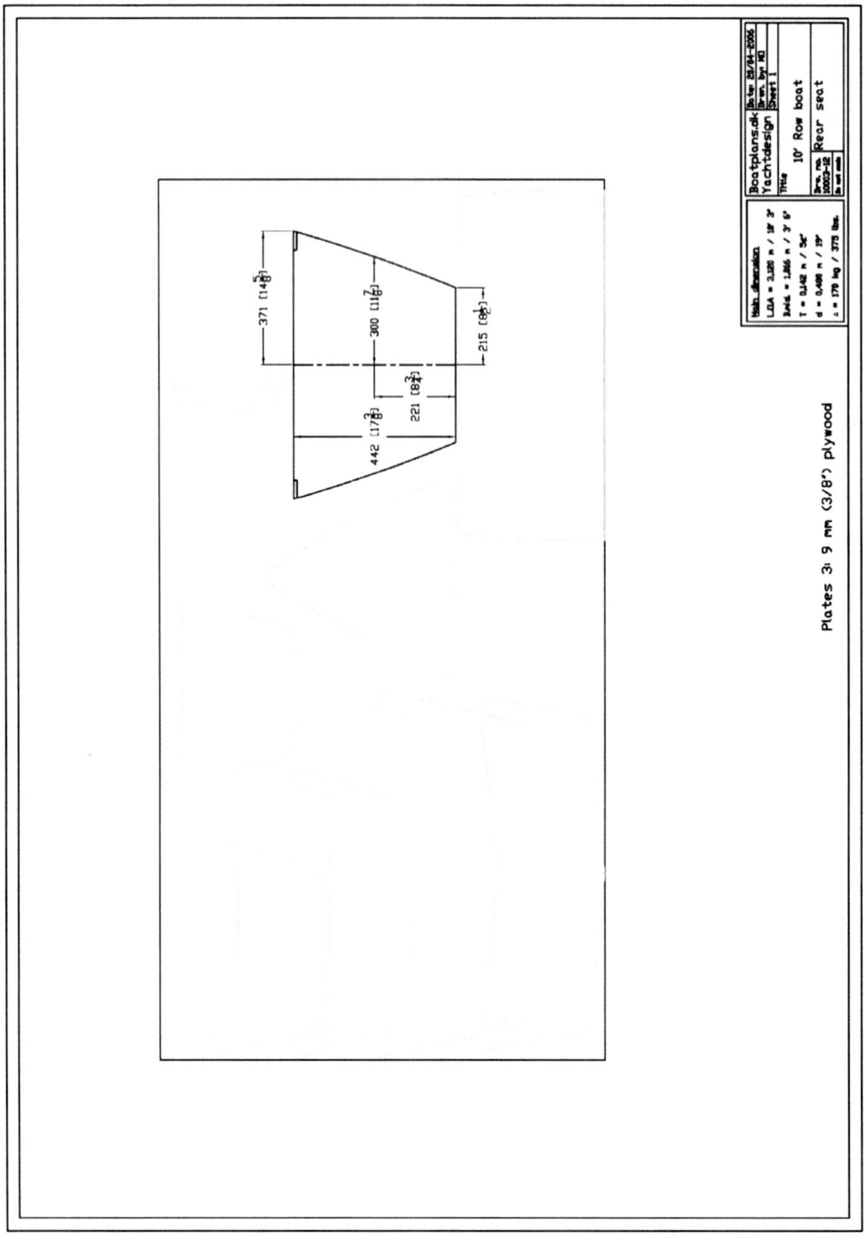

Boat Building Master Course

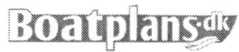

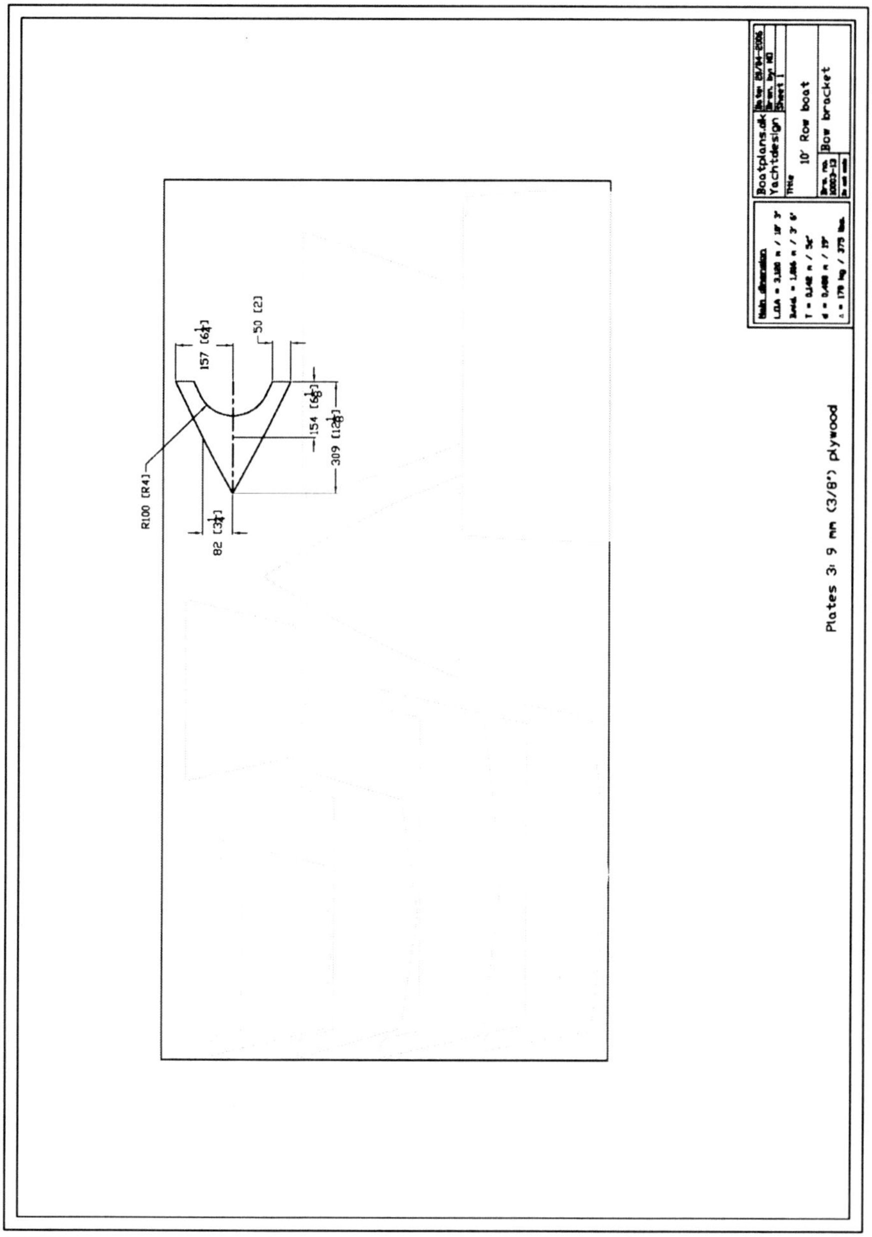
Boatplans.dk
Yachtdesign
10' Row boat
Bow bracket
157
50 [2]
154
309
R100 [R4]
82
Plates 3: 9 mm (3/8") plywood

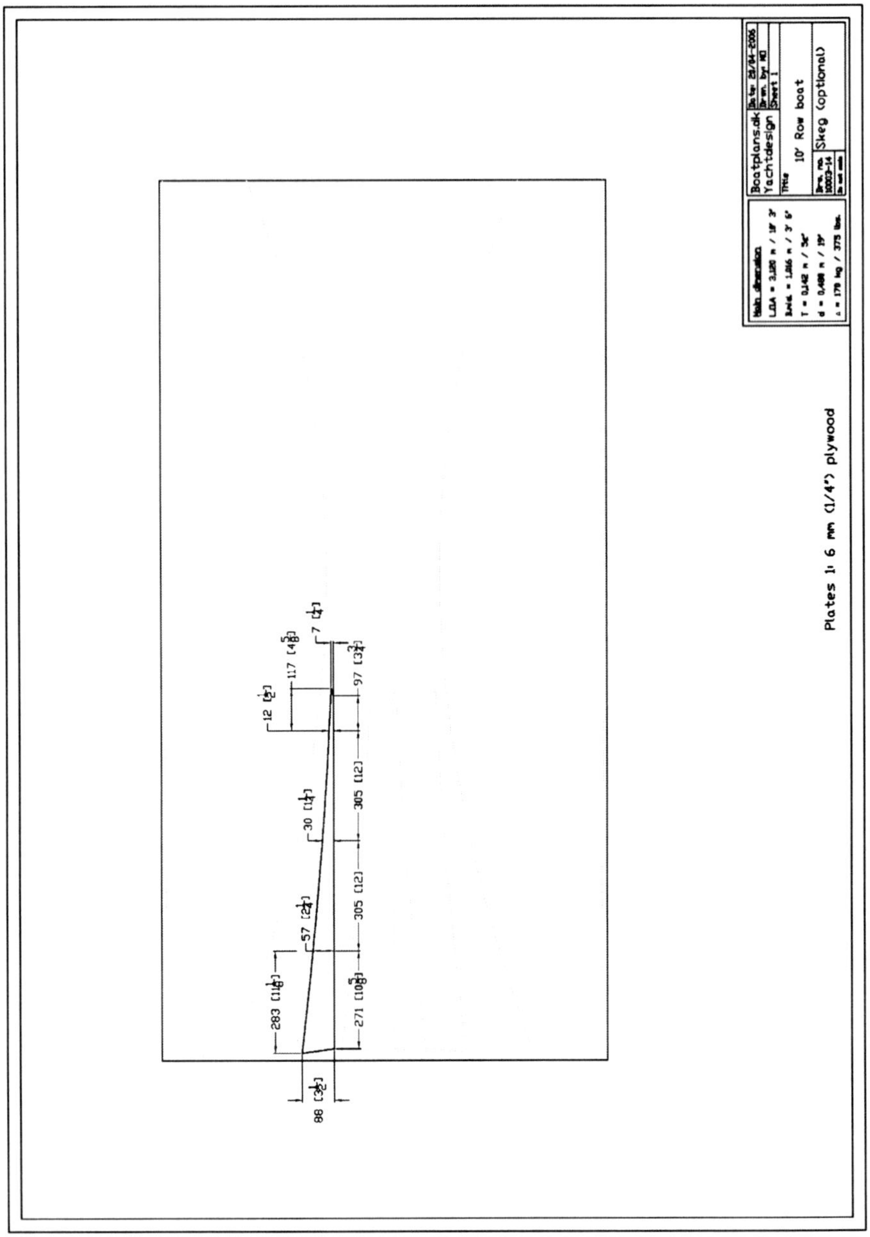

Boat Building Master Course

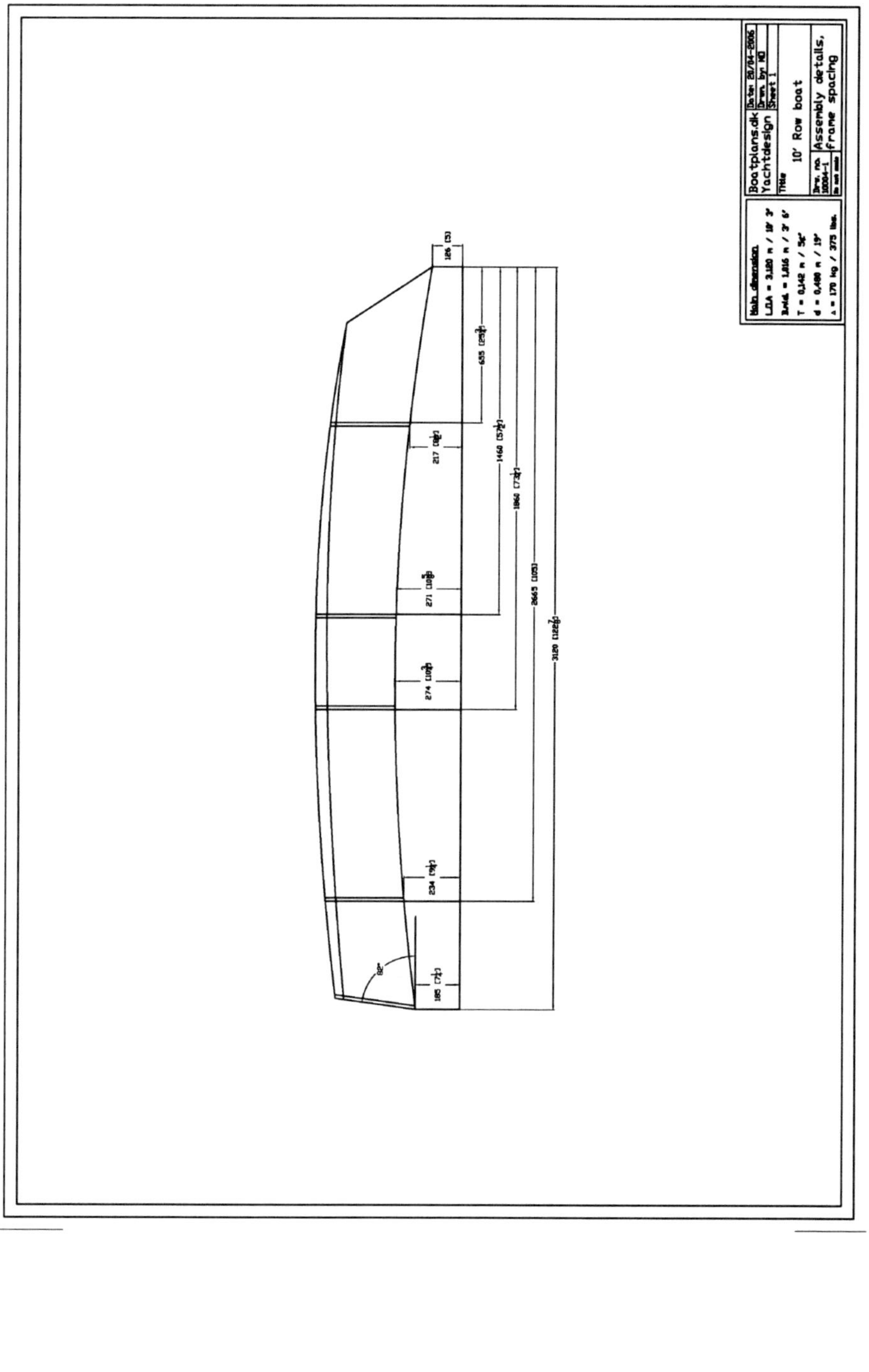

Boat Building Master Course

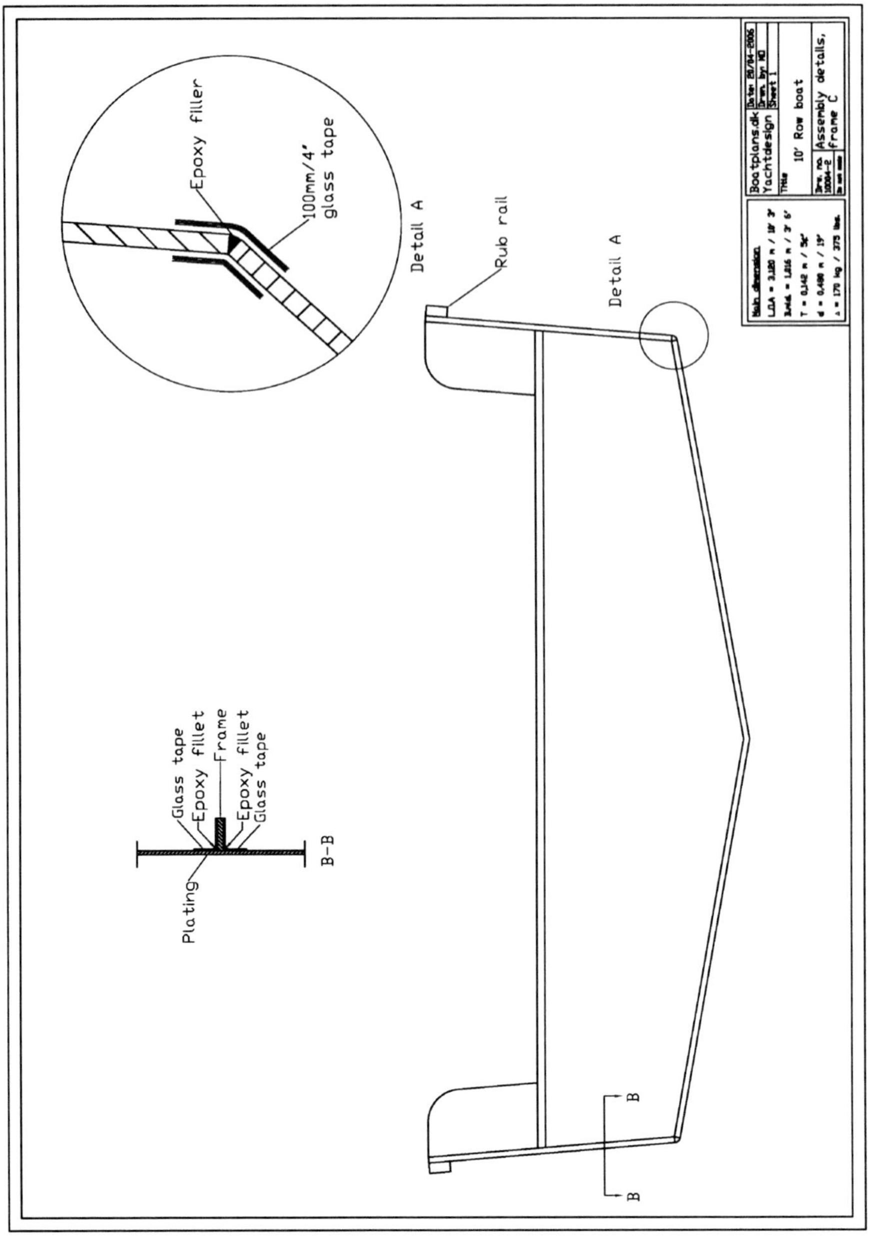

Boat Building Master Course

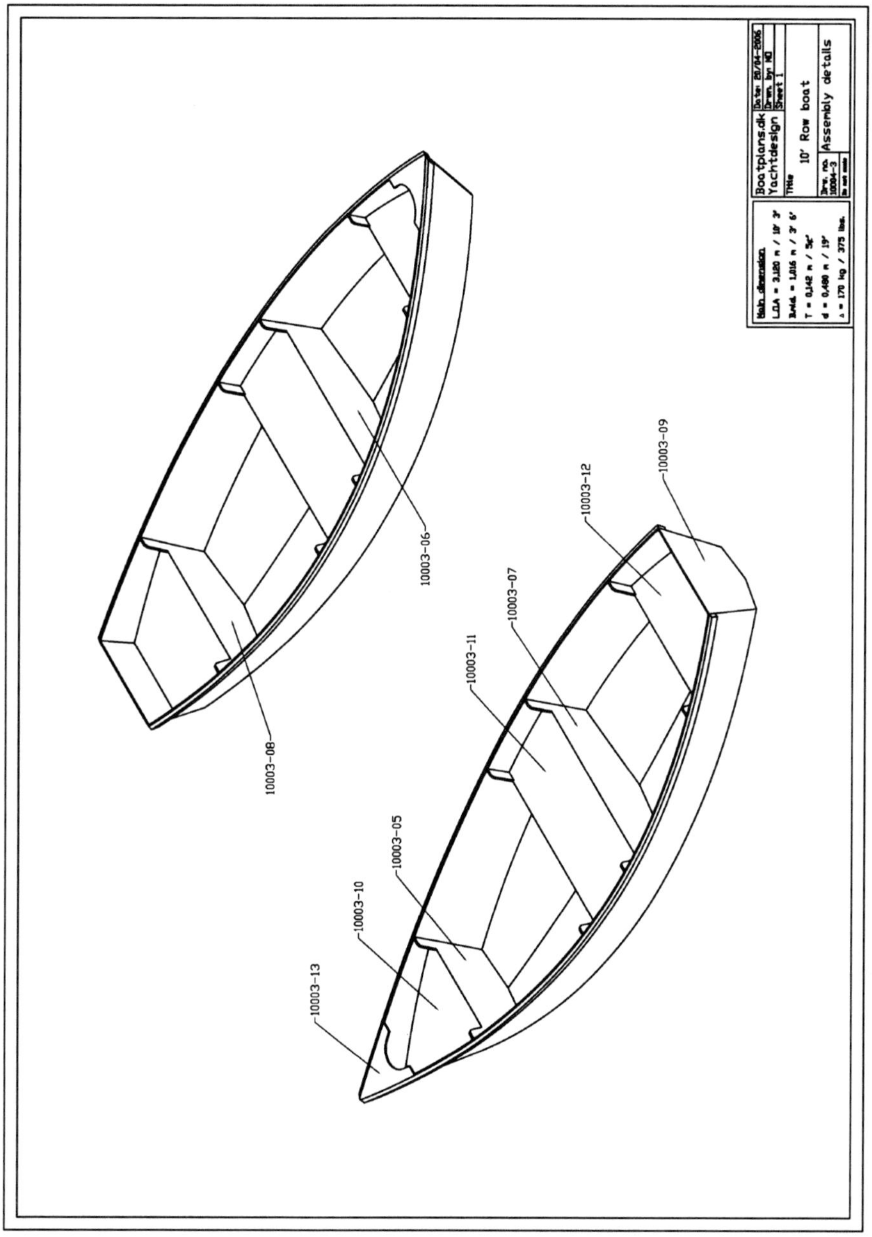

Boat Building Master Course

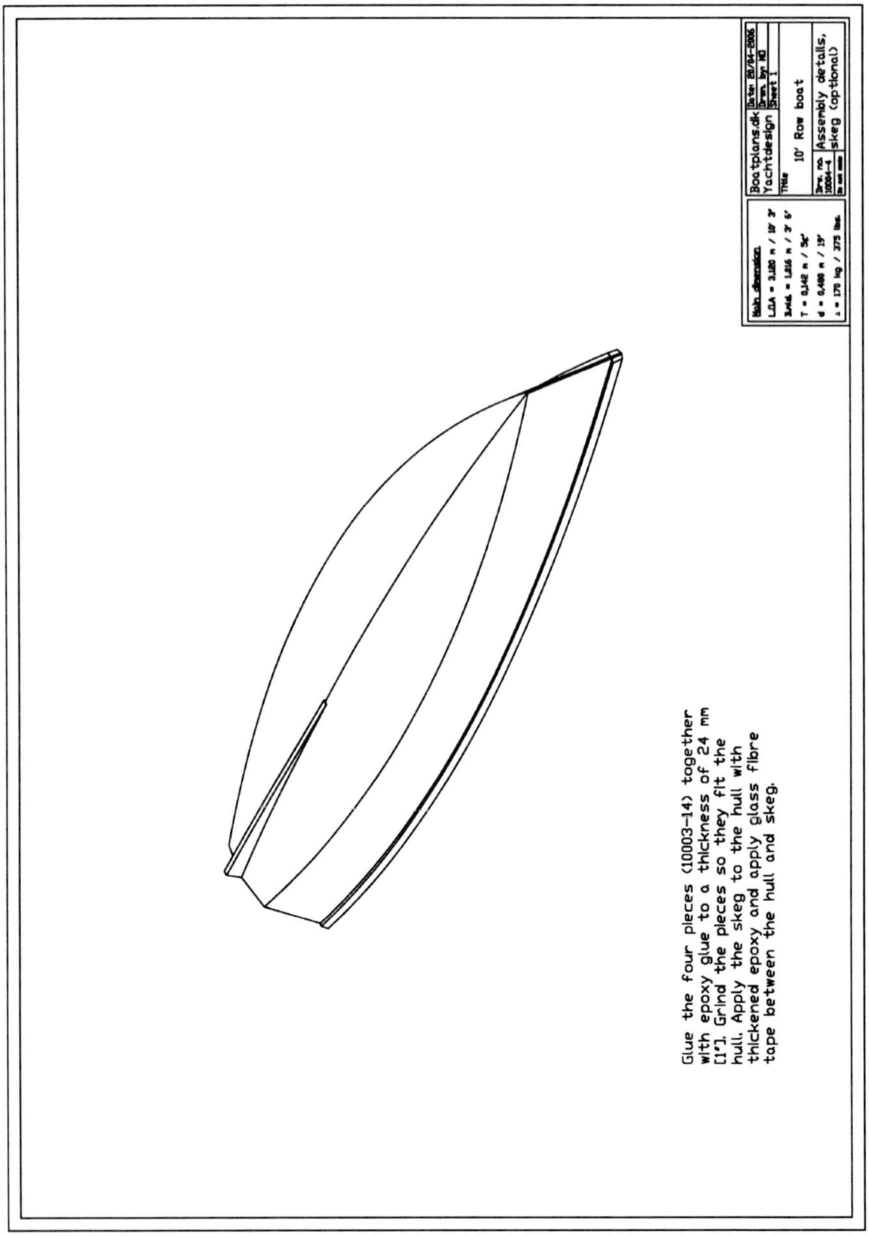

Boat Building Master Course

Glue the four pieces (10003-14) together with epoxy glue to a thickness of 24 mm (1"). Grind the pieces so they fit the hull. Apply the skeg to the hull with thickened epoxy and apply glass fibre tape between the hull and skeg.

Main dimensions
LOA = 3.05 m / 10' 2"
LWL = 2.85 m / 9' 6"
T = 0.142 m / 5¢
d = 0.488 m / 19"
Δ = 170 kg / 375 lbs.

Boatplans.dk — Date 25/01-2006
Yachtdesign — Drwn. by HG — Sheet 1
Title: 10' Row boat
Drwg. no. 10004-4 — Assembly details, skeg (optional)

Boat Building Master Course

Building instruction

Bill of Material

Plywood 2440x1220 / 8' x 4'
2 sheets 6 mm / 1/4"
1 sheet 9 mm / 3/8"

Wood
2 x 4,0 m [4.3 yd.] 15x25 mm [5/8"x1"] pine for rub rail

Fibreglass
44 m [48 yd.] 100mm [4"] glass fibre tape 170 g/m^2 [6 oz.]

Resin
Epoxy total 3,5 kg [0.9 gallon]

Wood flour
500 g (1 lbs.) filler

General

This design is the copyright of Boatplans.dk – Yacht design. The plans are made available for all who wants to build the boat. The plans may not be made a subject of trade for any third party persons.

All plywood used should be Marine or Exterior grade but of cause the choice is yours. For all natural wood use spruce, fir or pine.

Remember to use marine glue wherever glue is needed. For all seams in the chine hull use 100 mm fibreglass tapes with epoxy resin. For all stitching use copper wire or cable ties.

Construction sequence

The hull panels are drawn. Use the dimensions on the drawings 10003-01 to 10003-13. Use standard plywood sheets 2440 x 1220

Boat Building Master Course

(8'x4'). There are to be used 2 sheets of 6 mm (1/4") plywood and one sheet of 9 mm [3/8"] plywood. Mark the edges of the hull panels and use a thin wood batten held to the marks by nails or weights and draw the lines.

All the panels are in two or more parts. Joint the parts with 100 mm wide fibreglass tape (e.g. cut it yourself from a piece of fibreglass) and epoxy resin. The dimensions shown on the drawing are made for butt joints. If you wish to joint the hull panels with a scarf joint changes are to be made in the dimensions.

Once the hull panels are dried and the frames and transom are cut the assembly of the hull can start. Set up the frames A, B, C and D on a flat surface. Use the dimensions on drawing 10004-1. Alternately you can build a jig. It is necessary to make some temporary supports for the frames and transom.

Place the bottom panels and fasten it to the frames with screws or nails. When the bottom panel is laid out stitch the bottom panels in the centre line. Stitch the two side panels to the bottom panel. At this stage do not over tighten the stitches so adjustments can be made. The side panels can be fastened to the frames with screws or nails. Assemble the transom with some screws or nails.

Now the hull is assembled and the time is to check the hull geometry. Make absolutely sure that the hull is not twisted and the shape is correct. As the hull is checked tighten up the stitches.

When the hull is checked it is time for sealing the seams. Start with the outside seams and use epoxy filler to make the curvature between the panels smooth. When done use the glass tape and epoxy resin for reinforcement of the seams. For the use of epoxy remember to follow the instruction from your supplier. It is also important to prime the wood with epoxy before the tape is laid. Remember to wet out the tape completely when laying the final layer. Also make sure to clean up any resin runs before it cures, it is very difficult to remove afterwards.

Boat Building Master Course

Now it is time to turn the hull upright. Finish the inside seams using epoxy filler before you put on the tape and epoxy. Remember to fasten the frames and transom with tape and epoxy as well. Use large epoxy fillets to glue frames and transom to the hull.

With the hull turned upright it is now time to assemble the seats. There might be some adjustments to make before the seats fits. Glue and glass the seats to the hull and frames.

Assemble the bow bracket and fasten it with epoxy and glass fibre tape. You can choose to apply the skeg to the hull. The advantage for the skeg is better tracking. Follow the instruction on drawing 10004-4 for details on assembly.

Watertight hatches can be mounted in the frames thus making the compartments suitable for storage. The easiest is to buy some standard watertight hatches from your normal supplier.

It is not from a strength point of view necessary to cover the entire hull with epoxy and fabric. But it is recommended to at least prime the plywood with epoxy resin for better waterproof properties.

The hull may be finished with paint or varnish (for normal use, a good quality exterior house paint/varnish is sufficient).

Good luck with the building of your new boat.

Morten Olesen
Boatplans.dk

Boat Building Master Course

Appendix B, Boat plans for the 13' J – Skiff

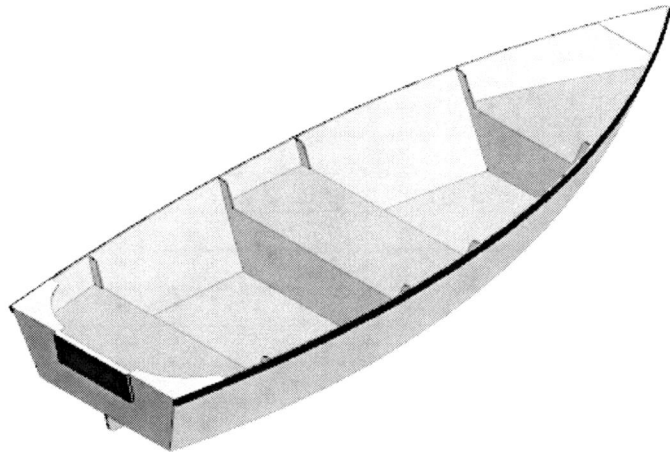

This 13' flat bottom skiff is a real workboat. It is so easy to build that you can build it in a day (maybe add a few days for fairing and painting ;-).

The 13' J - Skiff is not a lightweight boat, but it is for sure stable and will do very well for both fishing and sailing with friends. In fact this boat is so stable that you can even use it as a drift boat.

The boat will go well with an outboard engine between 4 and 12 hp. With only 5 sheets of plywood this boat is very affordable to build and the real easy building process makes no excuse for not getting started building right away.

Drawing list

Drawing no.	Title	File
10000	Line drawing	10000.pdf
10001	General arrangement	10001.pdf
10002	Overview 9 mm plate	10002.pdf
10003-01	Bottom panel rear part	10003-01.pdf
10003-02	Bottom panel front part	10003-02.pdf
10003-03	Side panel front part	10003-03.pdf
10003-04	Side panel rear part	10003-04.pdf
10003-05	Frame A	10003-05.pdf
10003-06	Frame B	10003-06.pdf
10003-07	Frame C	10003-07.pdf
10003-08	Frame D	10003-08.pdf
10003-09	Transom	10003-09.pdf
10003-10	Front seat	10003-10.pdf
10003-11	Middle seat	10003-11.pdf
10003-12	Rear seat	10003-12.pdf
10003-13	Bow bracket	10003-13.pdf
10003-14	Transom bracket	10003-14.pdf
10003-15	Skeg	10003-15.pdf
10003-16	Rub plates	10003-16.pdf
10004-1	Assembly details, frame spacing	10004-1.pdf
10004-2	Assembly details, frame C	10004-2.pdf
10004-3	Assembly details	10004-3.pdf

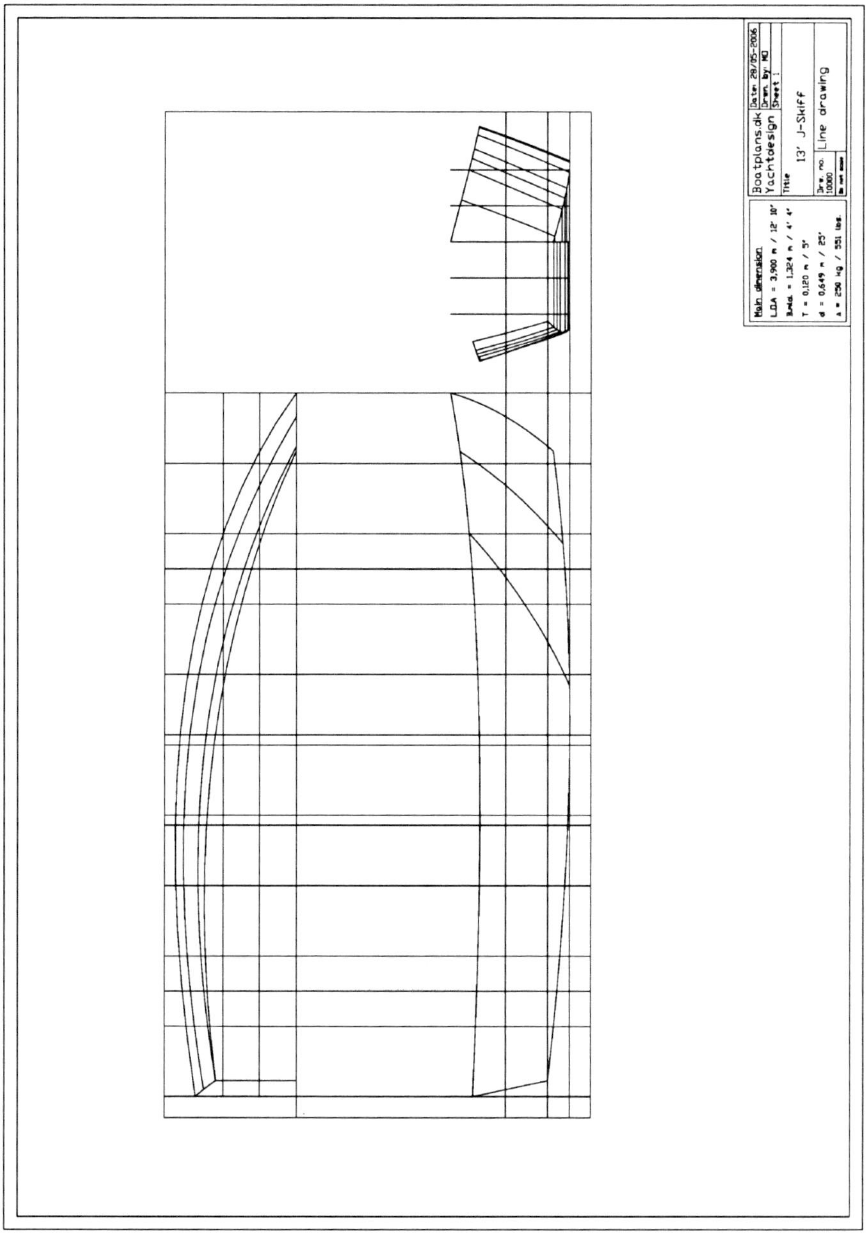

Boat Building Master Course

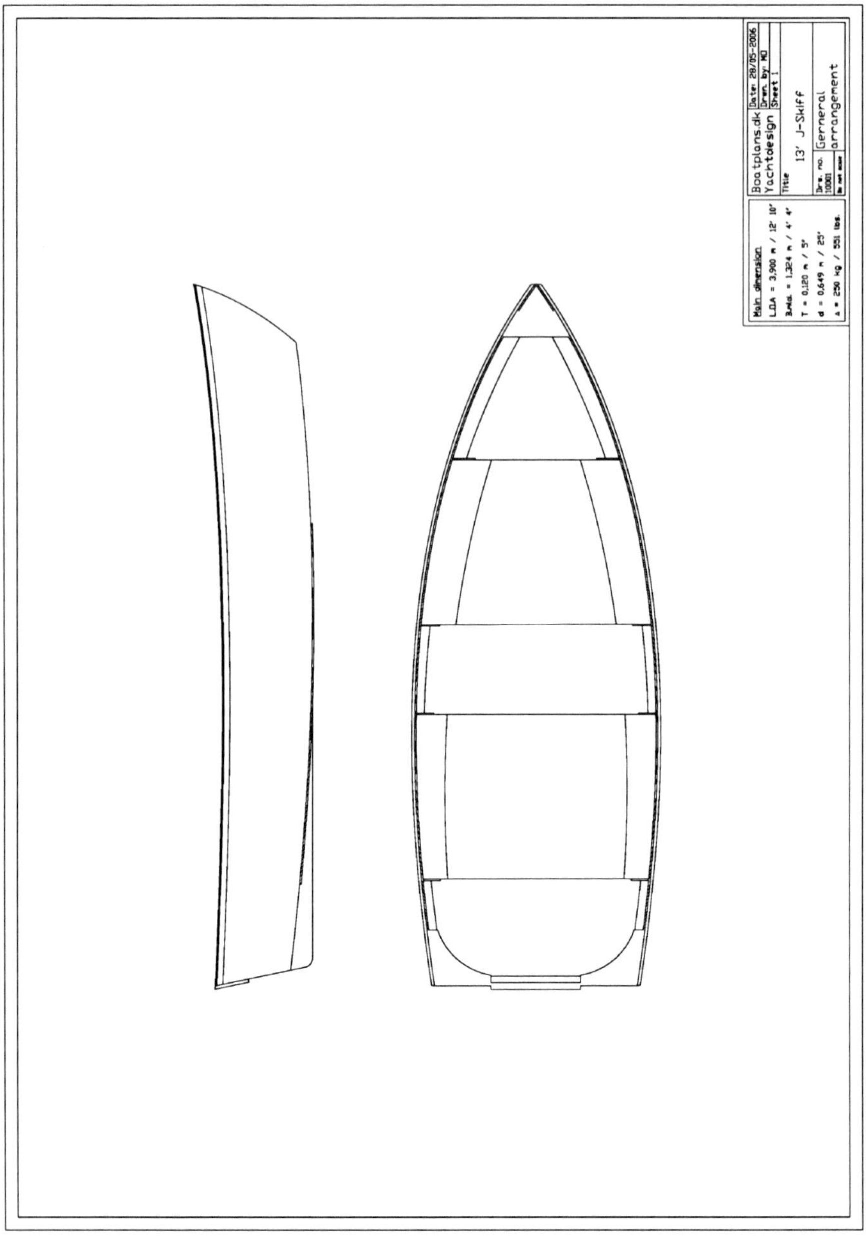

Boat Building Master Course

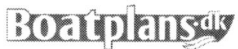

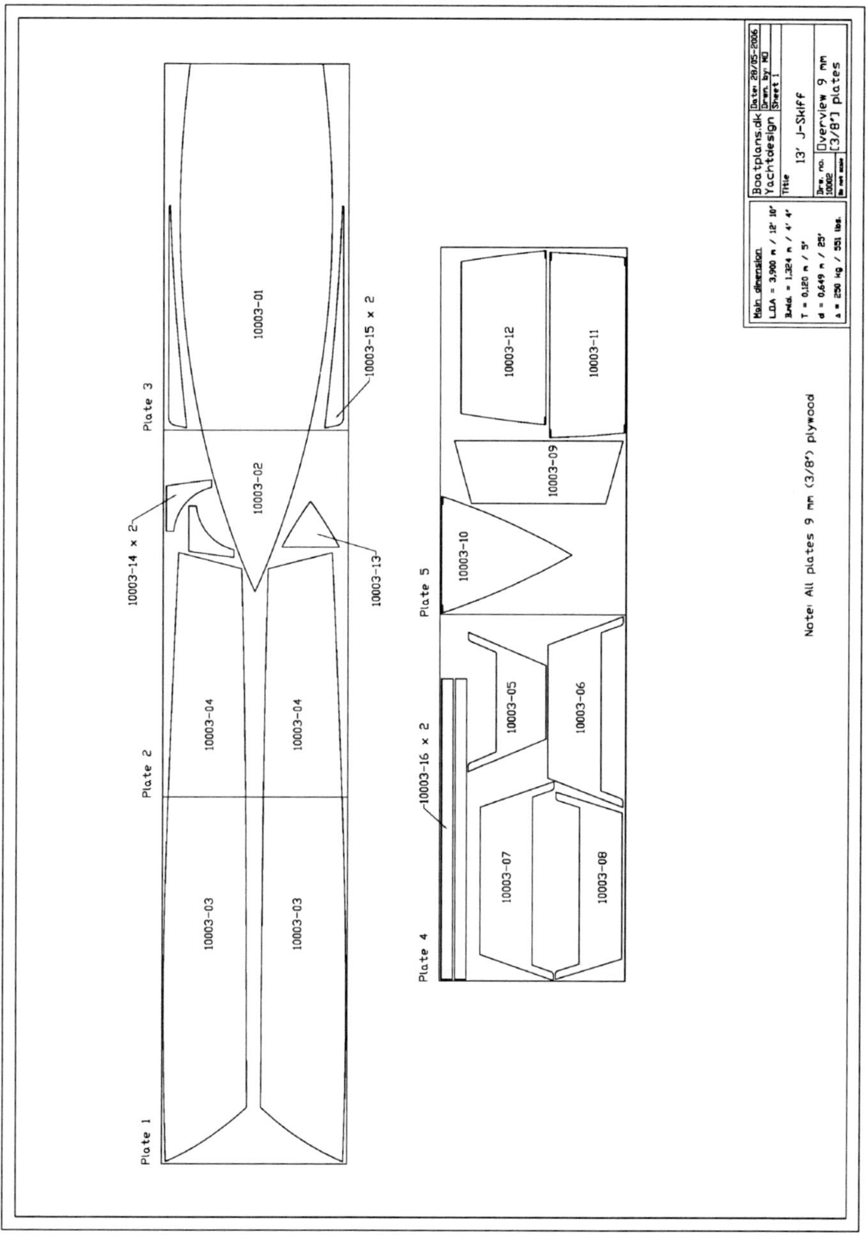
Boatplans.dk
Yachtdesign
Date: 28/05-2006
Drwn. by: MD
Sheet 1
Title
13' J-Skiff
Drw. no. 10002
Overview 9 mm [3/8"] plates
Main dimension
LOA = 3,900 m / 12' 10"
B.wld. = 1,324 m / 4' 4"
T = 0,120 m / 5"
d = 0,649 m / 25"
Δ = 250 kg / 551 lbs.
Note: All plates 9 mm (3/8") plywood
Plate 1
Plate 2
Plate 3
Plate 4
Plate 5
10003-01
10003-02
10003-03
10003-03
10003-04
10003-04
10003-05
10003-06
10003-07
10003-08
10003-09
10003-10
10003-11
10003-12
10003-13
10003-14 x 2
10003-15 x 2
10003-16 x 2

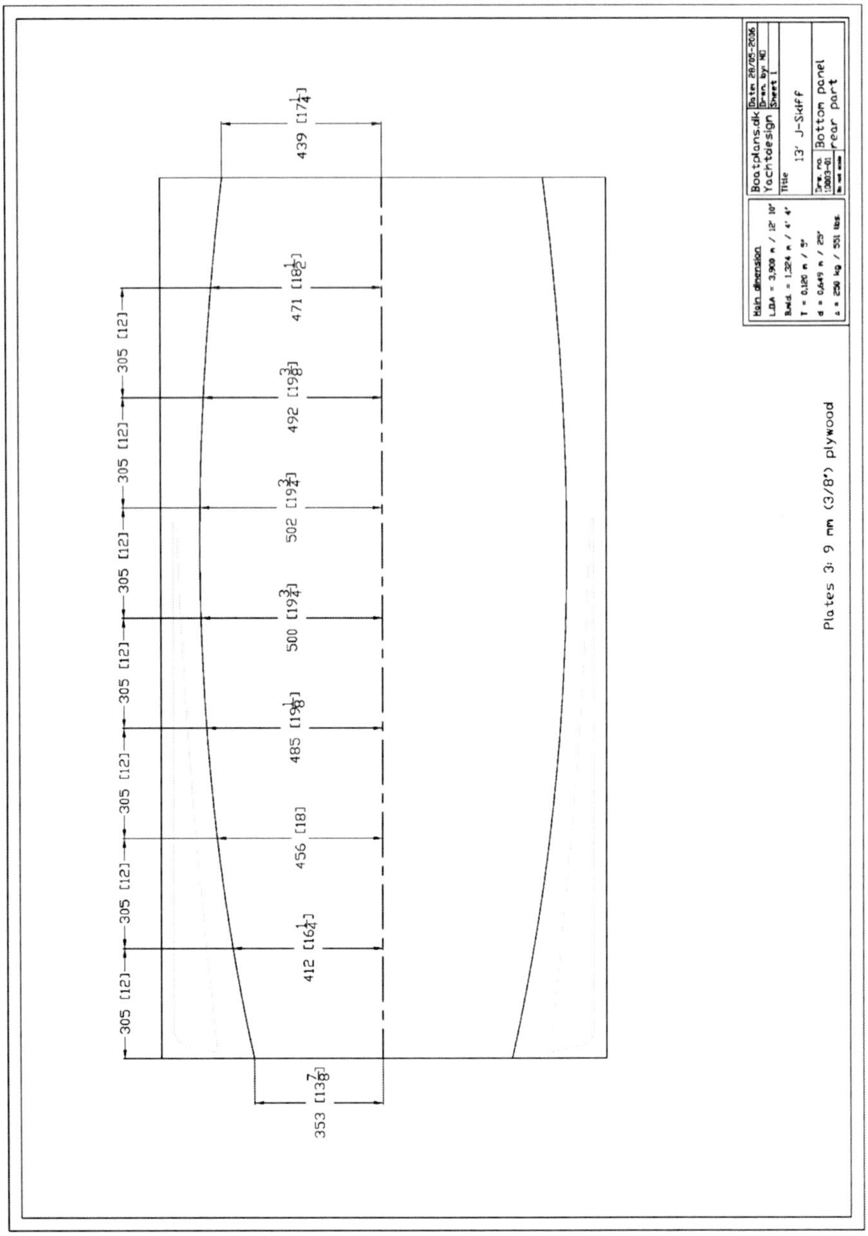

Boat Building Master Course

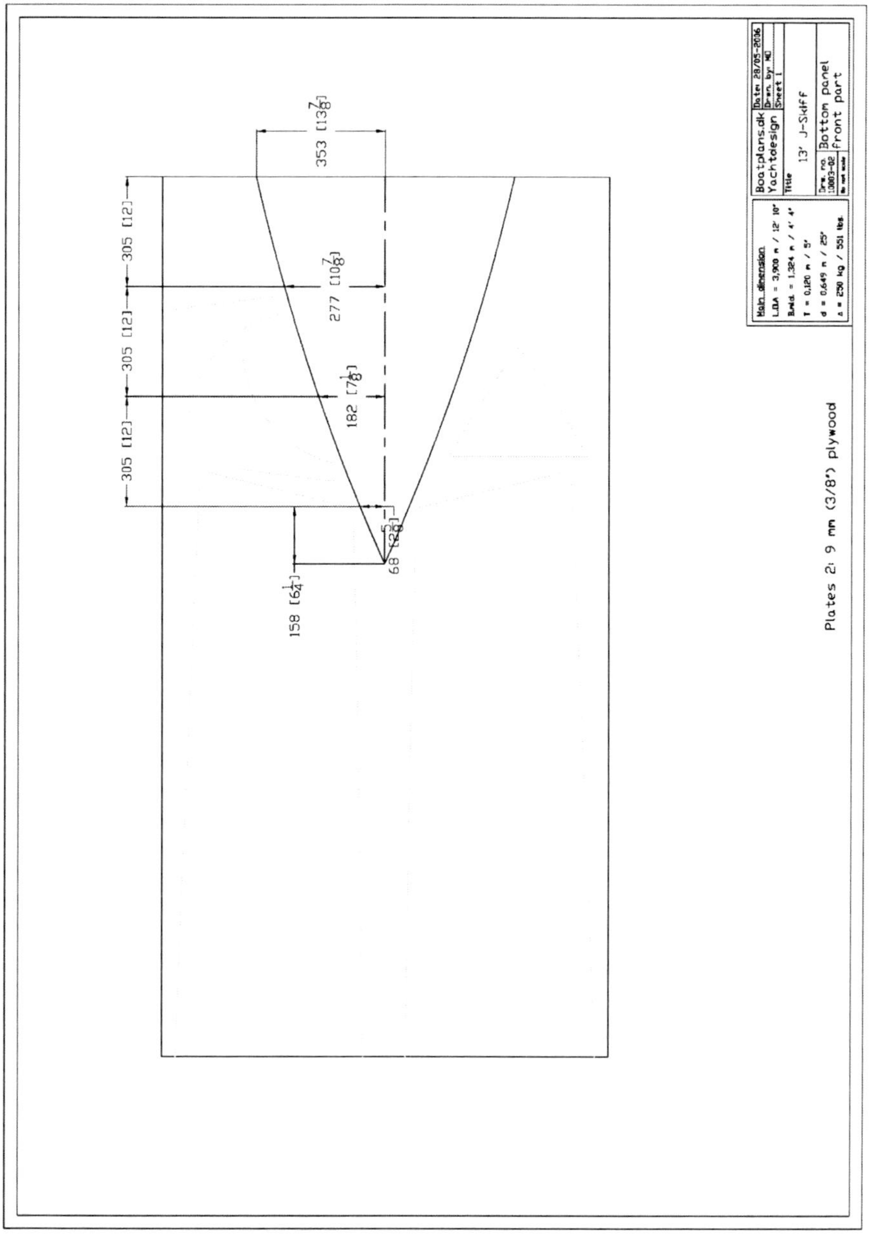

Boat Building Master Course

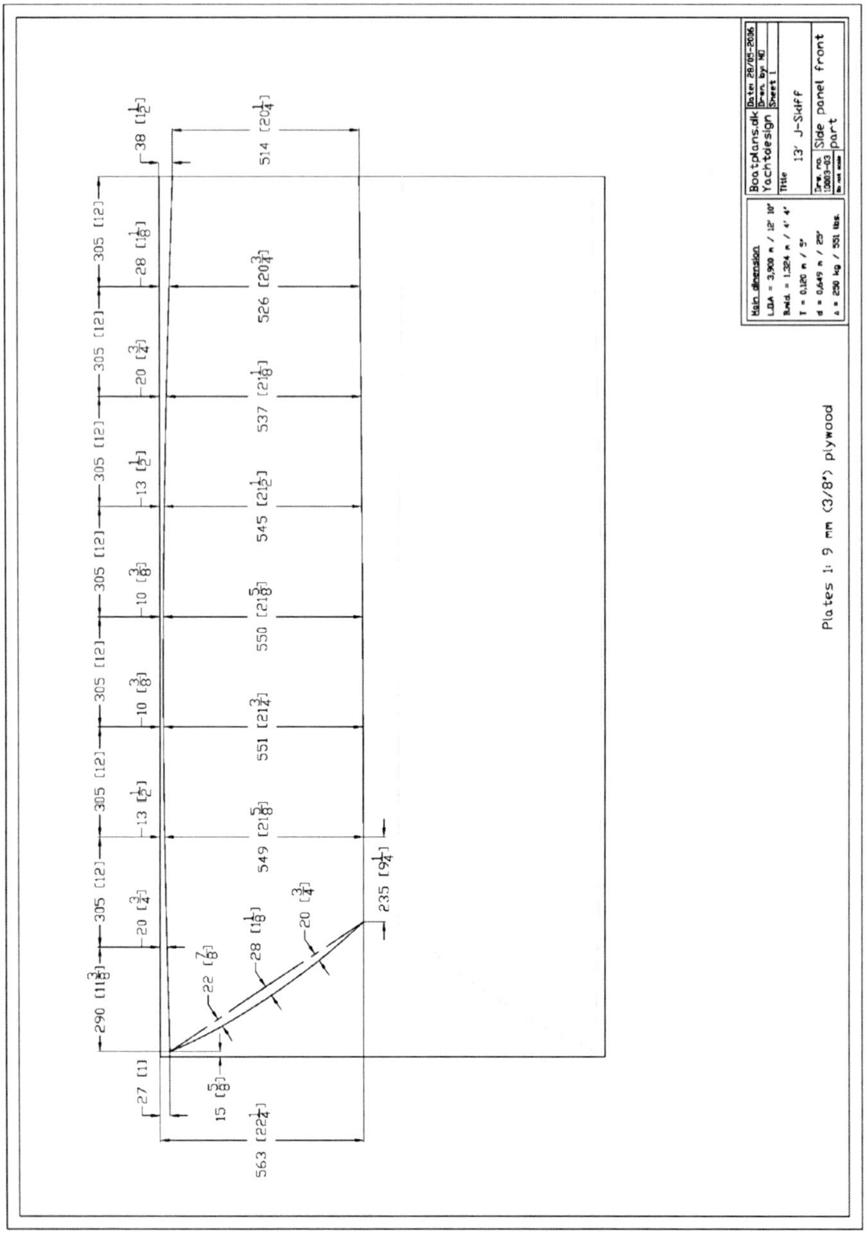

Boat Building Master Course

Boat Building Master Course

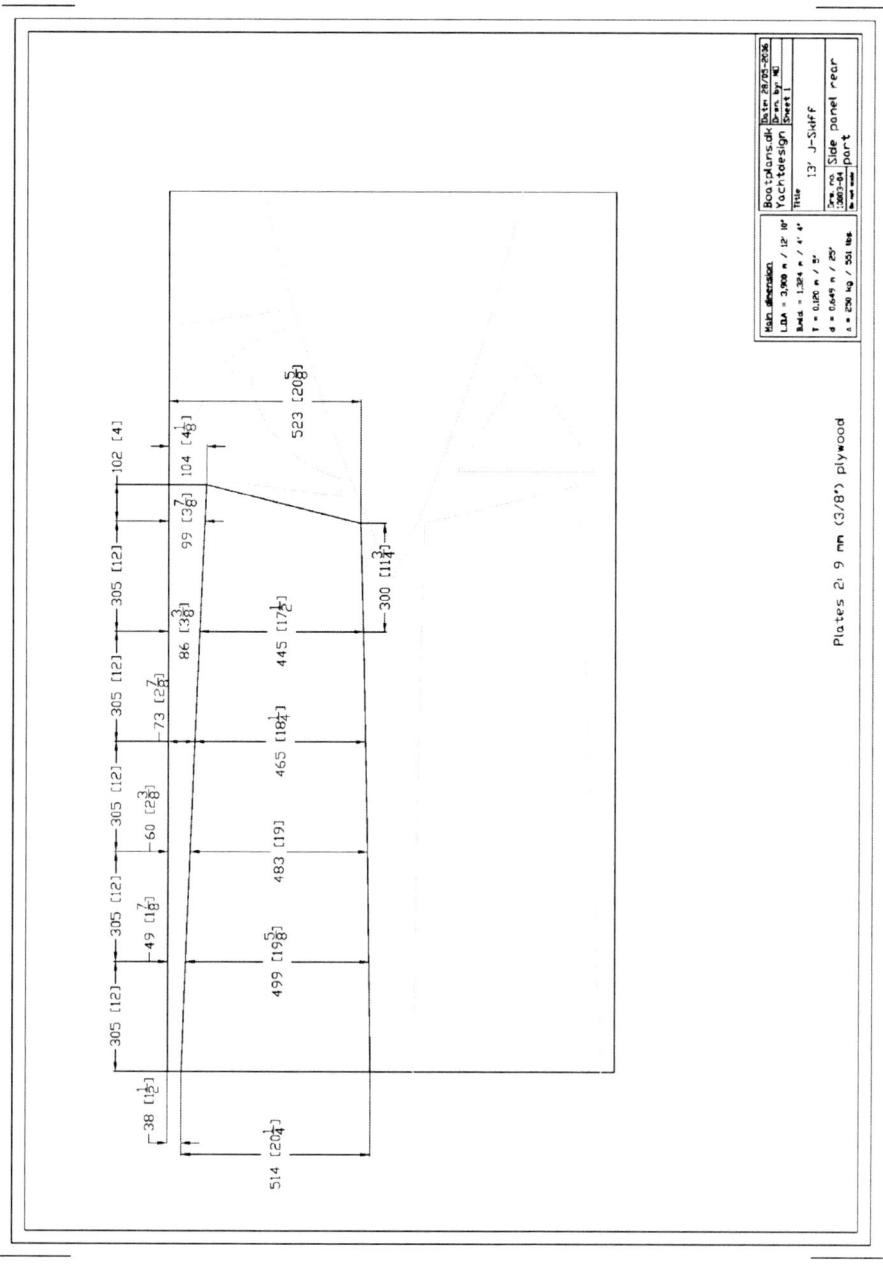

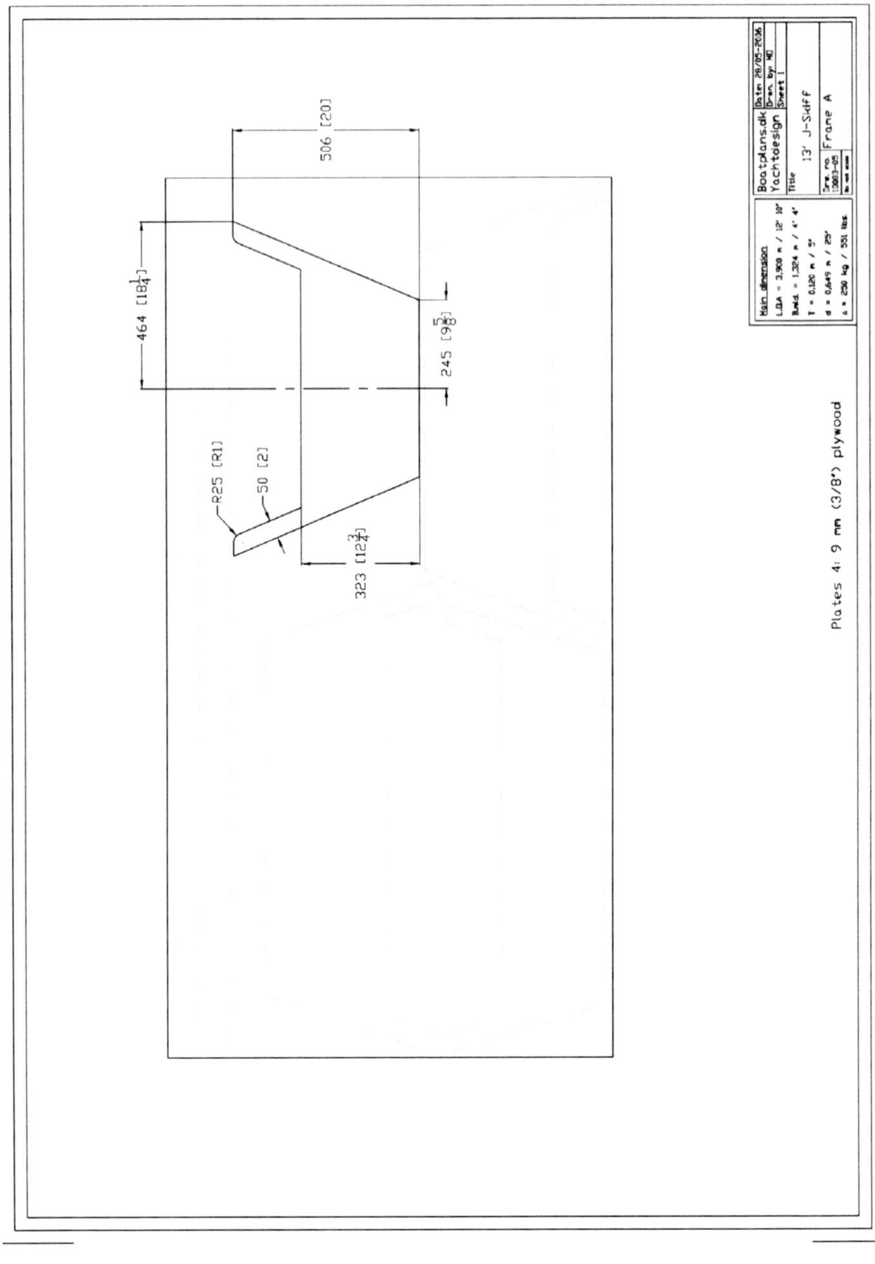

Boat Building Master Course

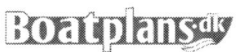

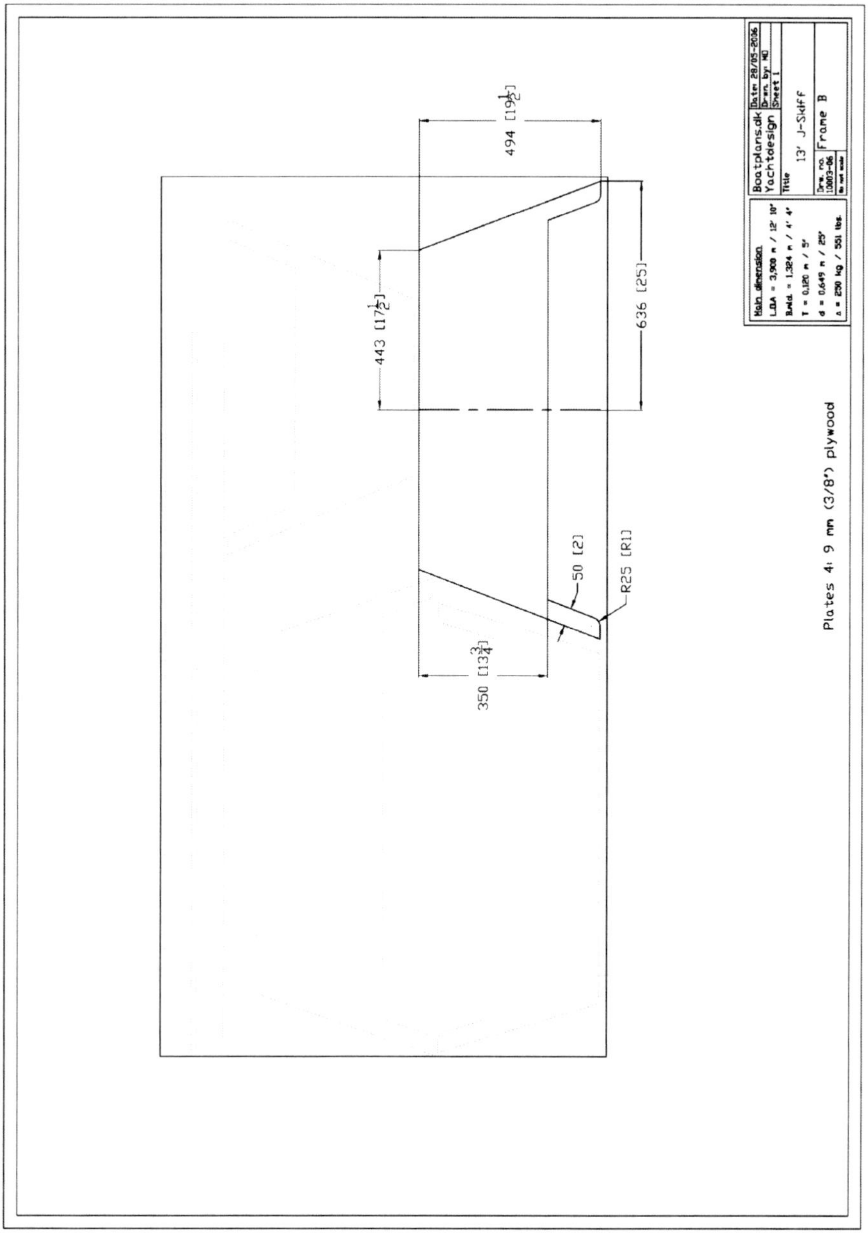
494 [19½]
443 [17½]
636 [25]
50 [2]
R25 [R1]
350 [13¾]
Main dimension
LOA = 3,900 m / 12' 10"
Bmld. = 1,324 m / 4' 4"
T = 0,120 m / 5"
d = 0,649 m / 25"
Δ = 250 kg / 551 lbs.
Boatplans.dk Yachtdesign
Date: 28/05-2006
Drw. by: MD
Sheet 1
Title
13' J-Skiff
Drw. no. 10003-06
Frame B
Plates 4: 9 mm (3/8") plywood

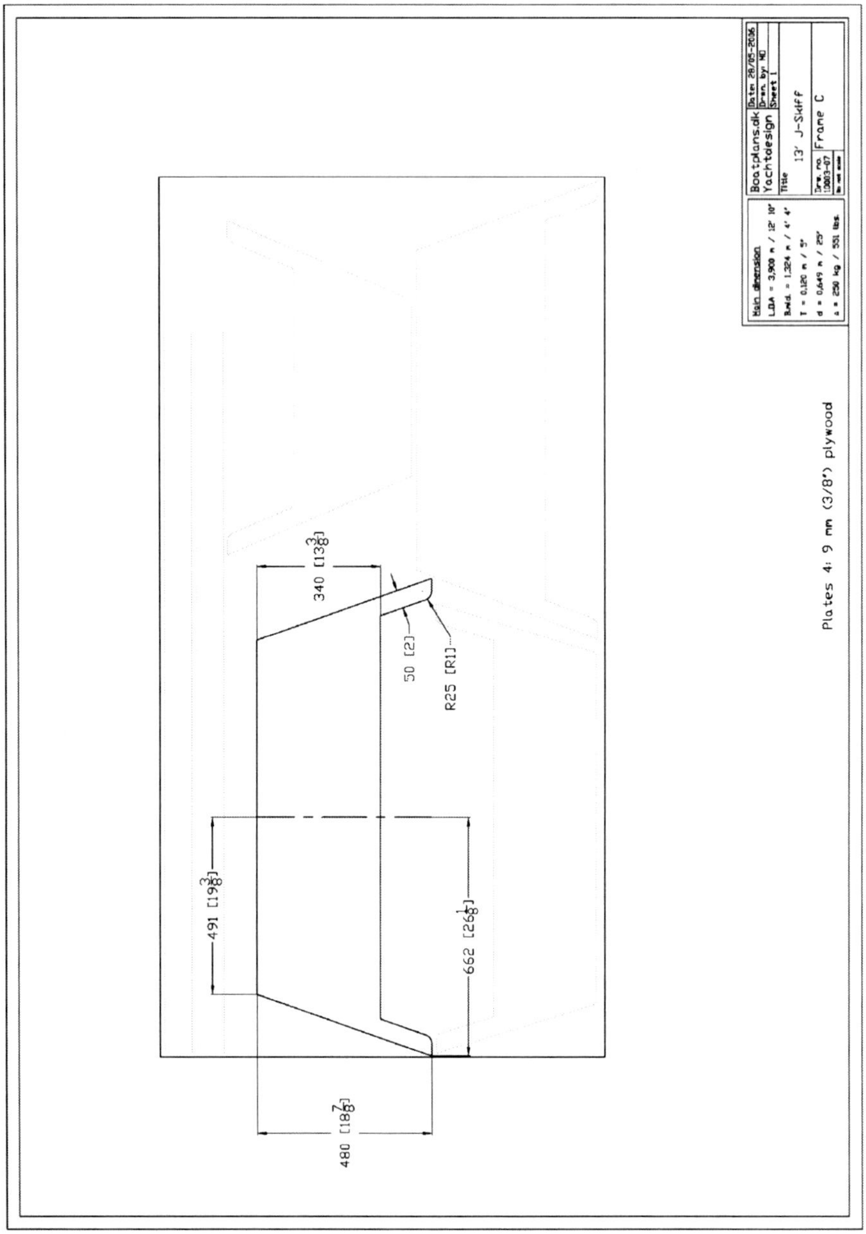

Boat Building Master Course

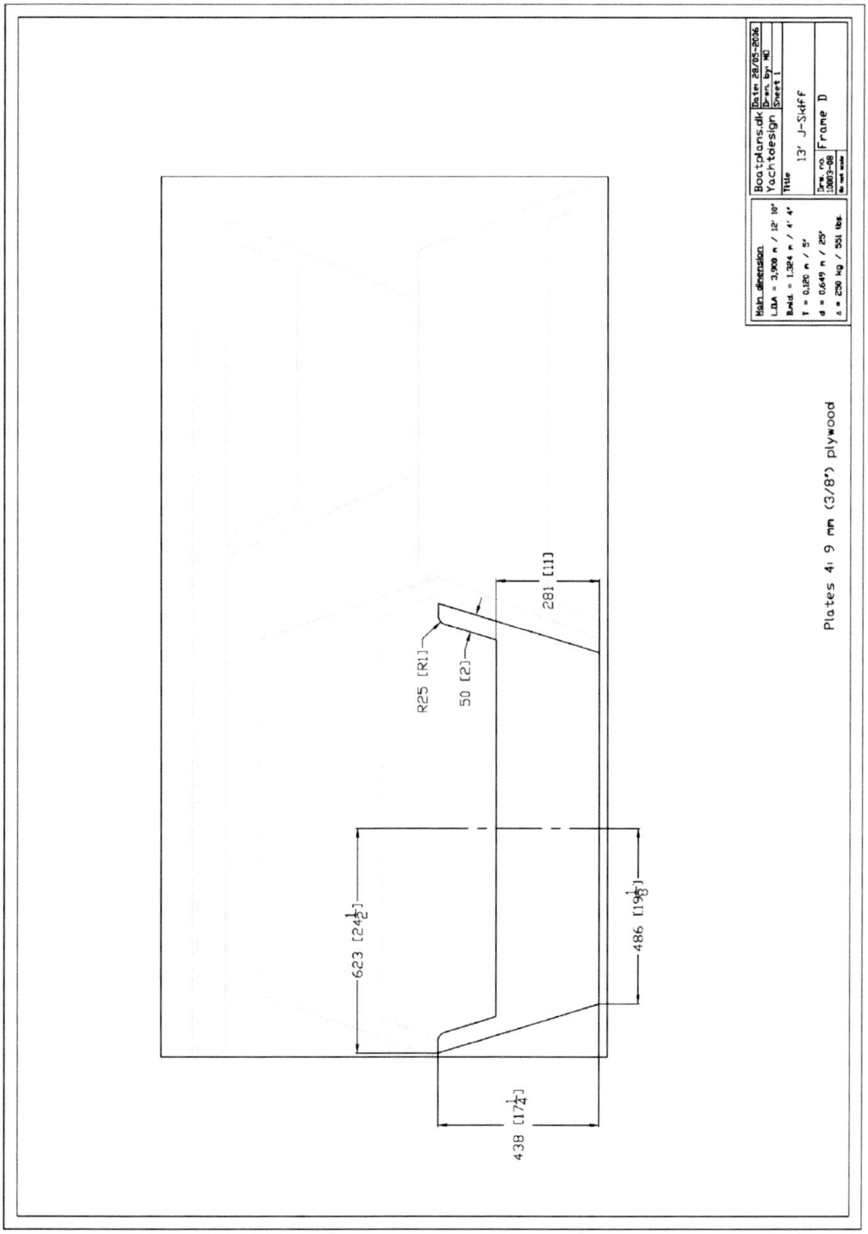

Boat Building Master Course

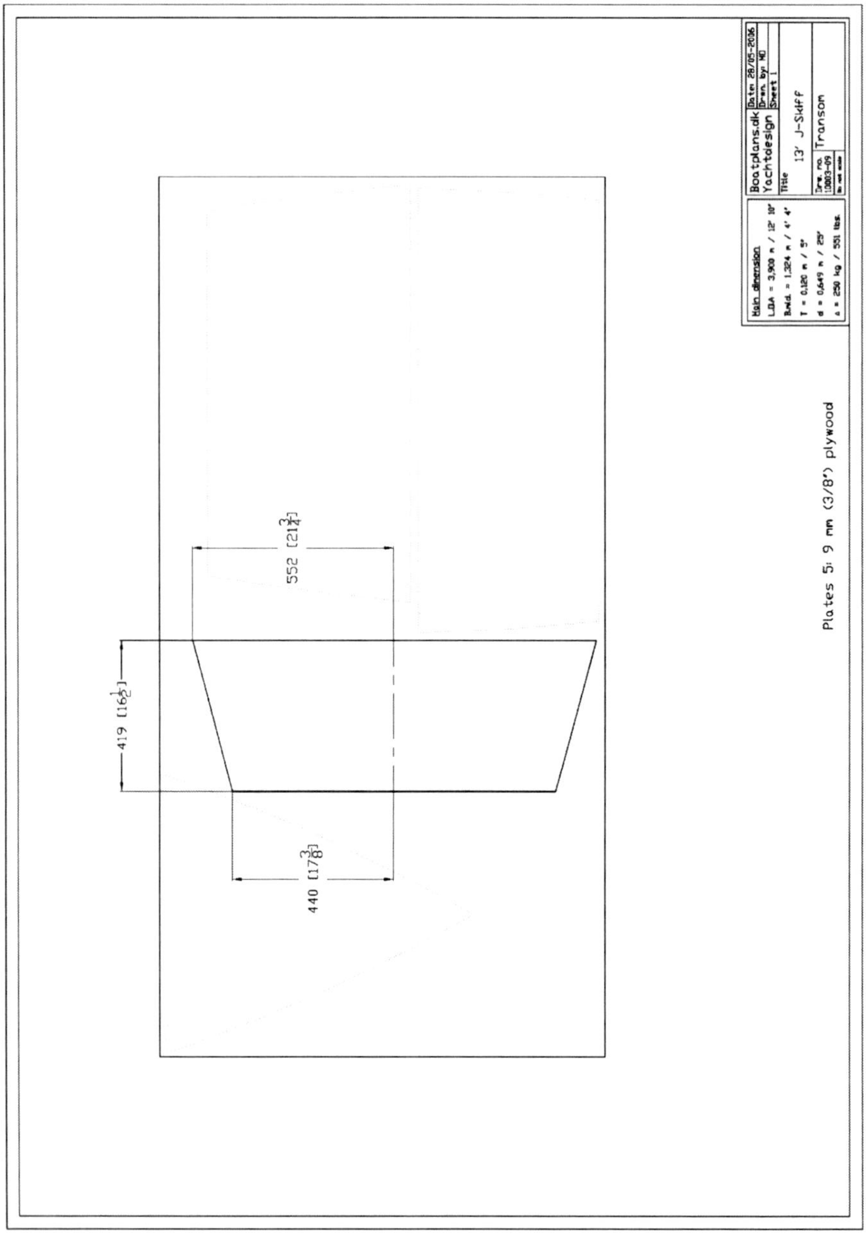

Boat Building Master Course

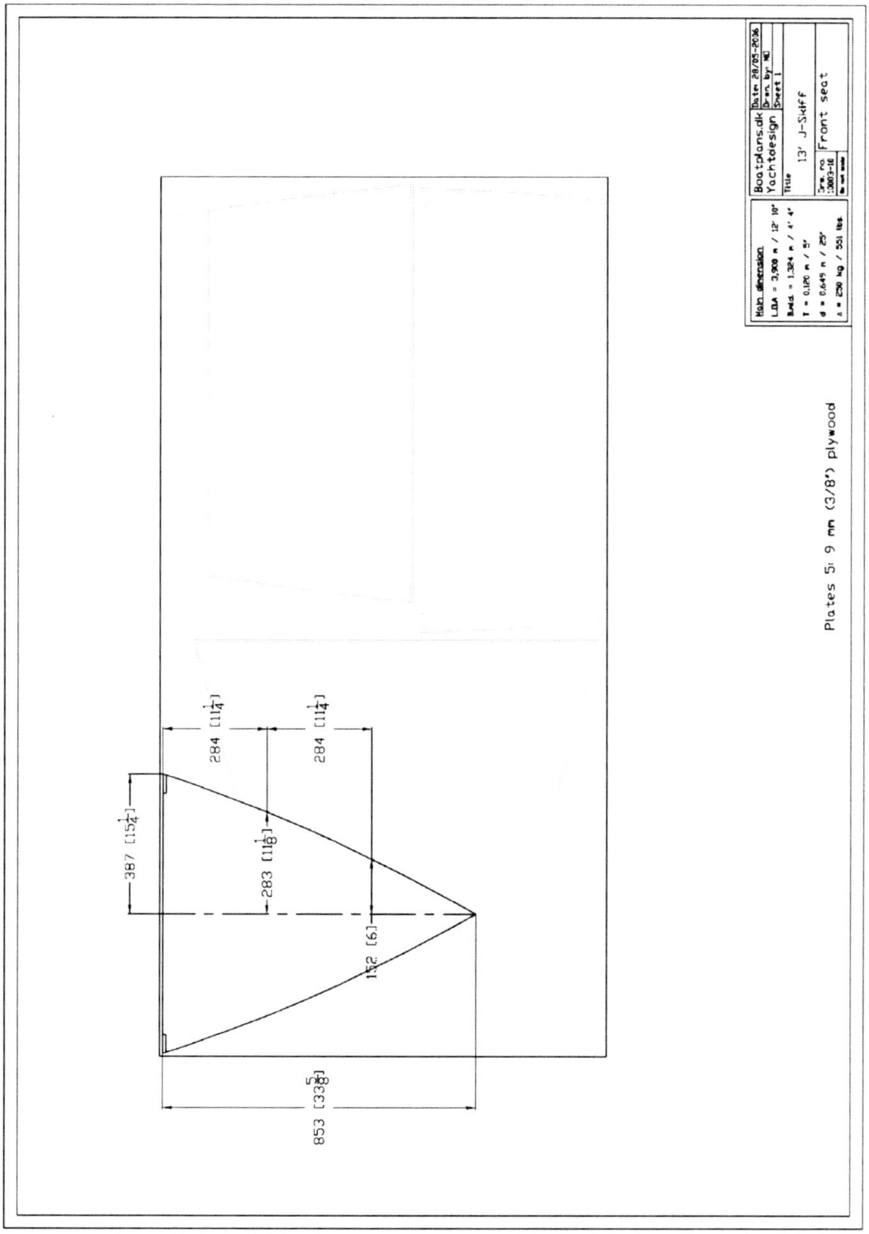

Boat Building Master Course

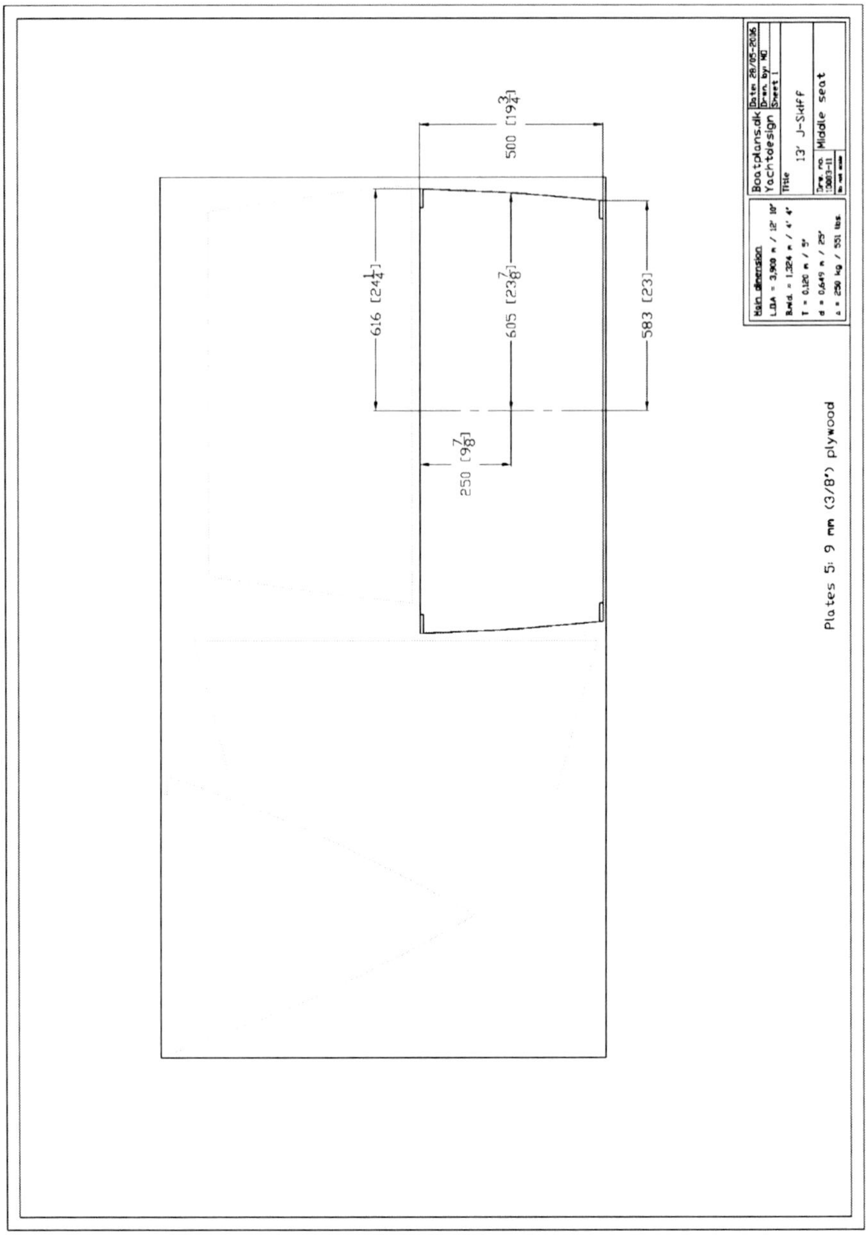

Boat Building Master Course

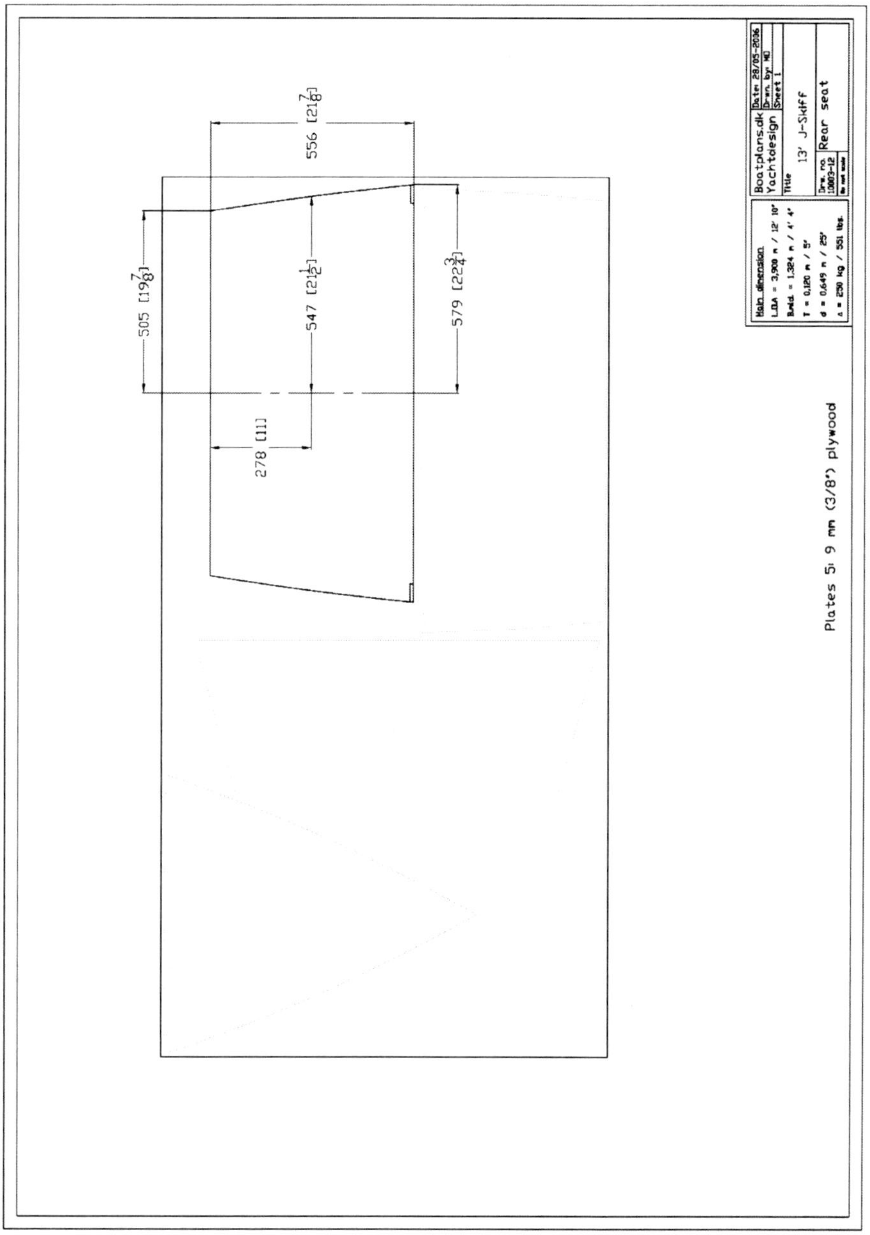

Boat Building Master Course

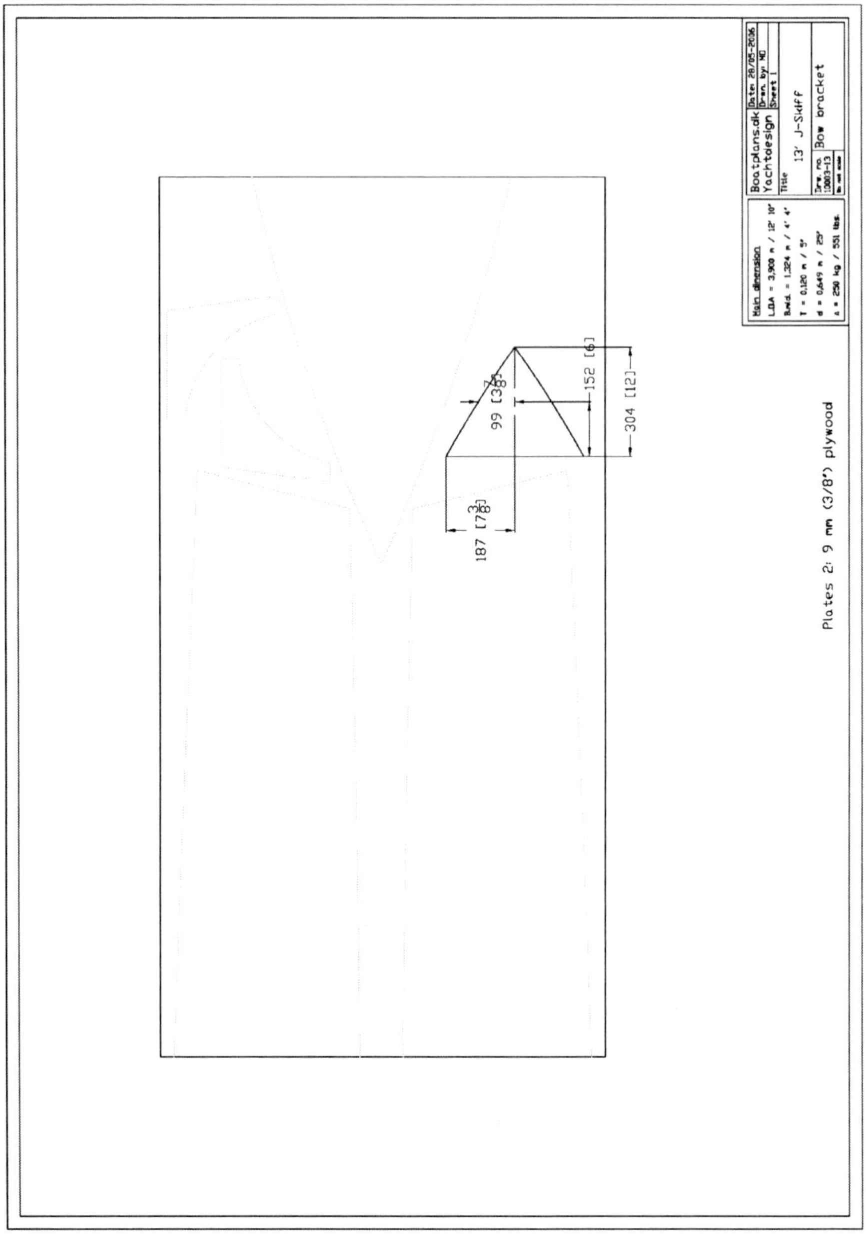

Boat Building Master Course

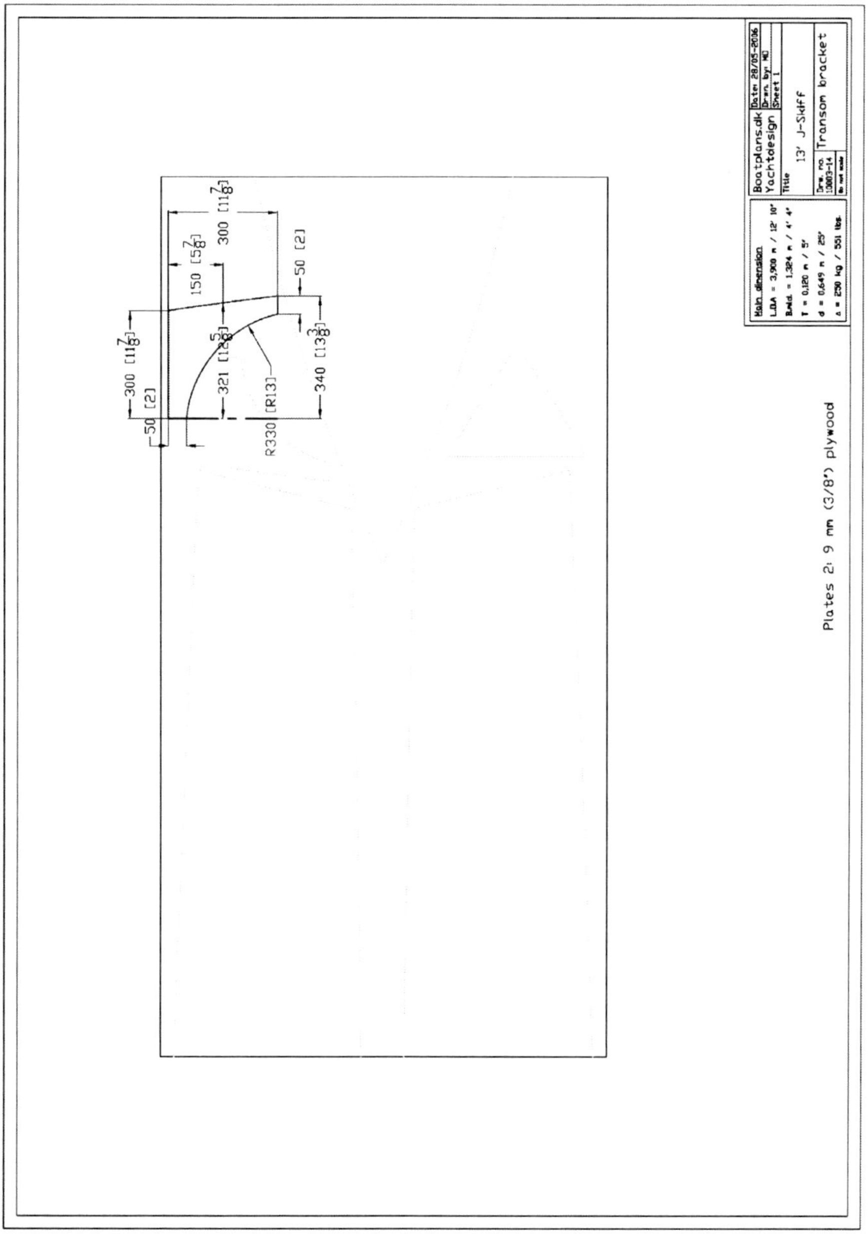

Boat Building Master Course

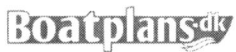

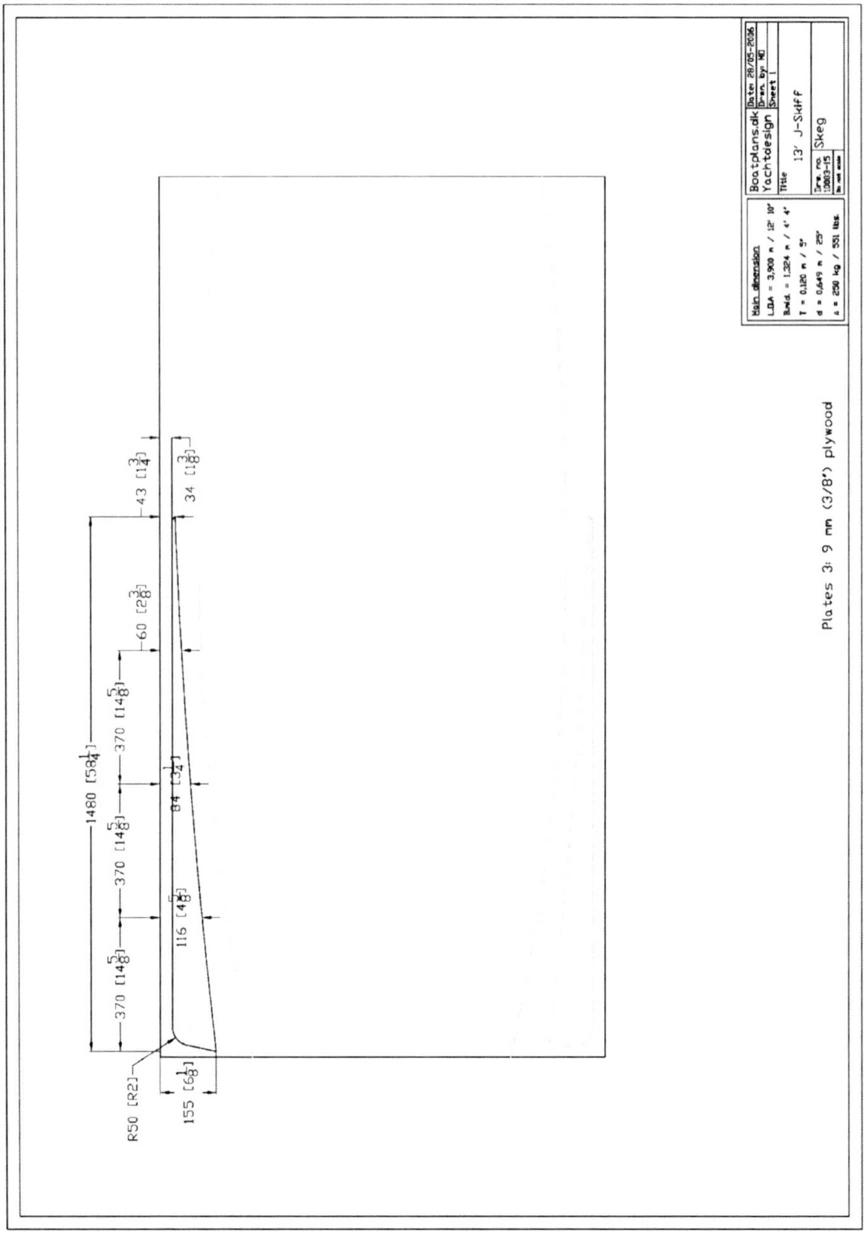
Boatplans.dk
Yachtdesign
13' J-Skiff
Skeg
Plates 3: 9 mm (3/8") plywood
1480 [58¼]
370 [14⅝]
R50 [R2]
155 [6⅛]

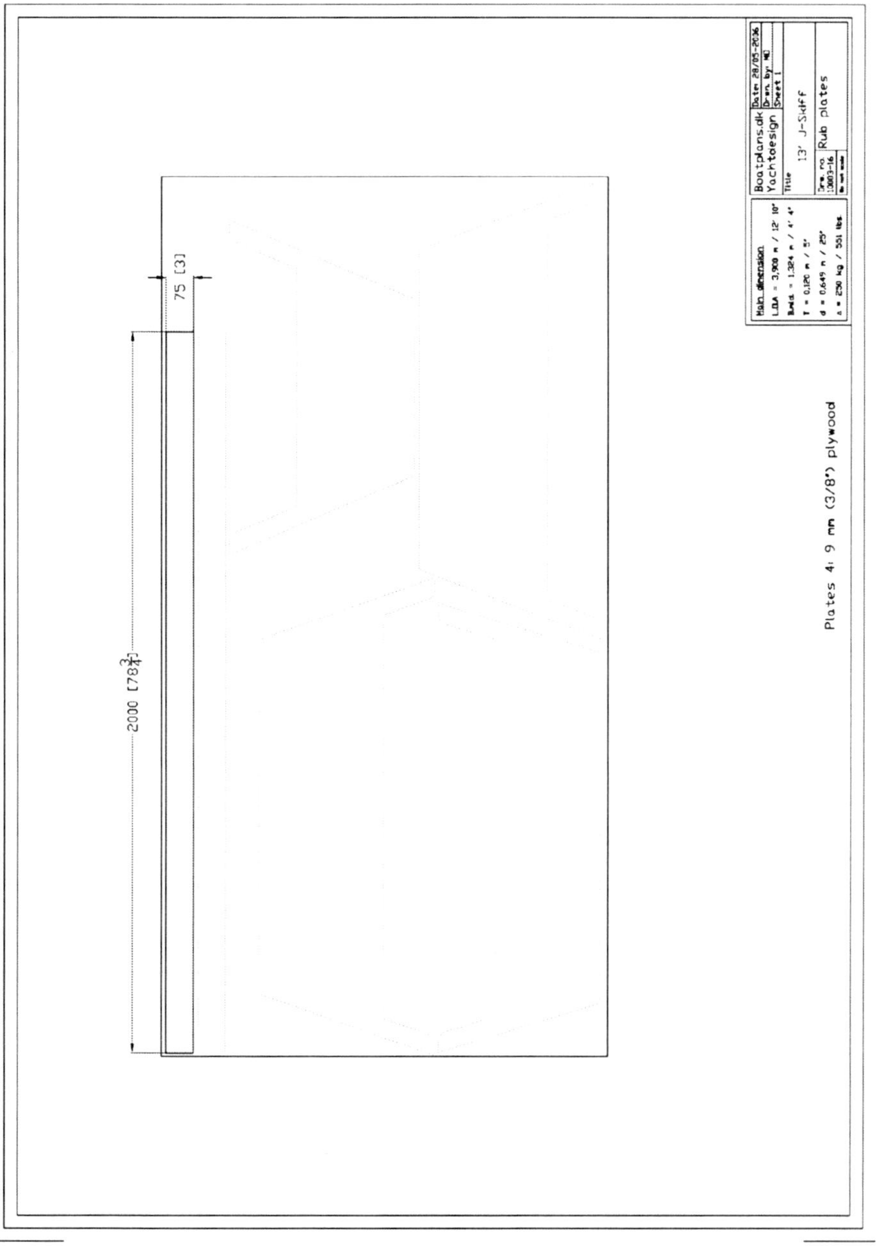

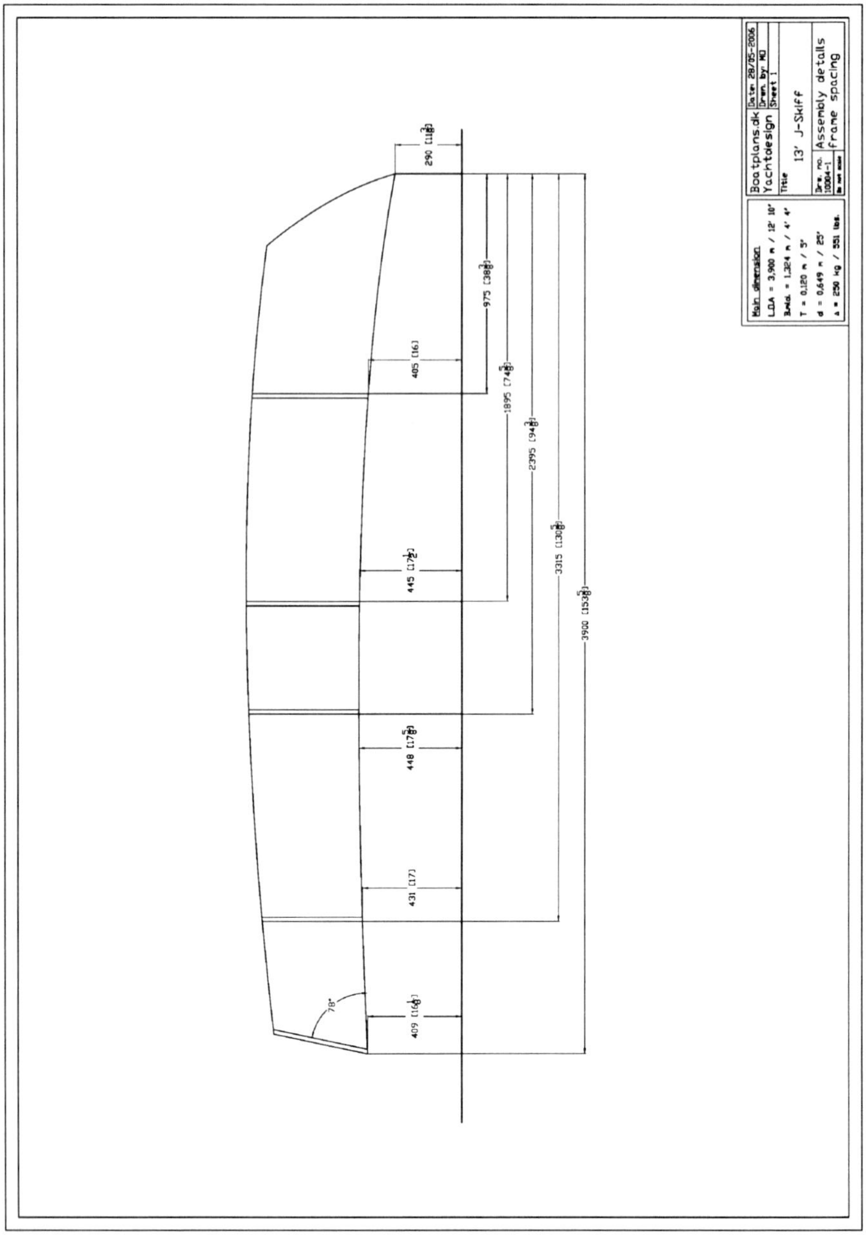

Boat Building Master Course

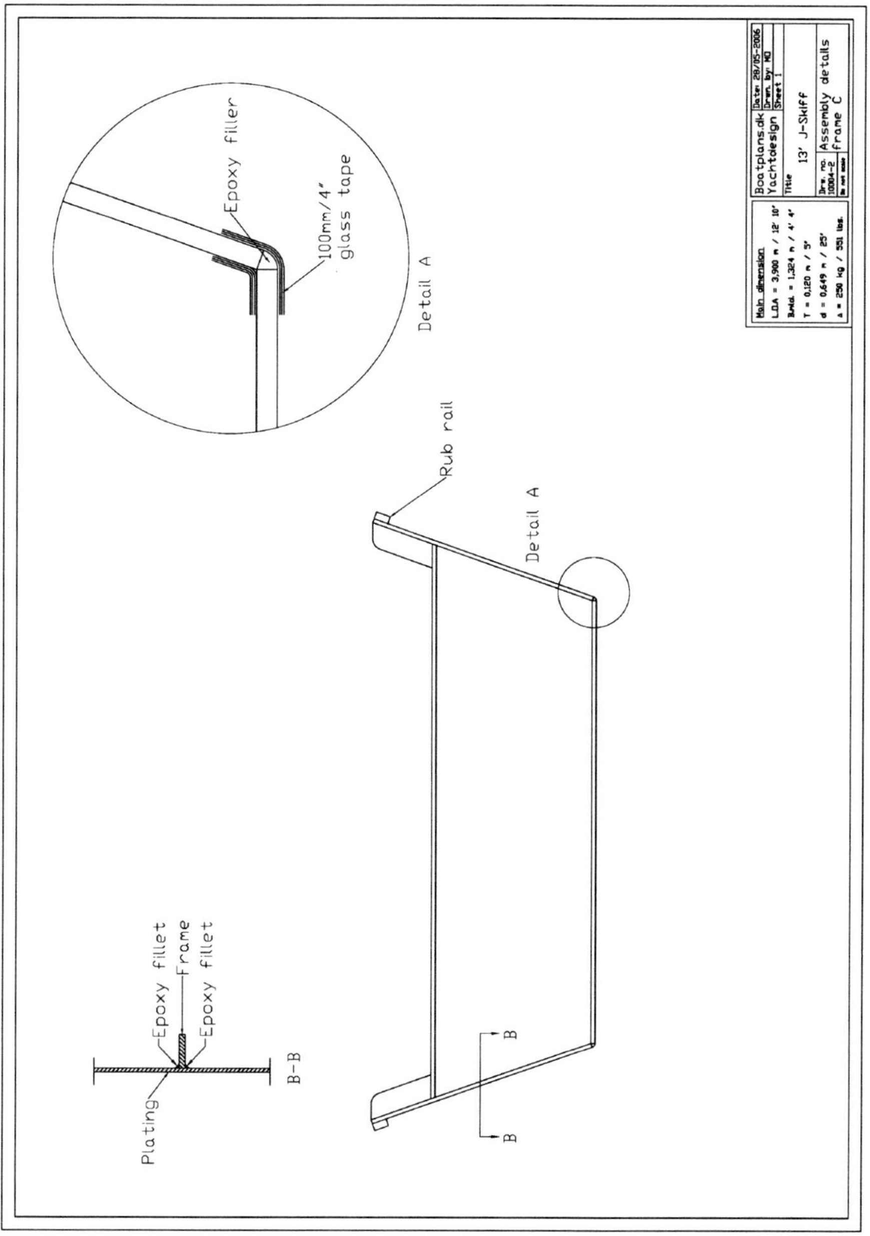

Boat Building Master Course

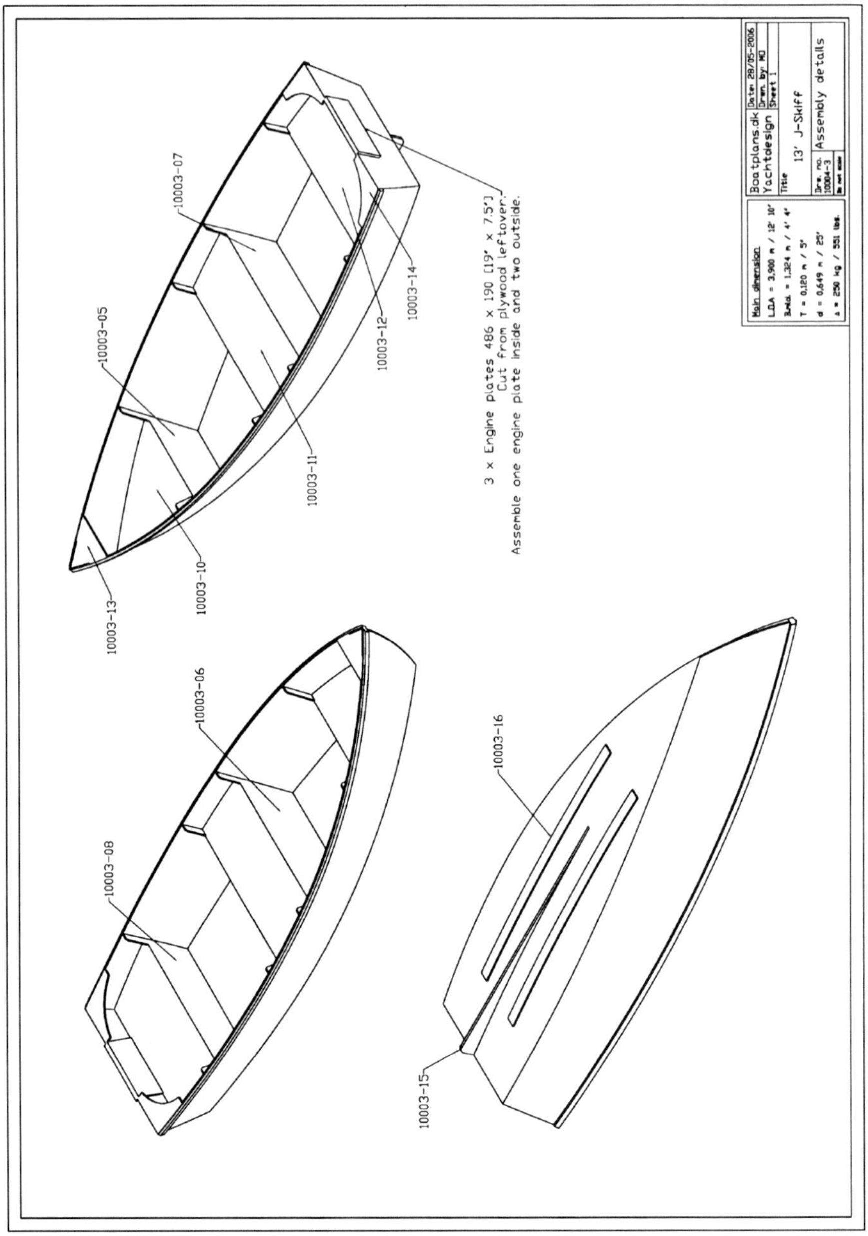

Boat Building Master Course

Boat Building Master Course

Building instruction

Bill of Material

Plywood 2440x1220 (8' x 4')
5 sheets 9 mm (3/8")

Wood
2 x 4,2 m (4.6 yd) 16x32 mm (5/8x5/4") pine for rub rail

Fibreglass
55 m (60 yd) 100mm (4") glass fibre tape

Resin
Epoxy total 7 litre (1.8 gallon)

Wood flour
500 g (1 lbs.) filler

General

This design is the copyright of Boatplans.dk – Yacht design. The plans are made available for all who wants to build the dingy. The plans may not be made a subject of trade for any third party persons.

All plywood used should be Marine or Exterior grade but of cause the choice is yours. For all natural wood use spruce, fir or pine.

Remember to use marine glue wherever glue is needed. For all seams in the chine hull use 100 mm fibreglass tapes with epoxy resin. For all stitching use copper wire or cable ties.

Construction sequence

The hull panels are drawn. Use the dimensions on the drawings 10003-01 to 10003-16. Use standard plywood sheets 2440 x 1220 (8'x4'). There are to be used 5 sheets of 9 mm (3/8") plywood. Mark the edges of the hull panels and use a thin wood batten held to the marks by nails or weights and draw the lines.

All the panels are in two parts. Joint the parts with 200 mm [8"] wide fibreglass tape (e.g. cut it yourself from a piece of fibreglass) and epoxy resin. The dimensions shown on the drawing are made for butt joints. If you wish to joint the hull panels with a scarf joint changes are to be made in the dimensions.

Once the hull panels are dried and the frames, stringers and transom are cut the assembly of the hull can start. Set up the frames A, B, C and D on a flat surface. Use the dimensions on drawing 10004-1. Alternately you can build a jig. It is necessary to make some temporary supports for the frames.

Place the bottom panel and fasten it to the frames with screws or nails. The side panels can be fastened to the frames with screws or nails. Stitch them to the bottom panel. At this stage do not over tighten the stitches so adjustments can be made. The transoms are now assembled. Use screws, nails or cable ties for fastening the transoms.

Now the hull is assembled and the time is to check the hull geometry. Make absolutely sure that the hull is not twisted and the shape is correct. As the hull is checked tighten up the stitches.

When the hull is checked it is time for sealing the seams. Start with the outside seams and use epoxy filler to make the curvature between the panels smooth. When done use the glass tape and epoxy resin for reinforcement of the seams. For the use of epoxy remember to follow the instruction from your supplier. It is also important to prime the wood with epoxy before the tape is laid. Remember to wet out the tape completely when laying the final layer. Also make sure to clean up any resin runs before it cures, it is very difficult to remove afterwards.

Before the hull is turned it is advisable to coat the plywood with epoxy.

Now it is time to turn the hull upright. Finish the inside seams using epoxy filler before you put on the tape and epoxy. Remember to fasten the frames and transom with thickened epoxy. Use large epoxy fillets to glue frames and transom to the hull.

With the hull turned upright it is now time to assemble the seats. There might be some adjustments to make before the seats fits. Glue the seats to the hull and frames with thickened epoxy. It is advisable to mount the outboard engine plates after the hull is finished. They are made for the engine bracket and therefore it is best if they can be replaced if damaged.

It is possible to install hatches so the space under the seats can be used for storage. It is advisable to use watertight hatches so the compartments at the same time can act as flotation. Choose appropriate hatches from your local hardware store or marine supplier.

It is not from a strength point of view necessary to cover the entire hull with epoxy and fabric. But it is recommended to at least coat the plywood with epoxy resin for better waterproof properties.

The hull may be finished with paint or varnish (for normal use, a good quality exterior house paint/varnish is sufficient).

Good luck with the building of your new boat.

Morten Olesen
Boatplans.dk

 **Boat Building Master Course**

Appendix C, Boat plans for the 16' Ozarks float boat

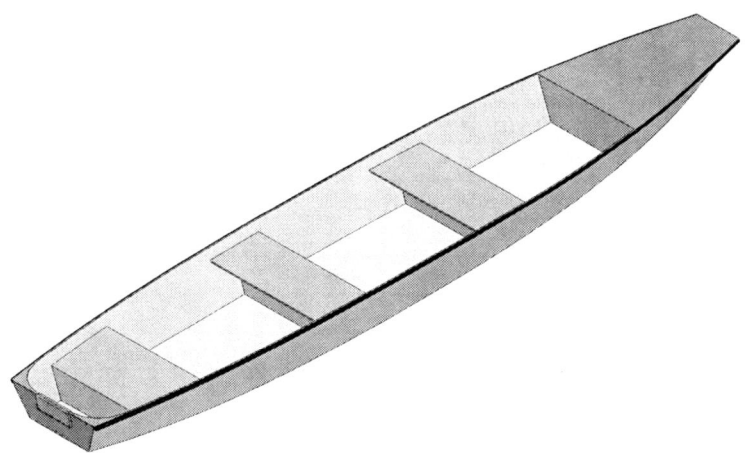

Based on the design of a flat-bottom boat used by people of the Ozarks in the 19th century, this float boat (sometimes called a Johnboat) is the perfect all-round fishing boat.

Take her out on the flats or canyons. Drop anchor and find fish -- bass, blue fish or trout – without a trip to the tropics. Paddle along creeks, ponds and rivers. Attach a small outboard motor or electric trolling engine and cruise easily across the lake or bay.

Wherever you take this boat you can be sure she'll handle even the roughest waters with ease, and give you (and your friends or family) the opportunity to experience hours of fun and adventure on the water.

Boat Building Master Course

Drawing list

Drawing no.	Title	File
10000	Line drawing	10000.pdf
10001	General arrangement	10001.pdf
10002-1	Overview 9 mm plate	10002-1.pdf
10003-01	Bottom panel rear part	10003-01.pdf
10003-02	Bottom panel middle part	10003-02.pdf
10003-03	Bottom panel front part	10003-03.pdf
10003-04	Side panel rear part	10003-04.pdf
10003-05	Side panel front part	10003-05.pdf
10003-06	Stem transom	10003-06.pdf
10003-07	Frame A	10003-07.pdf
10003-08	Frame B	10003-08.pdf
10003-09	Frame C	10003-09.pdf
10003-10	Frame D	10003-10.pdf
10003-11	Frame E	10003-11.pdf
10003-12	Transom	10003-12.pdf
10003-13	Front deck	10003-13.pdf
10003-14	Seat 1	10003-14.pdf
10003-15	Seat 2	10003-15.pdf
10003-16	Seat 3	10003-16.pdf
10003-17	Transom brackets	10003-17.pdf
10003-18	Outboard engine plates	10003-18.pdf
10003-19	Bottom runners	10003-19.pdf
10004-1	Assembly details, frame spacing	10004-1.pdf
10004-2	Assembly details, frame C	10004-2.pdf
10004-3	Assembly details	10004-3.pdf
10005-1	Building jig	10005-1.pdf

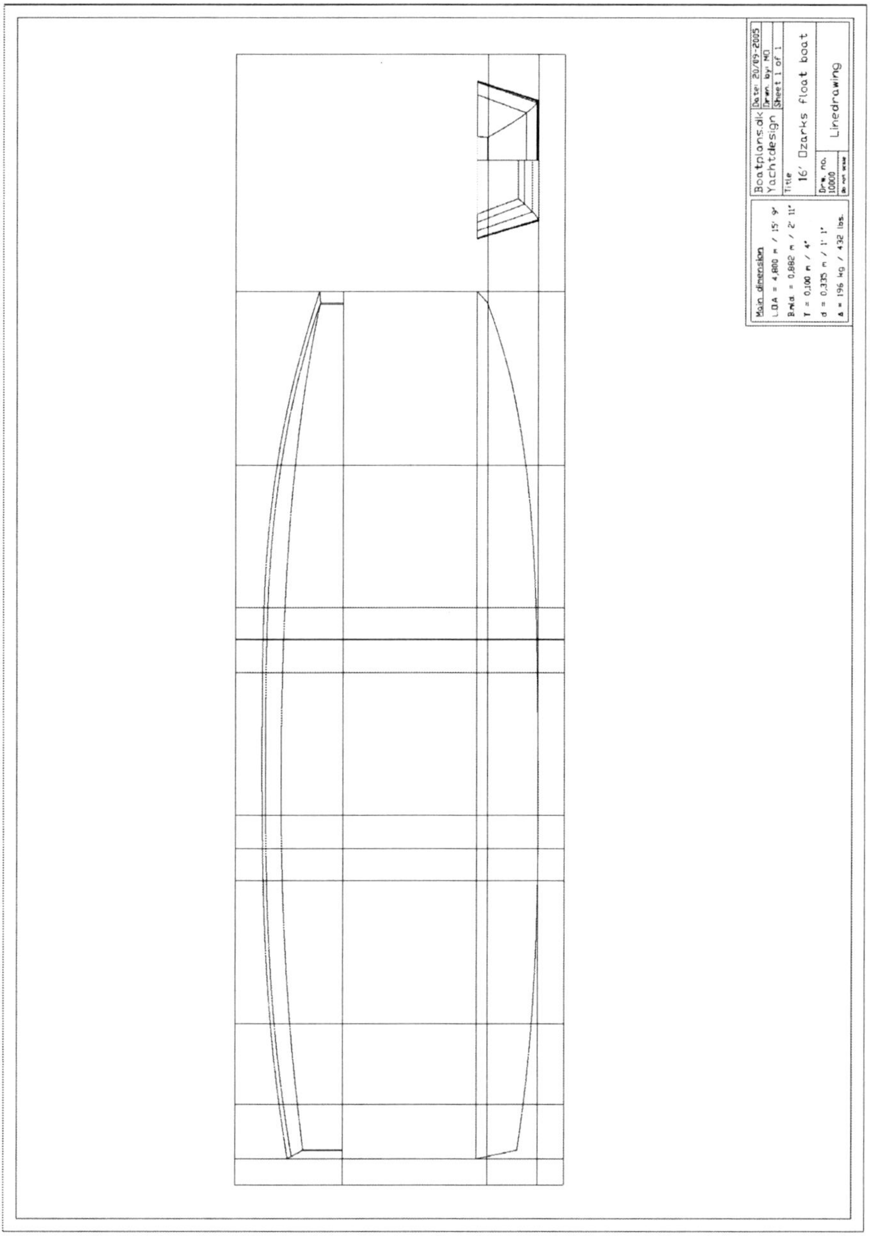

Boat Building Master Course

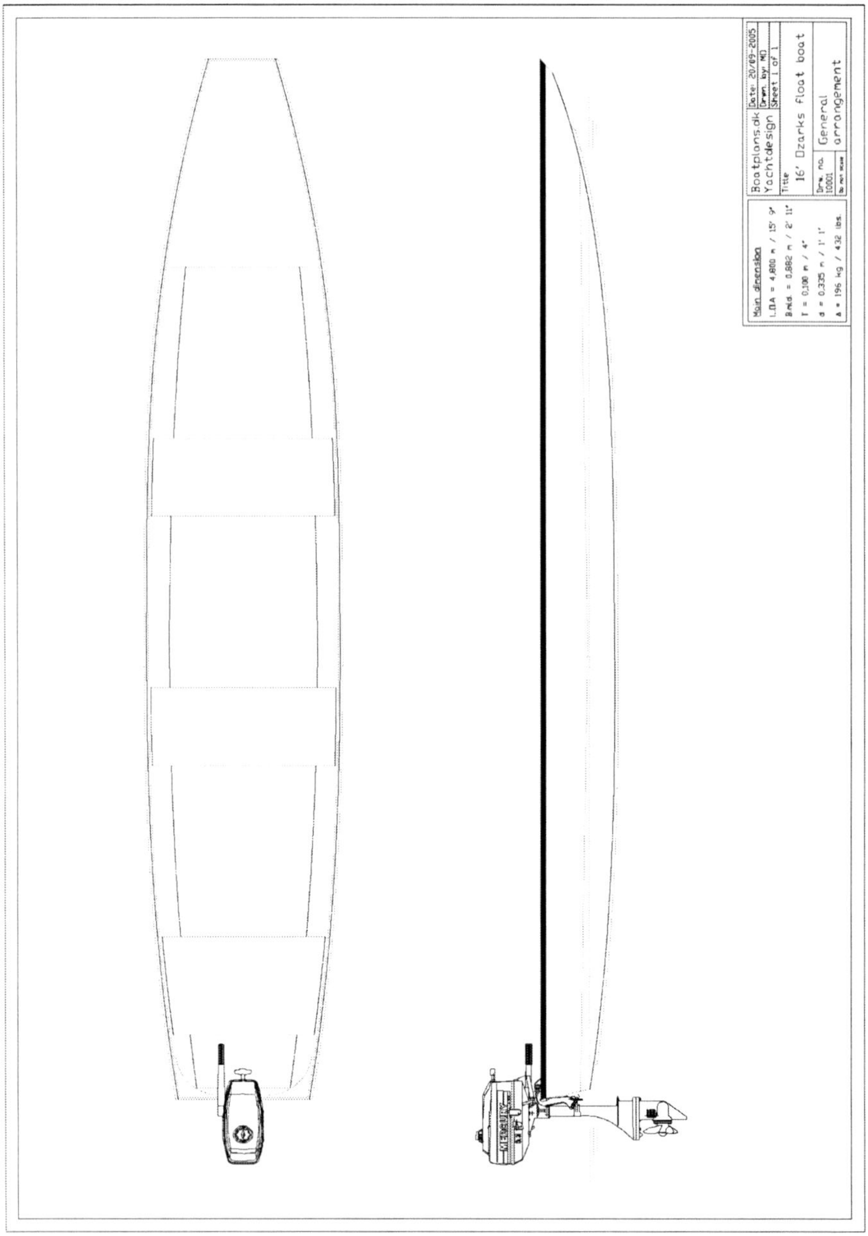

Boat Building Master Course

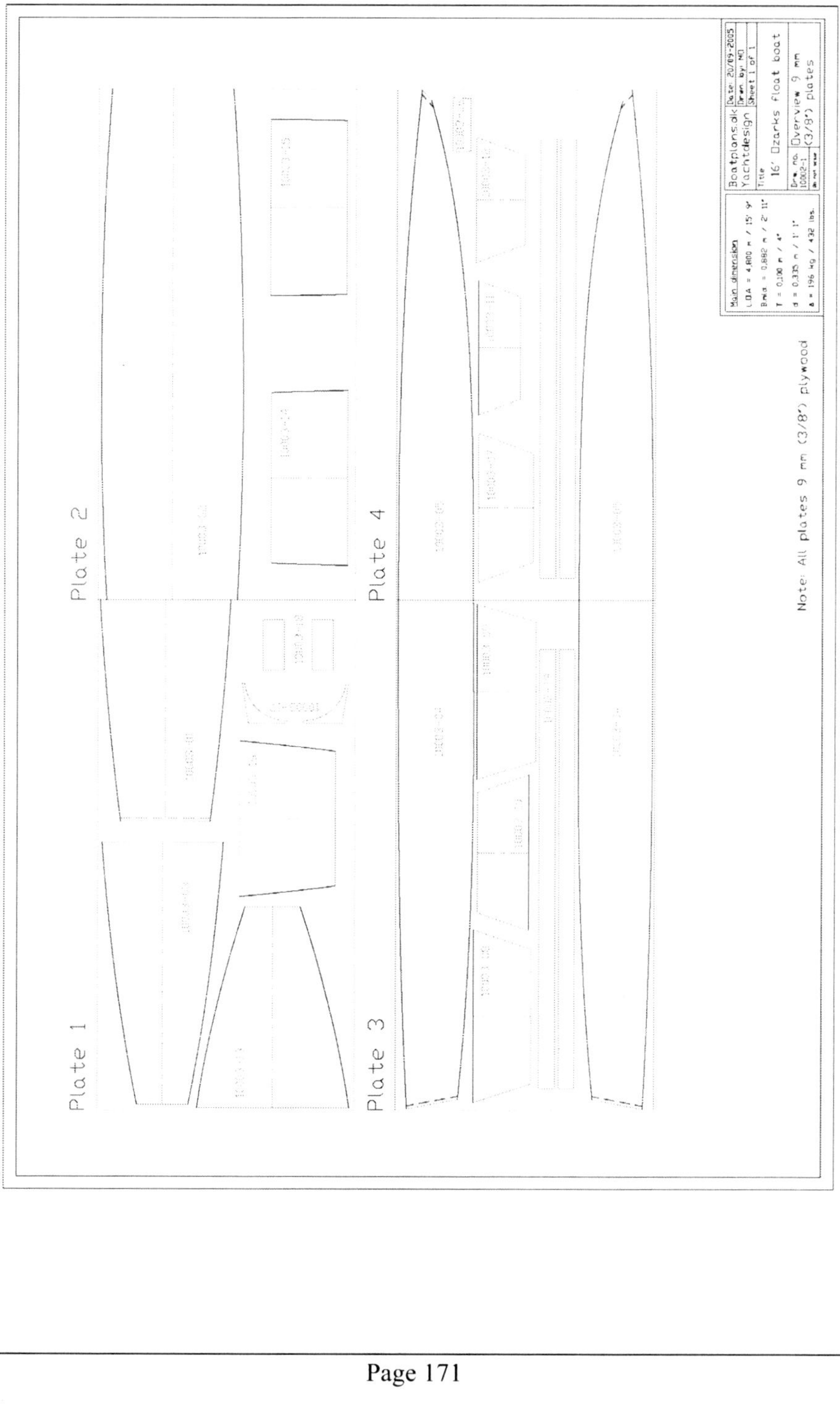

Boat Building Master Course

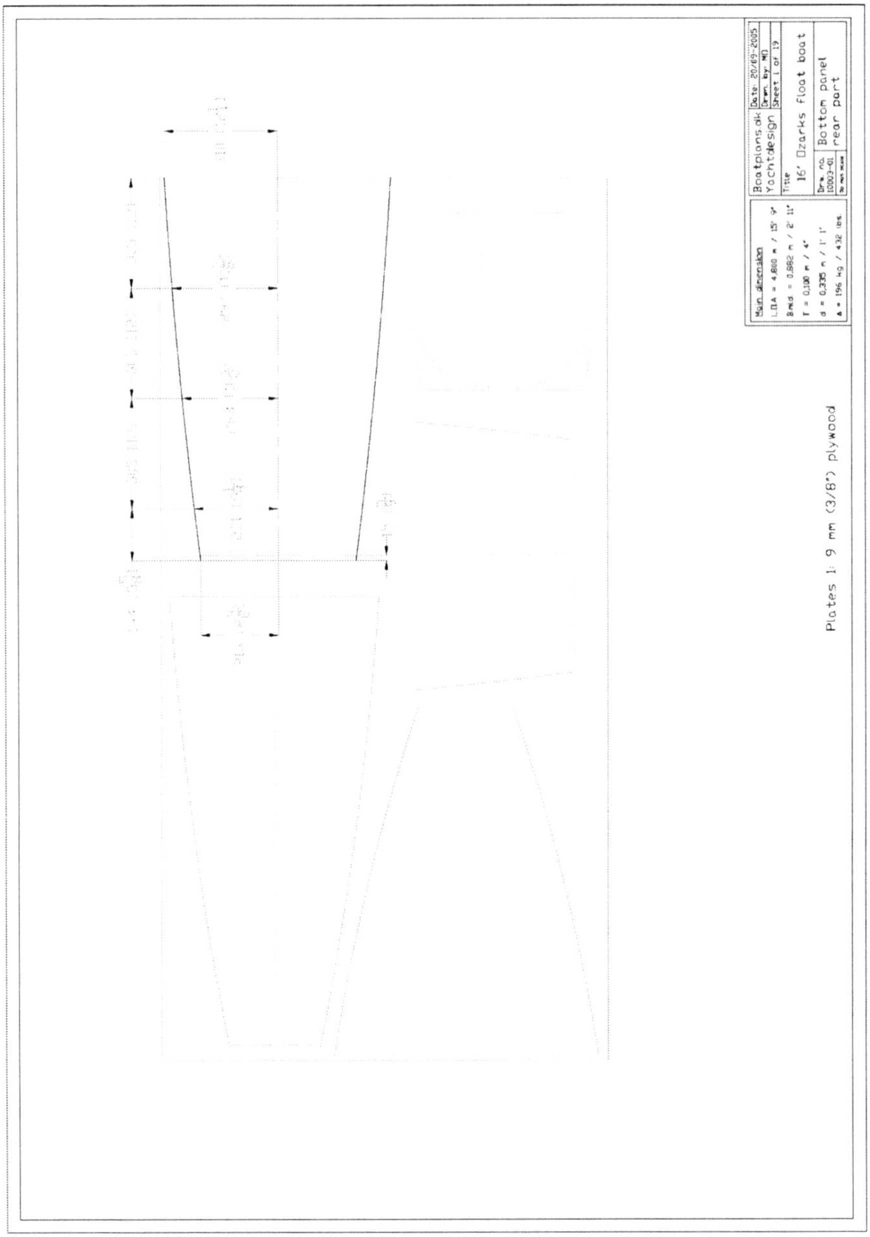

Boat Building Master Course

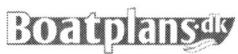

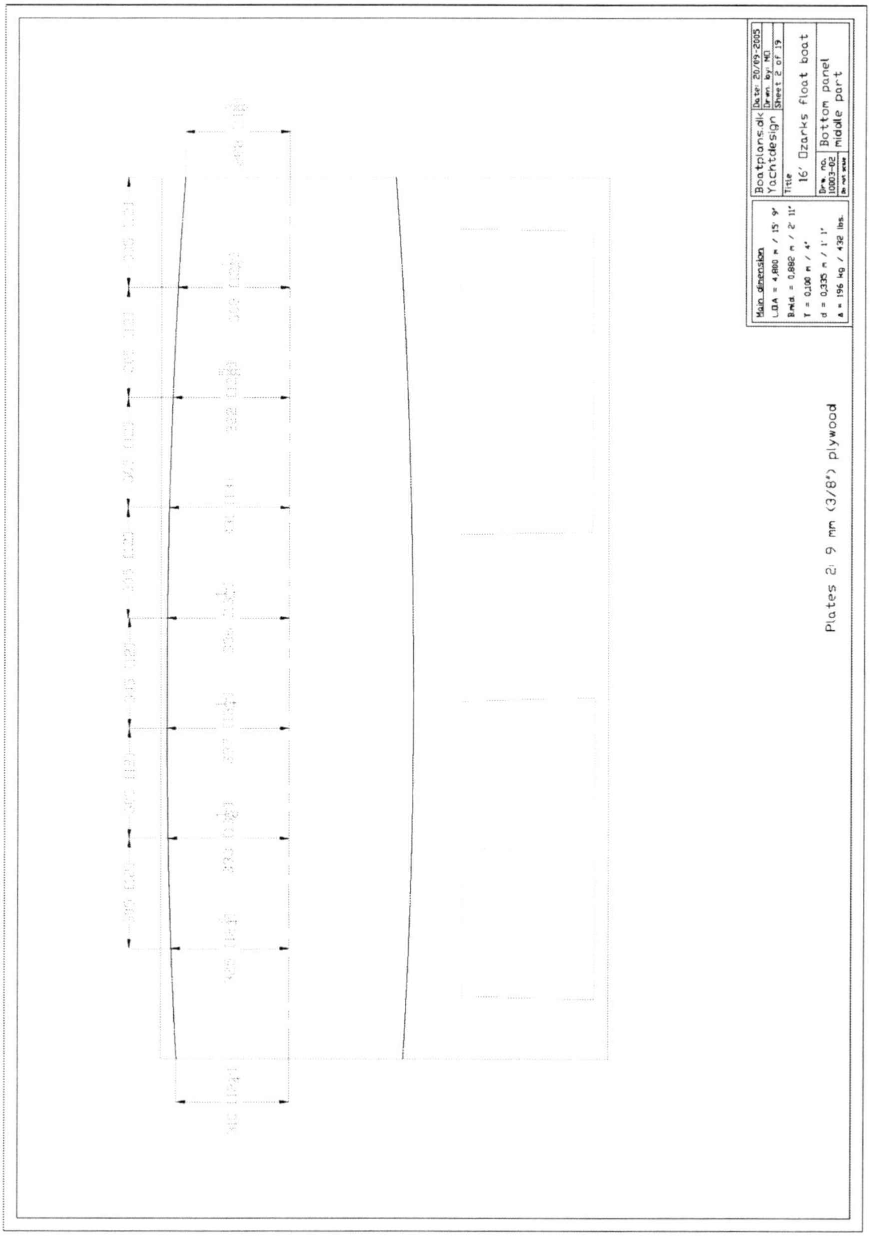
Main dimension
LOA = 4,800 m / 15' 9"
B.mid. = 0,882 m / 2' 11"
T = 0,100 m / 4"
d = 0,335 m / 1' 1"
Δ = 196 kg / 432 lbs.
Boatplans.dk
Yachtdesign
Date: 20/09-2005
Drwn. by: MO
Sheet 2 of 19
Title
16' Ozarks float boat
Drw. no.
10003-02
Bottom panel
middle part
Plates 2: 9 mm (3/8") plywood

# Boat Building Master Course

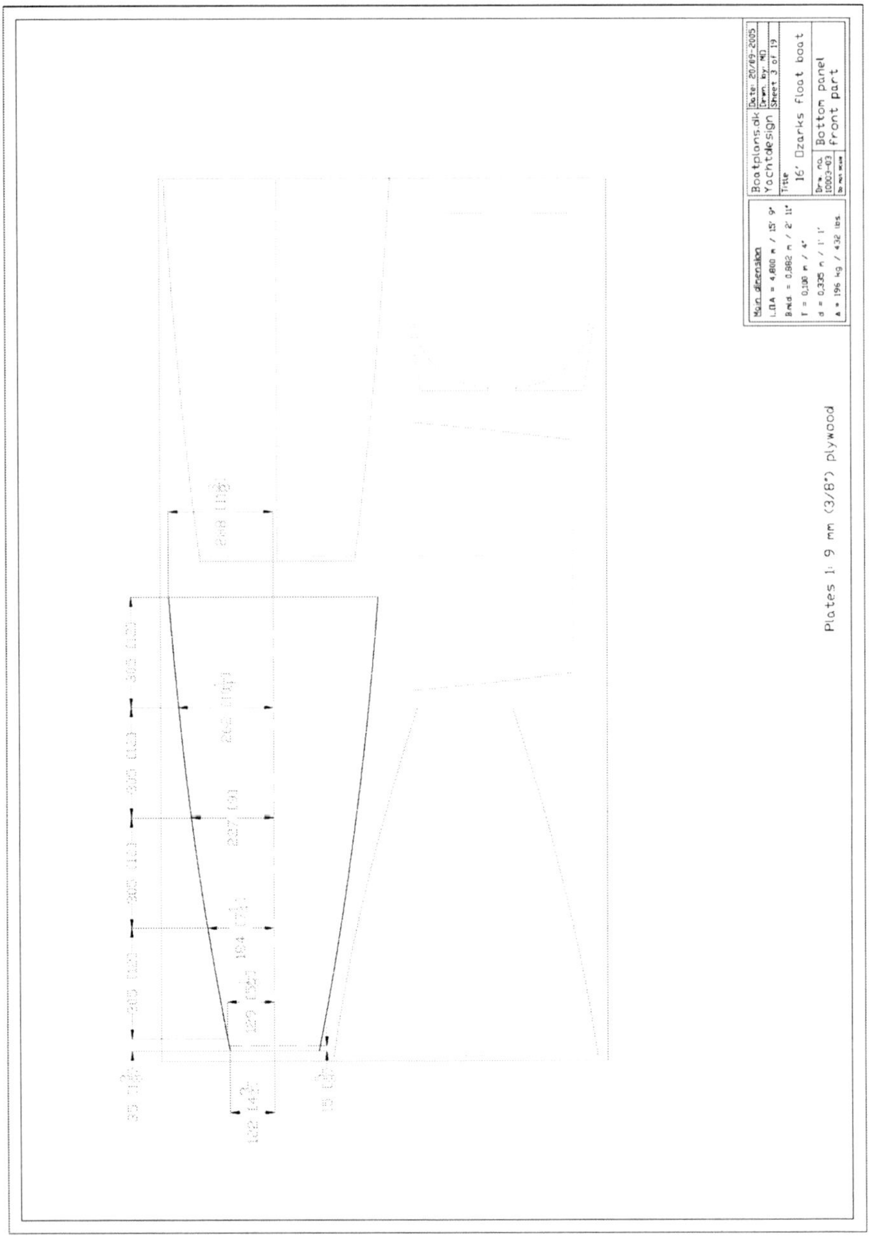

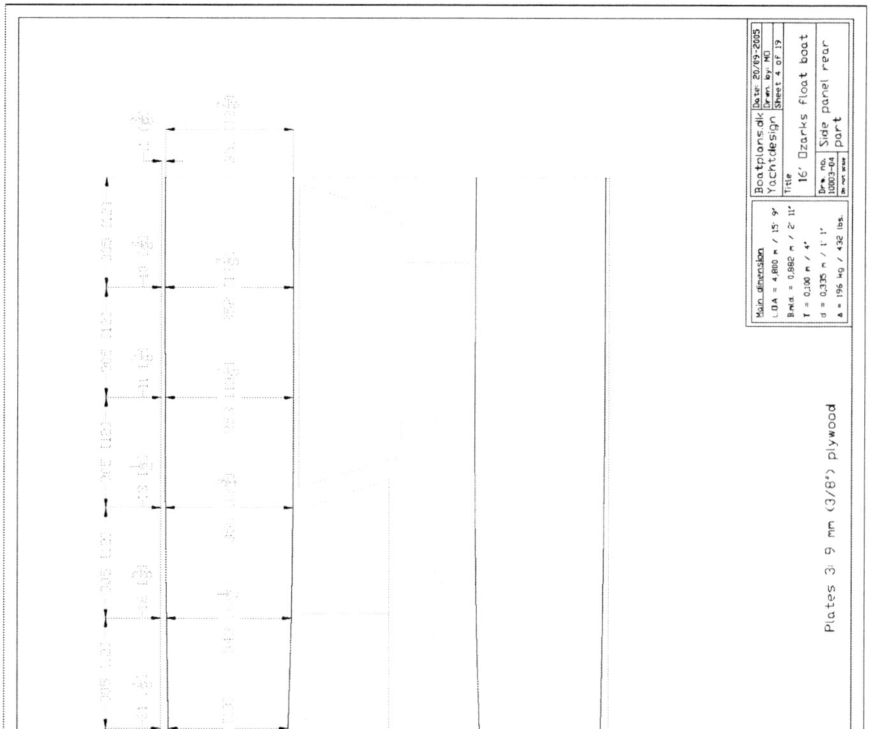

Boat Building Master Course

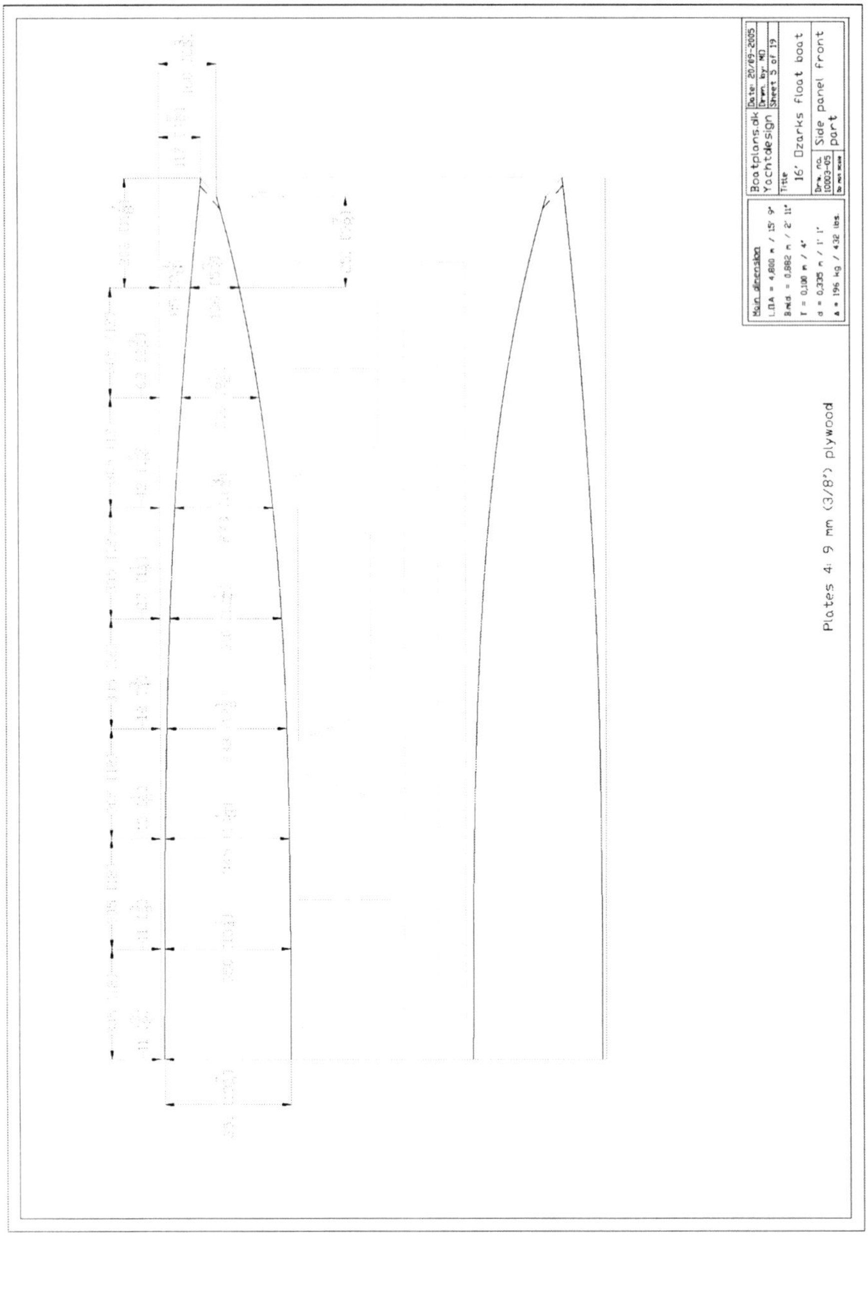

Boat Building Master Course

Boat Building Master Course

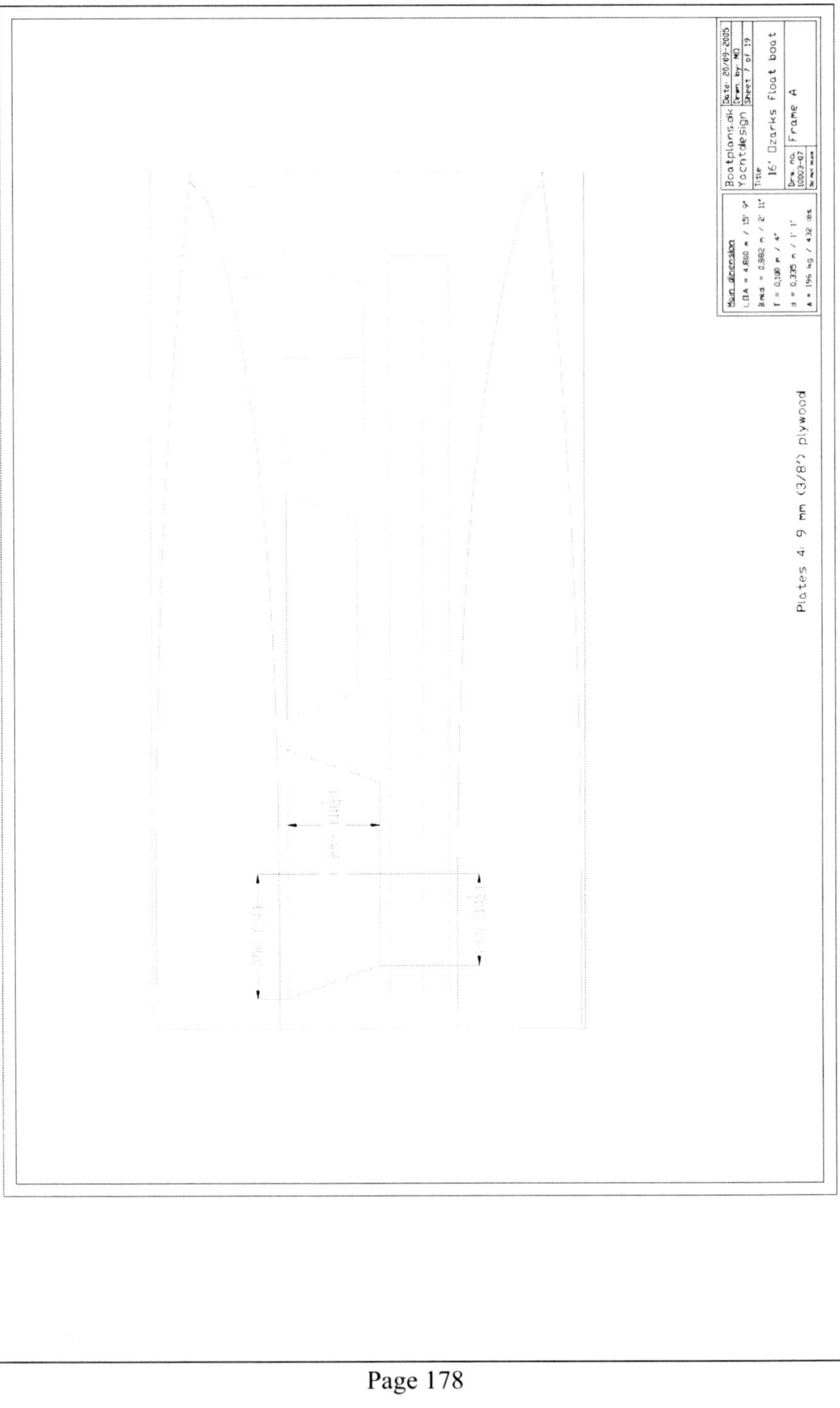

Boat Building Master Course

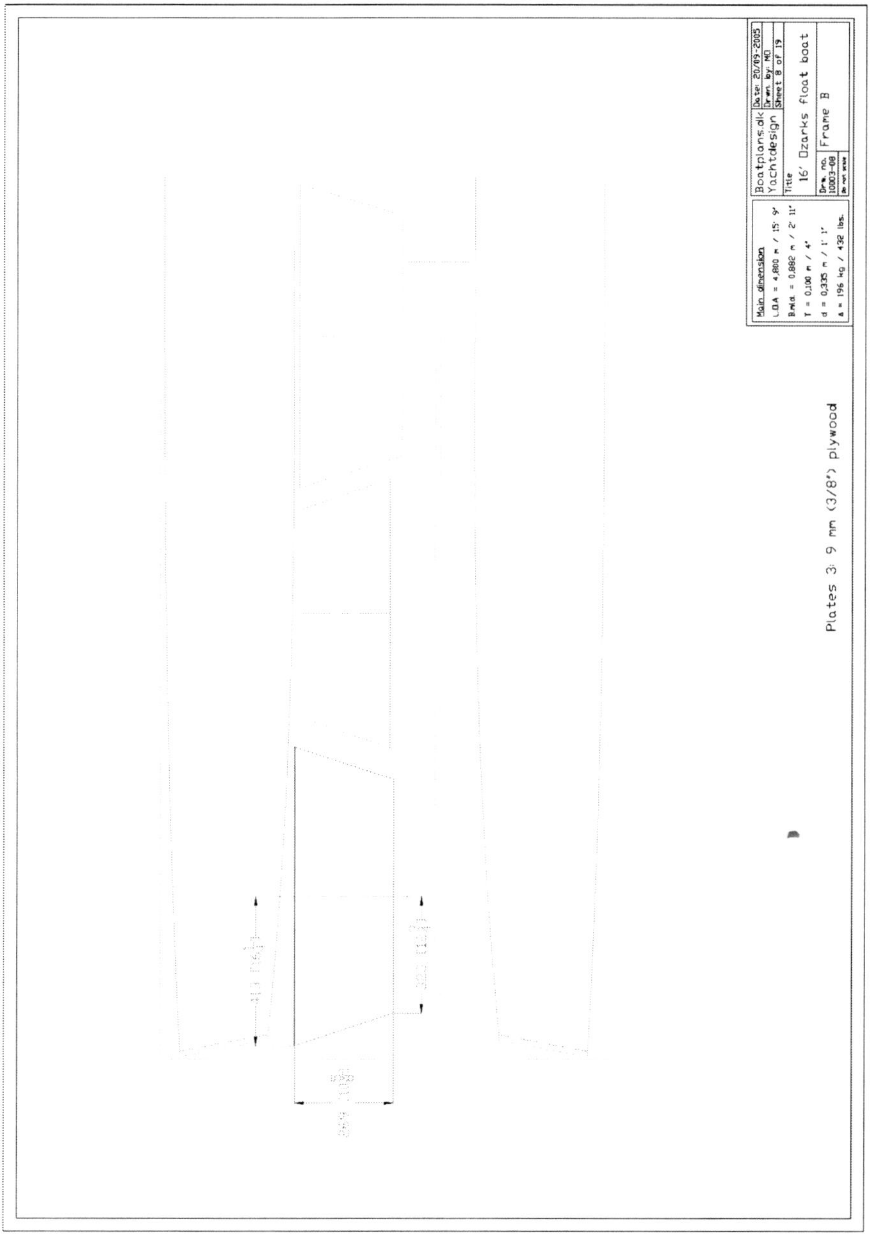

Boat Building Master Course

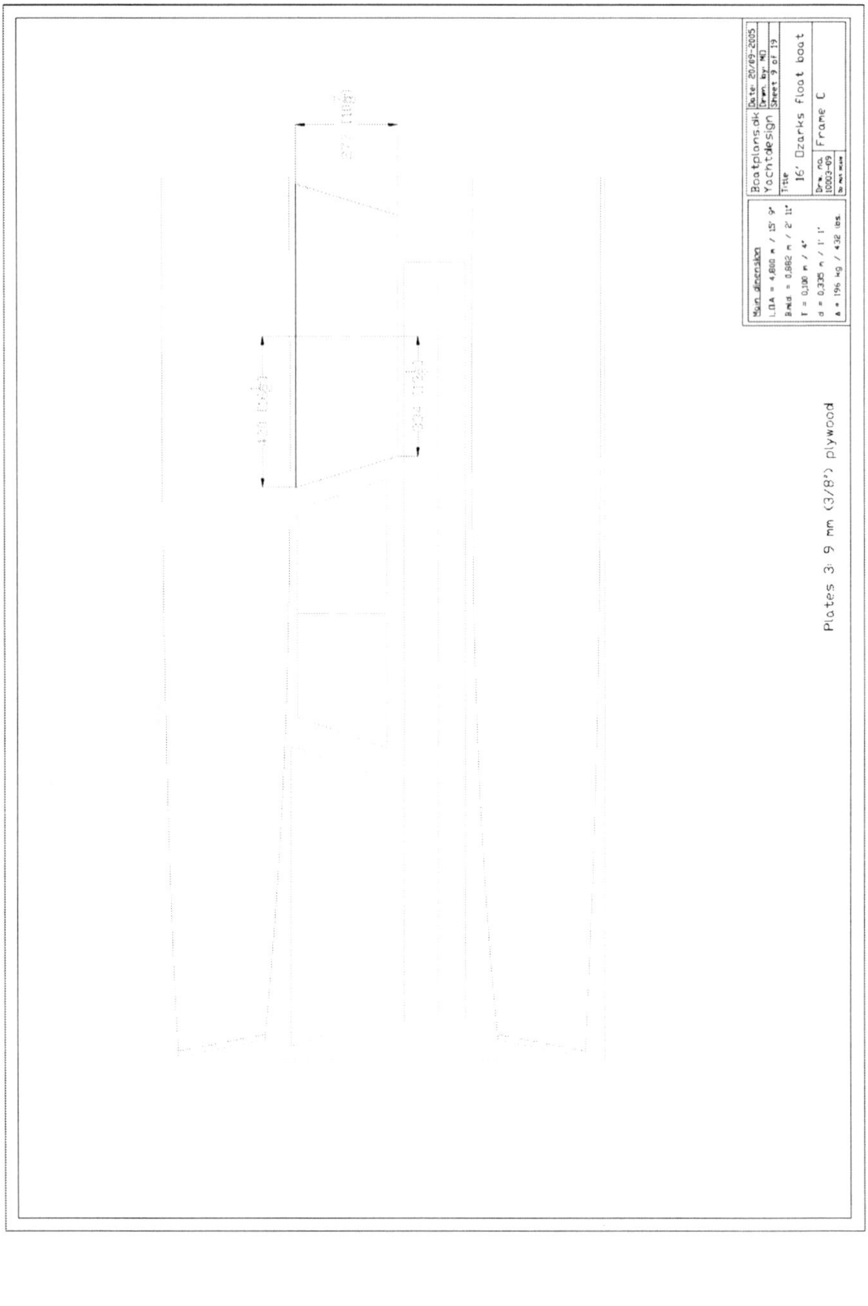

Boat Building Master Course

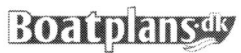

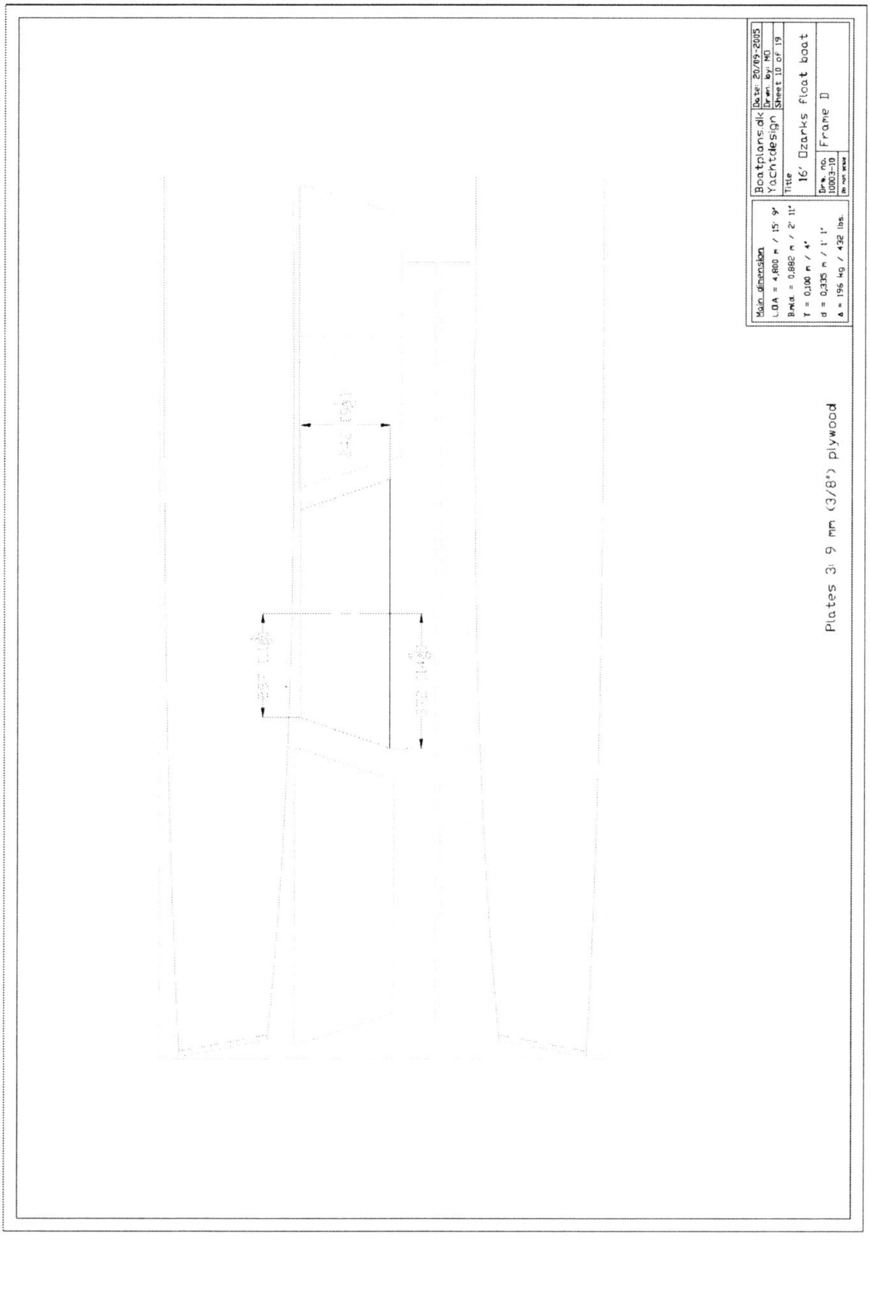
Main dimension
L.OA = 4,800 m / 15' 9"
B.mld. = 0,882 m / 2' 11"
T = 0,100 m / 4"
d = 0,335 m / 1' 1"
Δ = 196 kg / 432 lbs.
Boatplans.dk Yachtdesign
Date: 20/09-2005
Drwn by: MO
Sheet 10 of 19
Title
16' Ozarks float boat
Drw. no. 10003-10
Frame D
Plates 3: 9 mm (3/8") plywood

# Boat Building Master Course

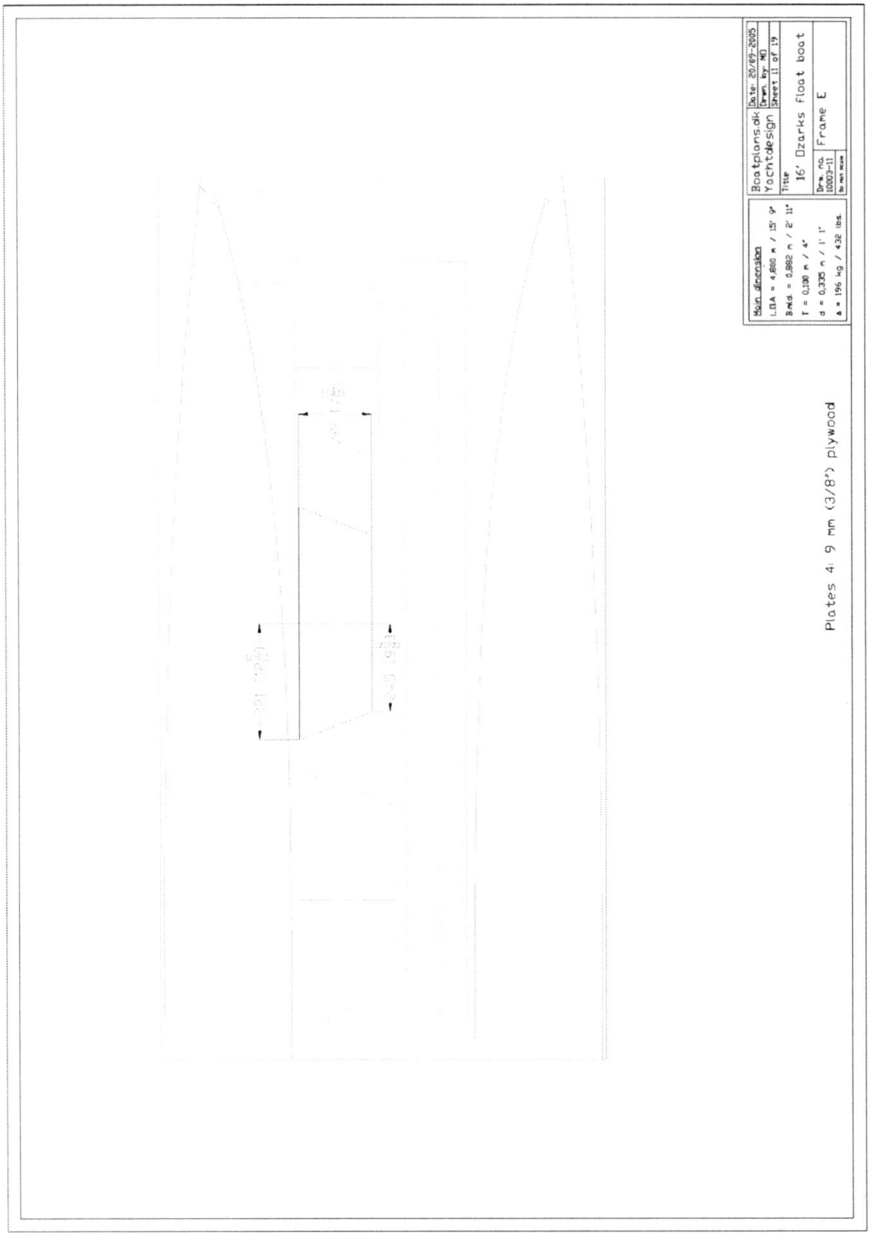

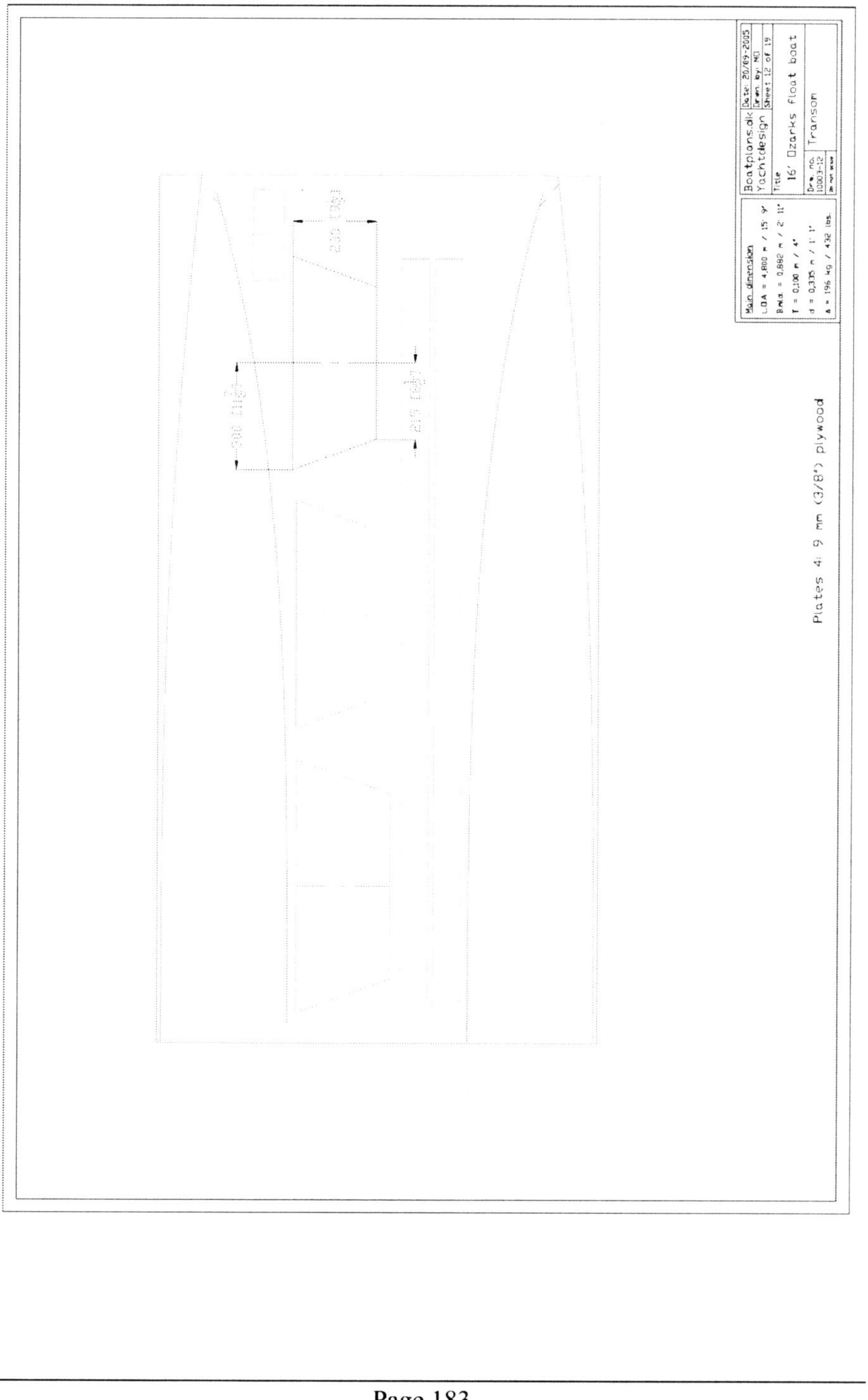

Boat Building Master Course

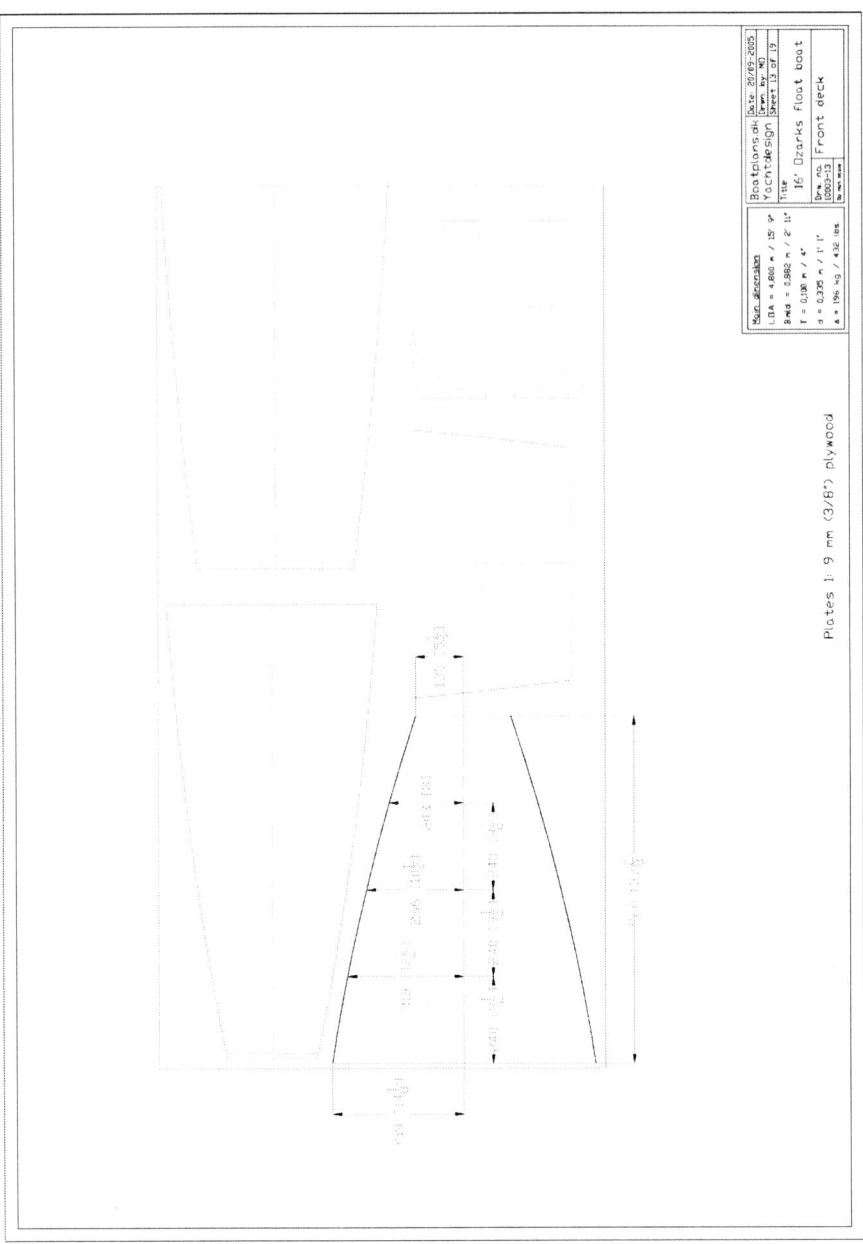

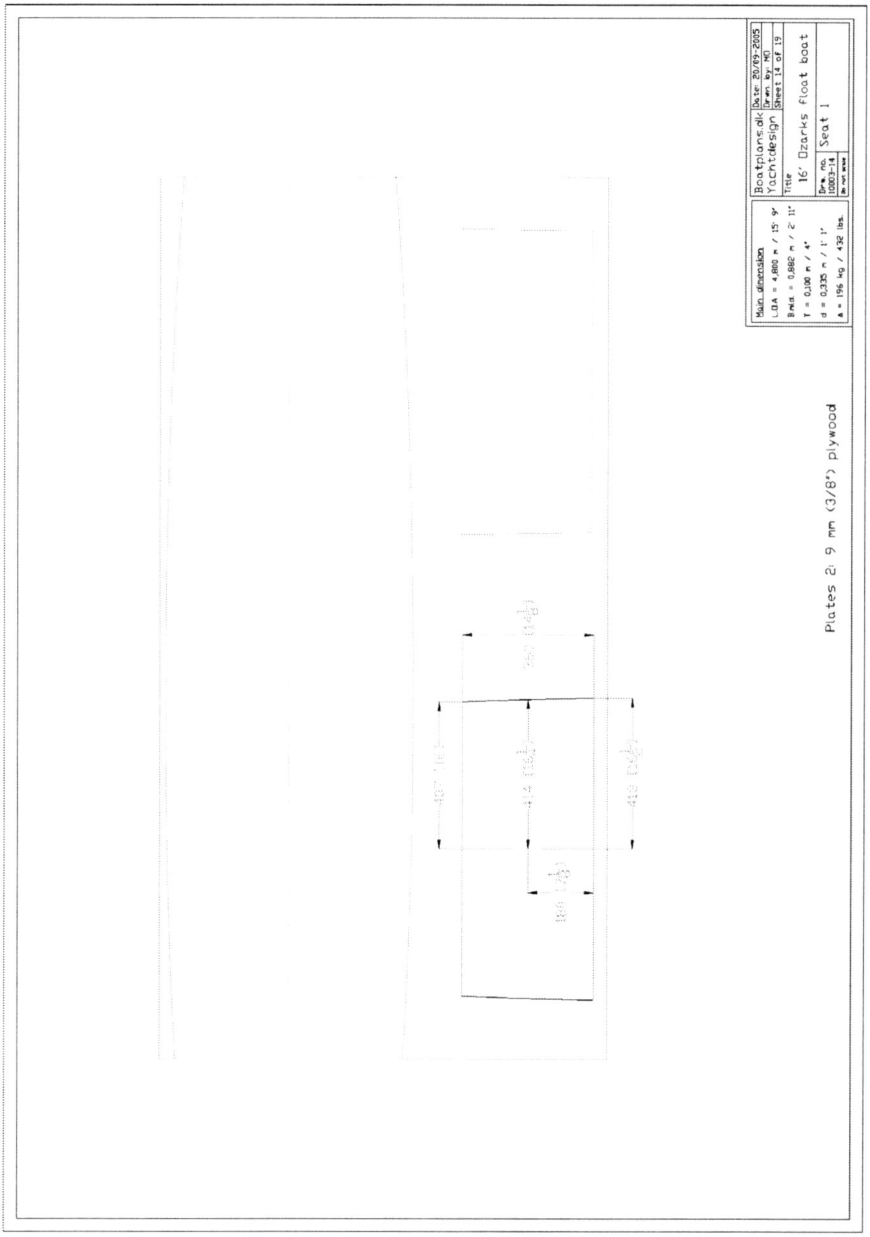

Boat Building Master Course

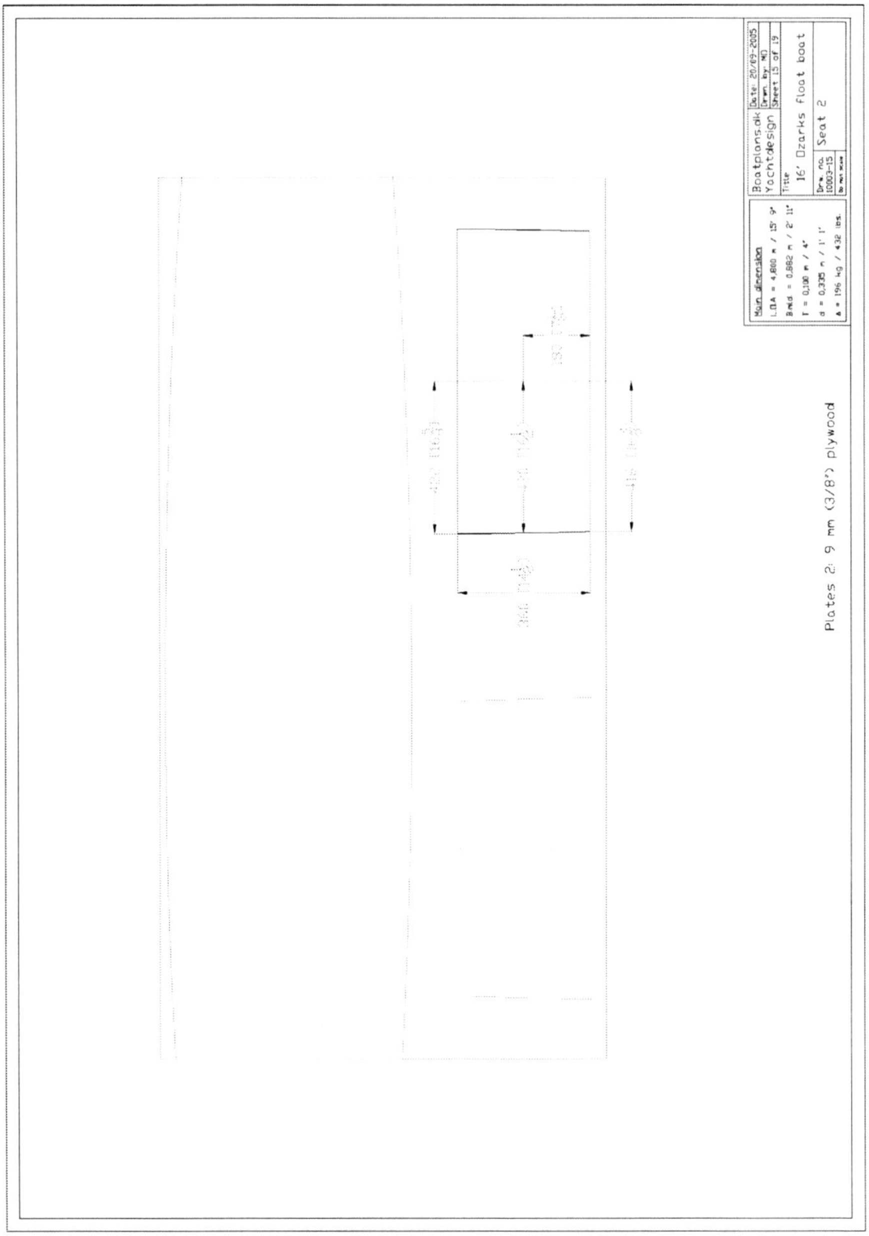

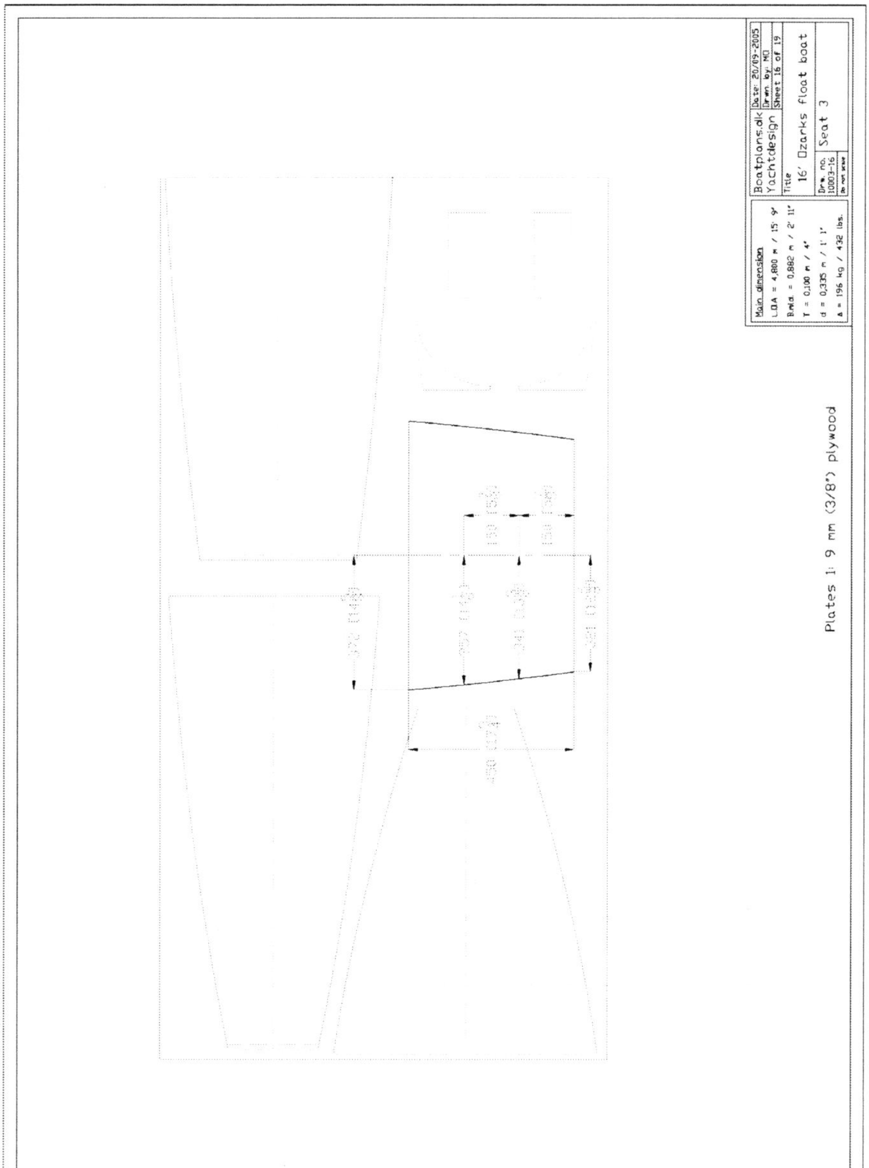

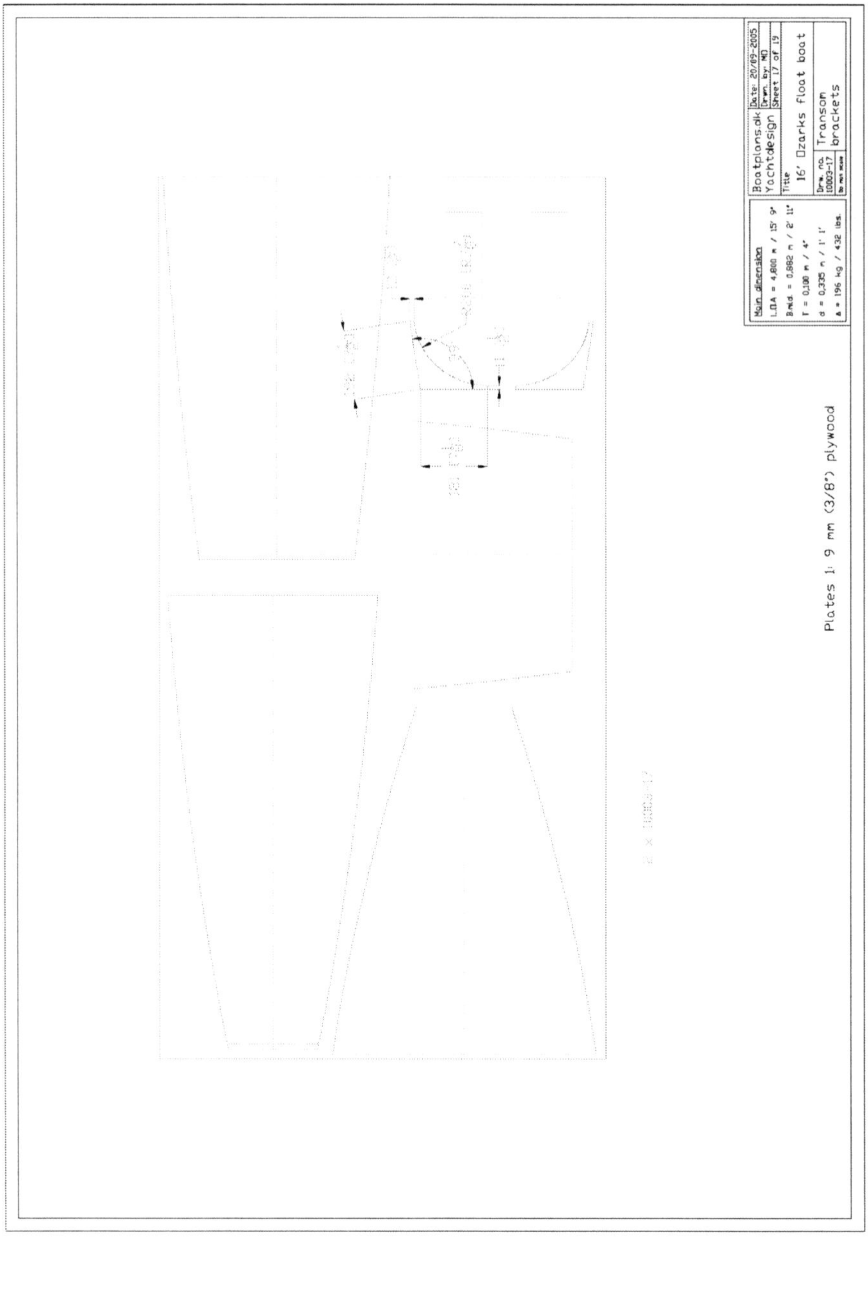

Boat Building Master Course

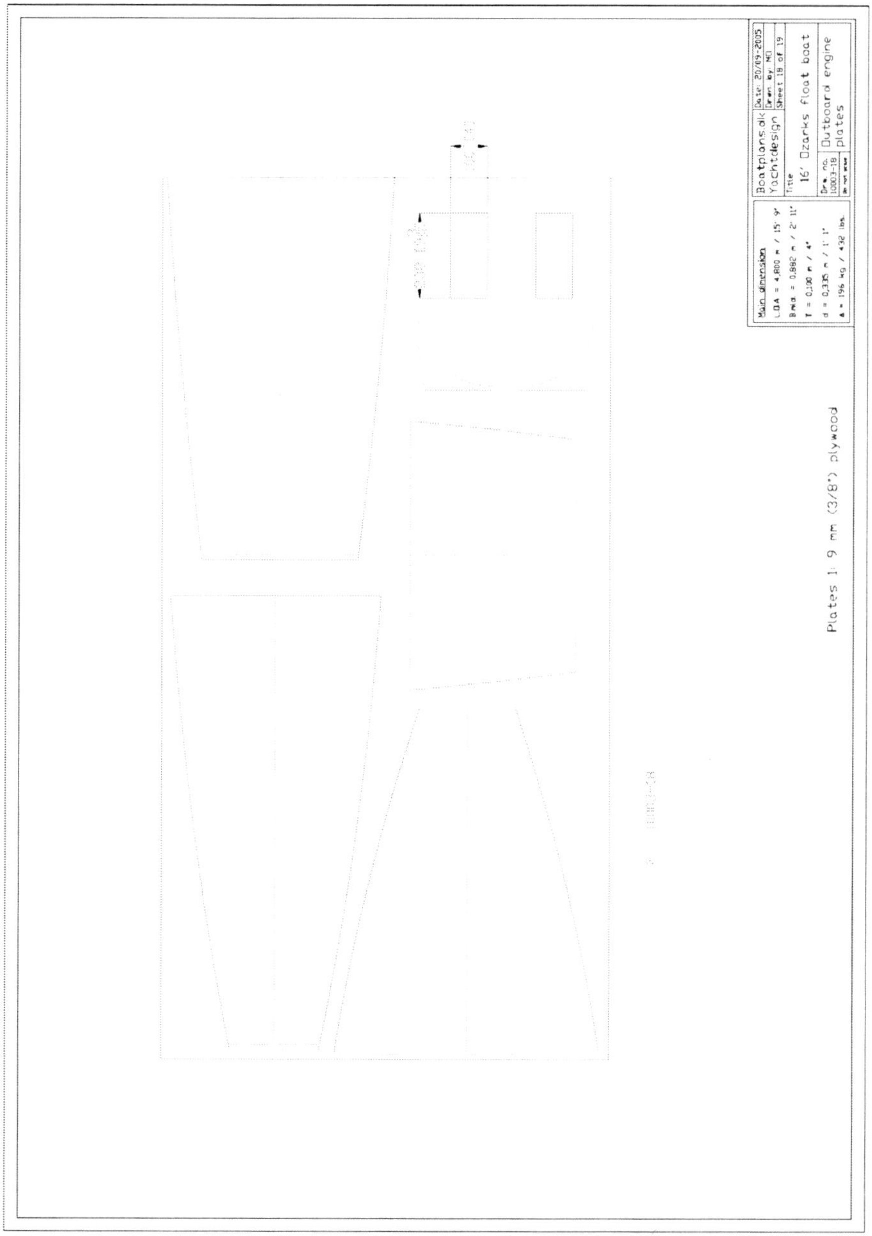

Boat Building Master Course

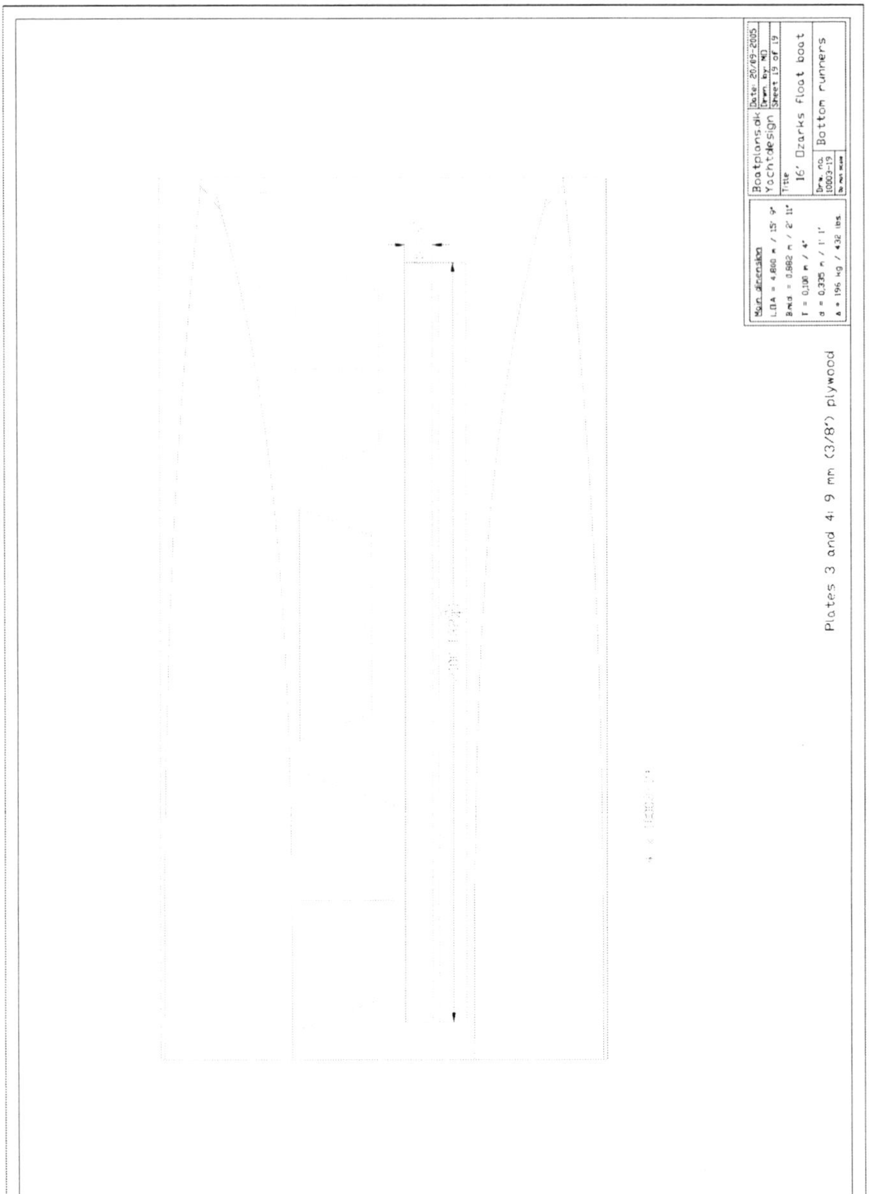

Boat Building Master Course

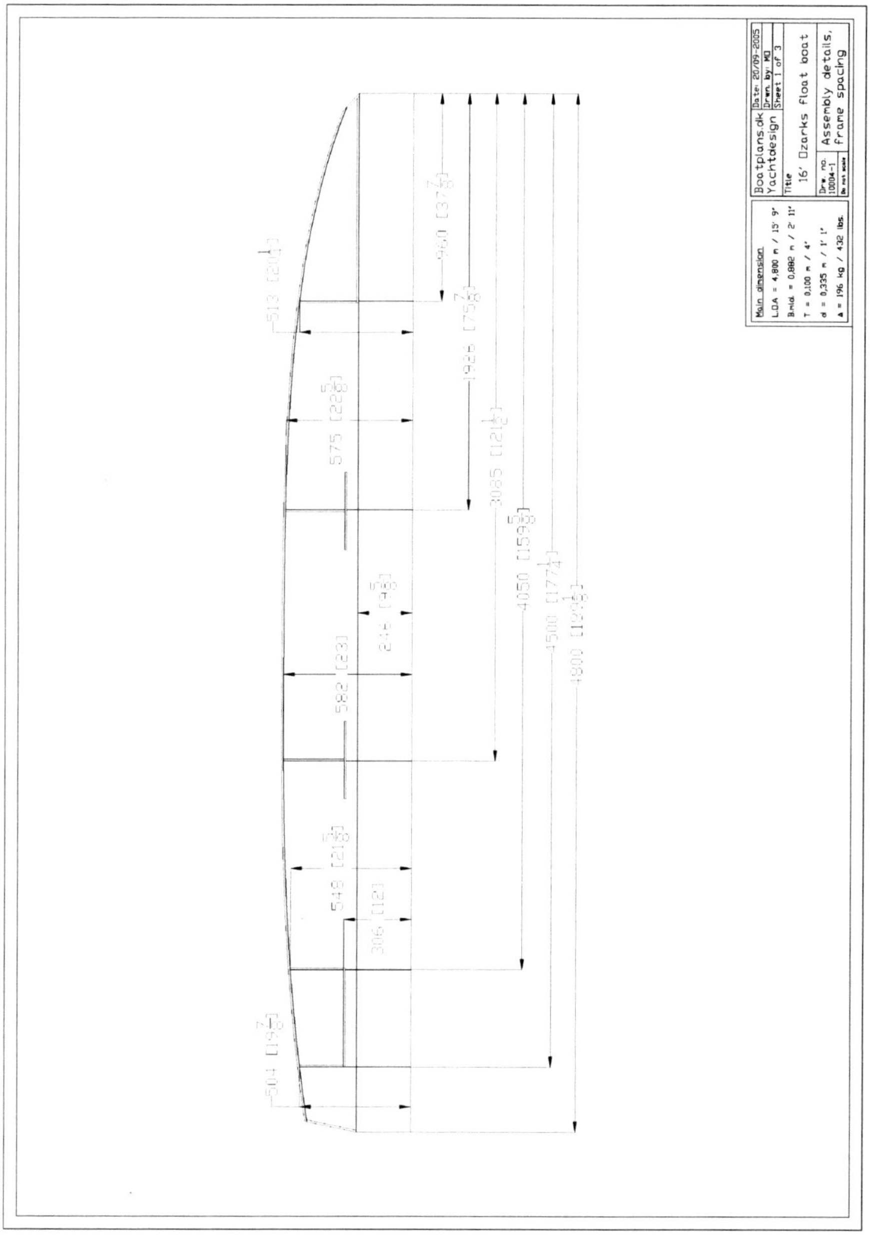

Boat Building Master Course

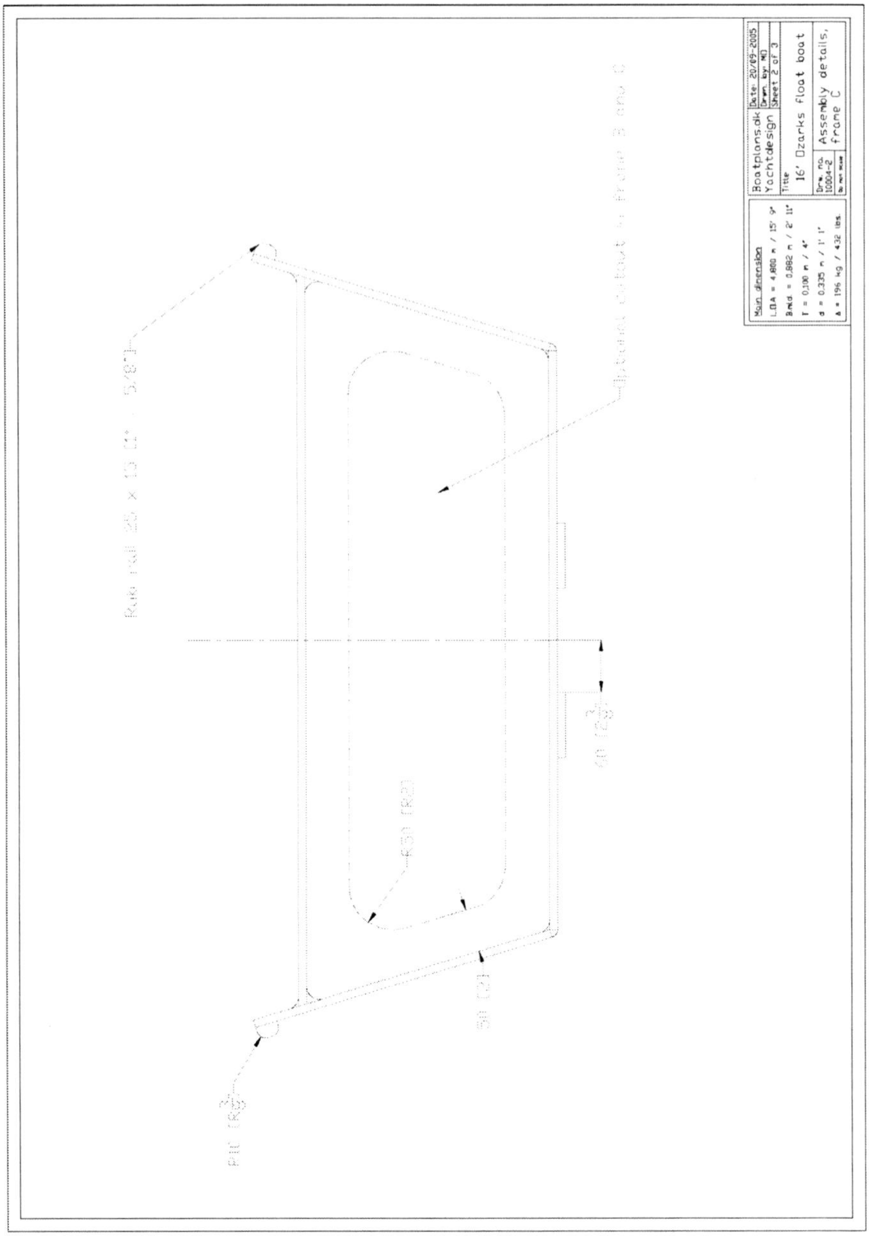

Boat Building Master Course

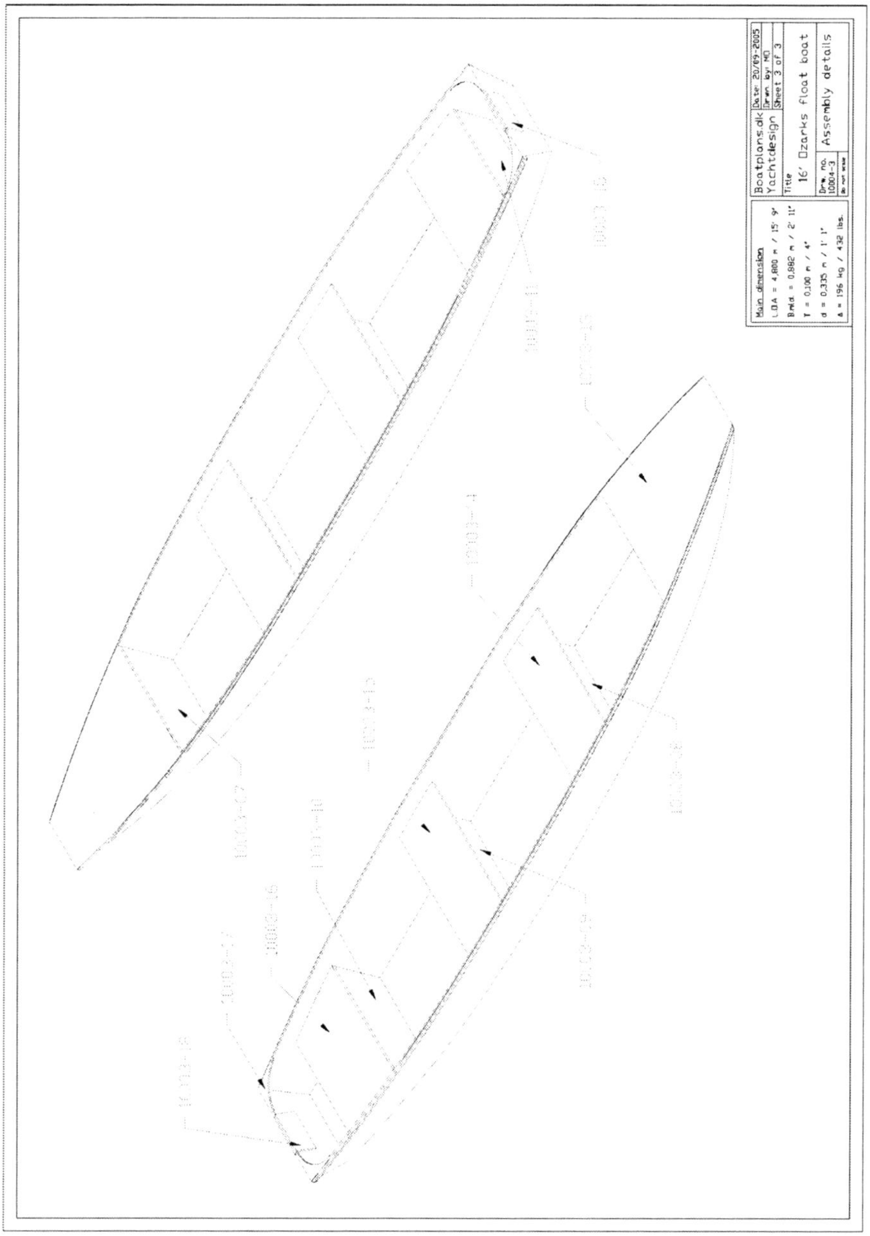

Boat Building Master Course

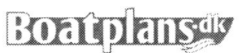

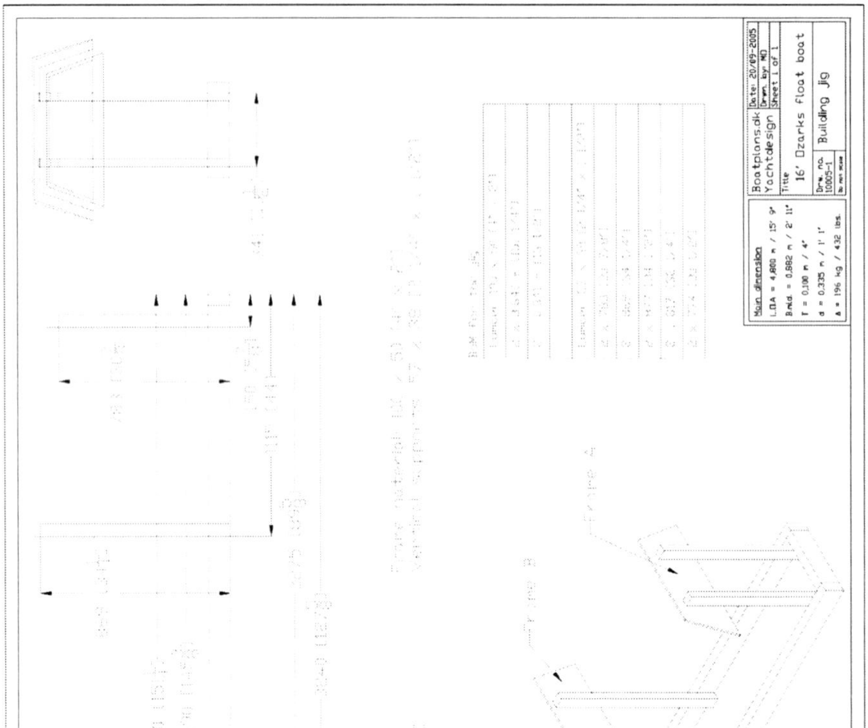
Main dimension
LOA = 4,800 m / 15' 9"
Bmld. = 0,882 m / 2' 11"
T = 0,100 m / 4"
d = 0,335 m / 1' 1"
Δ = 196 kg / 432 lbs.
Boatplans.dk
Yachtdesign
Date: 20/09-2005
Drwn. by: MD
Sheet 1 of 1
Title
16' Ozarks float boat
Building jig
Drw. no.
10005-1

Building instruction

Bill of Material

Plywood 2440x1220 [8' x 4']
4 sheet 9 mm (3/8")

Wood
2 x 5,2 m (2 x 5,7 yd) 25 x 15 (1" x 5/8") pine for rub rail

Fibreglass tape
50 m (55 yd) 100 mm (4") wide glass fibre tape 170 g/m^2

Resin
Epoxy total 4,5 kg (1 gallon)

Wood flour
500 g (1 lbs.) filler

General

This design is the copyright of Boatplans.dk – Yacht design. The plans are made available for all who wants to build the boat. The plans may not be made a subject of trade for any third party persons.

All plywood used should be Marine or Exterior grade but of cause the choice is yours. For all natural wood use spruce, fir or pine.

Remember to use marine glue wherever glue is needed. For all seams in the chine hull use 100 mm fibreglass tapes with epoxy resin. For all stitching use copper wire or plastic cable strips.

Construction sequence

The hull panels are drawn. Use the dimensions on the drawings 10003-01 to 10003-19. Use standard plywood sheets 2440 x 1220 (8'x4'). There are to be used 4 sheets of 9 mm (3/8") plywood. Mark the edges of the hull panels and use a thin wood batten held to the marks by nails or weights and draw the lines.

 **Boat Building Master Course**

All the panels are in two or more parts. Joint the parts with 100 mm wide fibreglass tape (e.g. cut it yourself from a piece of fibreglass) and epoxy resin. The dimensions shown on the drawing are made for butt joints. If you wish to joint the hull panels with a scarf joint changes are to be made in the dimensions.

Once the hull panels are dried and the frames, stringers and transom are cut the assembly of the hull can start. Set up the frames A, B, C, D, E and the transoms on a flat surface. Use the dimensions on drawing 10004-1. Alternately you can build a jig like shown on drawing 10005-1. It is necessary to make some temporary supports for the frames and transom.

Place the bottom panel and fasten it to the frames with screws or nails. When the bottom panel is laid out place the side panels in both sides. Stitch the two side panels to the bottom panel. At this stage do not over tighten the stitches so adjustments can be made. The side panels can be fastened to the frames with screws or nails.

It is now time to assemble the transoms. Be aware that the bottom and side panels are 15 mm [3/8"] longer in both ends. It is necessary to trim the panels after the transoms are positioned correctly.

Now the hull is assembled and the time is to check the hull geometry. Make absolutely sure that the hull is not twisted and the shape is correct. As the hull is checked tighten up the stitches.

When the hull is checked it is time for sealing the seams. Start with the outside seams and use epoxy filler to make the curvature between the panels smooth. When done use the glass tape and epoxy resin for reinforcement of the seams. For the use of epoxy remember to follow the instruction from your supplier. It is also important to prime the wood with epoxy before the tape is laid. Remember to wet out the tape completely when laying the final layer. Also make sure to clean up any resin runs before it cures, it is very difficult to remove afterwards.

Now it is time to turn the hull upright. Finish the inside seams using epoxy filler before you apply on the tape and epoxy. Remember to fasten the frames and transom with tape and epoxy as well. Use large epoxy fillets to glue frames and transom to the hull.

With the hull turned upright it is now time to assemble front deck and the seats. Gluing and glassing the deck from the inside can be a bit difficult, thus there is not much room for working. There might be some adjustments to make before the seats fits. Glue and glass the seats to the hull and frames.

It is possible to make the compartments in the bow and stern watertight. It is recommended dependant on your sailing waters to have some kind of flotation. The watertight compartments can be fitted with watertight hatches so the compartments can be used for storage.

It is not from a strength point of view necessary to cover the entire hull with epoxy and fabric. But it is recommended to at least prime the plywood with epoxy resin for better waterproof properties.

The hull may be finished with paint or varnish (for normal use, a good quality exterior house paint/varnish is sufficient).

Good luck with the building of your new boat.

Morten Olesen
Boatplans.dk

Lightning Source UK Ltd.
Milton Keynes UK
UKOW031921160112

185513UK00006B/25/P